T0321906

Deep Learning Innovations and Their Convergence With Big Data

S. Karthik
SNS College of Technology, Anna University, India

Anand Paul
Kyungpook National University, South Korea

N. Karthikeyan
Mizan–Tepi University, Ethiopia

A volume in the Advances in Data
Mining and Database Management
(ADMDM) Book Series

Published in the United States of America by
    IGI Global
    Information Science Reference (an imprint of IGI Global)
    701 E. Chocolate Avenue
    Hershey PA, USA 17033
    Tel: 717-533-8845
    Fax: 717-533-8661
    E-mail: cust@igi-global.com
    Web site: http://www.igi-global.com

Library of Congress Cataloging-in-Publication Data

Names: Karthik, S., 1977- editor. | Paul, Anand, editor. | Karthikeyan, N.,
   1977- editor.
Title: Deep learning innovations and their convergence with big data / S.
   Karthik, Anand Paul, and N. Karthikeyan, editors.
Description: Hershey, PA : Information Science Reference, [2018] | Includes
   bibliographical references.
Identifiers: LCCN 2017011947| ISBN 9781522530152 (hardcover) | ISBN
   9781522530169 (ebook)
Subjects: LCSH: Machine learning--Technological innovations. | Big data.
Classification: LCC Q325.5 .D44 2018 | DDC 006.3/1--dc23 LC record available at https://lccn.loc.
gov/2017011947

This book is published in the IGI Global book series Advances in Data Mining and Database Management (ADMDM) (ISSN: 2327-1981; eISSN: 2327-199X)

British Cataloguing in Publication Data
A Cataloguing in Publication record for this book is available from the British Library.

All work contributed to this book is new, previously-unpublished material.
The views expressed in this book are those of the authors, but not necessarily of the publisher.

For electronic access to this publication, please contact: eresources@igi-global.com.

Advances in Data Mining and Database Management (ADMDM) Book Series

ISSN:2327-1981
EISSN:2327-199X

Editor-in-Chief: David Taniar, Monash University, Australia

MISSION

With the large amounts of information available to organizations in today's digital world, there is a need for continual research surrounding emerging methods and tools for collecting, analyzing, and storing data.

The **Advances in Data Mining & Database Management (ADMDM)** series aims to bring together research in information retrieval, data analysis, data warehousing, and related areas in order to become an ideal resource for those working and studying in these fields. IT professionals, software engineers, academicians and upper-level students will find titles within the ADMDM book series particularly useful for staying up-to-date on emerging research, theories, and applications in the fields of data mining and database management.

COVERAGE

- Factor Analysis
- Association Rule Learning
- Heterogeneous and Distributed Databases
- Database Testing
- Data Analysis
- Predictive analysis
- Text mining
- Data quality
- Data mining
- Enterprise systems

IGI Global is currently accepting manuscripts for publication within this series. To submit a proposal for a volume in this series, please contact our Acquisition Editors at Acquisitions@igi-global.com or visit: http://www.igi-global.com/publish/.

The Advances in Data Mining and Database Management (ADMDM) Book Series (ISSN 2327-1981) is published by IGI Global, 701 E. Chocolate Avenue, Hershey, PA 17033-1240, USA, www.igi-global.com. This series is composed of titles available for purchase individually; each title is edited to be contextually exclusive from any other title within the series. For pricing and ordering information please visit http://www.igi-global.com/book-series/advances-data-mining-database-management/37146. Postmaster: Send all address changes to above address. ©© 2018 IGI Global. All rights, including translation in other languages reserved by the publisher. No part of this series may be reproduced or used in any form or by any means – graphics, electronic, or mechanical, including photocopying, recording, taping, or information and retrieval systems – without written permission from the publisher, except for non commercial, educational use, including classroom teaching purposes. The views expressed in this series are those of the authors, but not necessarily of IGI Global.

Titles in this Series

For a list of additional titles in this series, please visit:
https://www.igi-global.com/book-series/advances-data-mining-database-management/37146

Data Visualization and Statistical Literacy for Open and Big Data
Theodosia Prodromou (University of New England, Australia)
Information Science Reference • ©2017 • 365pp • H/C (ISBN: 9781522525127) • US $205.00

Web Semantics for Textual and Visual Information Retrieval
Aarti Singh (Guru Nanak Girls College, Yamuna Nagar, India) Nilanjan Dey (Techno India
College of Technology, India) Amira S. Ashour (Tanta University, Egypt & Taif University,
Saudi Arabia) and V. Santhi (VIT University, India)
Information Science Reference • ©2017 • 290pp • H/C (ISBN: 9781522524830) • US $185.00

Advancing Cloud Database Systems and Capacity Planning With Dynamic Applications
Narendra Kumar Kamila (C.V. Raman College of Engineering, India)
Information Science Reference • ©2017 • 430pp • H/C (ISBN: 9781522520139) • US $210.00

Web Data Mining and the Development of Knowledge-Based Decision Support Systems
G. Sreedhar (Rashtriya Sanskrit Vidyapeetha (Deemed University), India)
Information Science Reference • ©2017 • 409pp • H/C (ISBN: 9781522518778) • US $165.00

Intelligent Multidimensional Data Clustering and Analysis
Siddhartha Bhattacharyya (RCC Institute of Information Technology, India) Sourav De (Cooch
Behar Government Engineering College, India) Indrajit Pan (RCC Institute of Information
Technology, India) and Paramartha Dutta (Visva-Bharati University, India)
Information Science Reference • ©2017 • 450pp • H/C (ISBN: 9781522517764) • US $210.00

Emerging Trends in the Development and Application of Composite Indicators
Veljko Jeremic (University of Belgrade, Serbia) Zoran Radojicic (University of Belgrade,
Serbia) and Marina Dobrota (University of Belgrade, Serbia)
Information Science Reference • ©2017 • 402pp • H/C (ISBN: 9781522507147) • US $205.00

Web Usage Mining Techniques and Applications Across Industries
A.V. Senthil Kumar (Hindusthan College of Arts and Science, India)
Information Science Reference • ©2017 • 424pp • H/C (ISBN: 9781522506133) • US $200.00

For an enitre list of titles in this series, please visit:
https://www.igi-global.com/book-series/advances-data-mining-database-management/37146

701 East Chocolate Avenue, Hershey, PA 17033, USA
Tel: 717-533-8845 x100 • Fax: 717-533-8661
E-Mail: cust@igi-global.com • www.igi-global.com

Table of Contents

Detailed Table of Contents

Chapter 1
Advanced Threat Detection Based on Big Data Technologies 1
    Madhvaraj M. Shetty, Mangalore University, India
    Manjaiah D. H., Mangalore University, India

Today constant increase in number of cyber threats apparently shows that current countermeasures are not enough to defend it. With the help of huge generated data, big data brings transformative potential for various sectors. While many are using it for better operations, some of them are noticing that it can also be used for security by providing broader view of vulnerabilities and risks. Meanwhile, deep learning is coming up as a key role by providing predictive analytics solutions. Deep learning and big data analytics are becoming two high-focus of data science. Threat intelligence becoming more and more effective. Since it is based on how much data collected about active threats, this reason has taken many independent vendors into partnerships. In this chapter, we explore big data and big data analytics with its benefits. And we provide a brief overview of deep analytics and finally we present collaborative threat Detection. We also investigate some aspects of standards and key functions of it. We conclude by presenting benefits and challenges of collaborative threat detection.

Chapter 2
A Brief Review on Deep Learning and Types of Implementation for Deep

    *Uthra Kunathur Thikshaja, Kyungpook National University, South
        Korea*
    Anand Paul, Kyungpook National University, South Korea

In recent years, there's been a resurgence in the field of Artificial Intelligence and deep learning is gaining a lot of attention. Deep learning is a branch of machine learning based on a set of algorithms that can be used to model high-level abstractions in data by using multiple processing layers with complex structures, or otherwise composed of multiple non-linear transformations. Estimation of depth in a Neural Network (NN) or Artificial Neural Network (ANN) is an integral as well as complicated process. These methods have dramatically improved the state-of-the-art in speech recognition, visual object recognition, object detection and many other domains such as drug discovery and genomics. This chapter describes the motivations for deep architecture, problem with large networks, the need for deep architecture and new implementation techniques for deep learning. At the end, there is also an algorithm to implement the deep architecture using the recursive nature of functions and transforming them to get the desired output.

Chapter 3
Big Spectrum Data and Deep Learning Techniques for Cognitive Wireless

    Punam Dutta Choudhury, Gauhati University, India
    Ankumoni Bora, Gauhati University, India
    Kandarpa Kumar Sarma, Gauhati University, India

The present world is data driven. From social sciences to frontiers of research in science and engineering, one common factor is the continuous data generation. It has started to affect our daily lives. Big data concepts are found to have significant impact in modern wireless communication systems. The analytical tools of big data have been identified as full scale autonomous mode of operation which necessitates a strong role to be played by learning based systems. The chapter has focused on the synergy of big data and deep learning for generating better efficiency in evolving communication frameworks. The chapter has also included discussion on machine learning and cognitive technologies w.r.t. big data and mobile communication. Cyber Physical Systems being indispensable elements of M2M communication, Wireless Sensor Networks and its role in CPS, cognitive radio networking and spectrum sensing have also been discussed. It is expected that spectrum sensing, big data and deep learning will play vital roles in enhancing the capabilities of wireless communication systems.

Big Data and deep computation are among the buzzwords in the present sophisticated digital world. Big Data has emerged with the expeditious growth of digital data. This chapter addresses the problem of employing deep learning algorithms in Big Data analytics. Unlike the traditional algorithms, this chapter comes up with various solutions to employ advanced deep learning mechanisms with less complexity and finally present a generic solution. The deep learning algorithms require less time to process the big amount of data based on different contexts. However, collecting the accurate feature and classifying the context into patterns using neural networks algorithms require high time and complexity. Therefore, using deep learning algorithms in integration with neural networks can bring optimize solutions. Consequently, the aim of this chapter is to provide an overview of how the advance deep learning algorithms can be used to solve various existing challenges in Big Data analytics.

Big Data Analytics has become an important paradigm that can help digital investigators to investigate cybercrimes as well as provide solutions to malware and threat prediction, detection and prevention at an early stage. Big Data Analytics techniques can use to analysis enormous amount of generated data from new technologies such as Social Networks, Cloud Computing and Internet of Things to understand the committed crimes in addition to predict the new coming severe attacks and crimes in the future. This chapter introduce principles of Digital Forensics and Big Data as well as exploring Big Data Analytics and Deep Learning benefits and advantages that can help the digital investigators to develop and propose new techniques and methods based on Big Data Analytics using Deep Learning techniques that can be adapted to the unique context of Digital Forensics as well as support performing digital investigation process in forensically sound and timely fashion manner.

 Sanjiban Sekhar Roy, VIT University, India
 Pulkit Kulshrestha, VIT University, India
 Pijush Samui, NIT Patna, India

Drought is a condition of land in which the ground water faces a severe shortage. This condition affects the survival of plants and animals. Drought can impact ecosystem and agricultural productivity, severely. Hence, the economy also gets affected by this situation. This paper proposes Deep Belief Network (DBN) learning technique, which is one of the state of the art machine learning algorithms. This proposed work uses DBN, for classification of drought and non-drought images. Also, k nearest neighbour (kNN) and random forest learning methods have been proposed for the classification of the same drought images. The performance of the Deep Belief Network(DBN) has been compared with k nearest neighbour (kNN) and random forest. The data set has been split into 80:20, 70:30 and 60:40 as train and test. Finally, the effectiveness of the three proposed models have been measured by various performance metrics.

 Muhammad Mazhar Ullah Rathore, Kyungpook National University,
  South Korea
 Awais Ahmad, Yeungnam University, South Korea
 Anand Paul, Kyungpook National University, South Korea

Geosocial network data provides the full information on current trends in human, their behaviors, their living style, the incidents and events, the disasters, current medical infection, and much more with respect to locations. Hence, the current geosocial media can work as a data asset for facilitating the national and the government itself by analyzing the geosocial data at real-time. However, there are millions of geosocial network users, who generates terabytes of heterogeneous data with a variety of information every day with high-speed, termed as Big Data. Analyzing such big amount of data and making real-time decisions is an inspiring task. Therefore, this book chapter discusses the exploration of geosocial networks. A system architecture is discussed and implemented in a real-time environment in order to process the abundant amount of various social network data to monitor the earth events, incidents, medical diseases, user trends and thoughts to make future real-time decisions as well as future planning.

Chapter 8

Sabitha Rajagopal, SNS College of Technology, Anna University, India

Data Science employs techniques and theories to create data products. Data product is merely a data application that acquires its value from the data itself, and creates more data as a result; it's not just an application with data. Data science involves the methodical study of digital data employing techniques of observation, development, analysis, testing and validation. It tackles the real time challenges by adopting a holistic approach. It 'creates' knowledge about large and dynamic bases, 'develops' methods to manage data and 'optimizes' processes to improve its performance. The goal includes vital investigation and innovation in conjunction with functional exploration intended to notify decision-making for individuals, businesses, and governments. This paper discusses the emergence of Data Science and its subsequent developments in the fields of Data Mining and Data Warehousing. The research focuses on need, challenges, impact, ethics and progress of Data Science. Finally the insights of the subsequent phases in research and development of Data Science is provided.

Chapter 9

Singaraju Jyothi, Sri Padmavati Mahila University, India
Bhargavi P, Sri Padmavati Mahila University, India

Data Science and Computational biology is an interdisciplinary program that brings together the domain specific knowledge of science and engineering with relevant areas of computing and bioinformatics. Data science has the potential to revolutionise healthcare, and respond to the increasing volume and complexity in biomedical and bioinformatics data. From genomics to clinical records, from imaging to mobile health and personalised medicine, the data volume in biomedical research presents urgent challenges for computer science. This chapter elevates the researchers in what way data science play important role in Computational Biology such as Bio-molecular Computation, Computational Photonics, Medical Imaging, Scientific Computing, Structural Biology, Bioinformatics and Bio-Computing etc. Big data analytics of biological data bases, high performance computing in large sequence of genome database and Scientific Visualization are also discussed in this chapter.

It is just now at the top of an aggregation point of globalization's era in terms of things and living creatures. And the communication methods including in many sorts of transfers like commodity, facility, information, system, thought, knowledge, human, etc. may cause many kinds of and many types of interactions among us. And those many kinds of and many types of interactions have been again causing many sorts of problems. Under these situations, Cloud has come out as a smart solution to these problems. However, "Cloud is the final ultimate solution to offer to these problems' solving?" On this chapter, this question is deeply concerned from various aspects. And it is studied on this regard for getting a new paradigm.

Chapter 11

In this modern Digital era, Technology is a key player in transforming the educational pedagogy for the benefit of students and society at large. Technology in the classroom allows the teacher to deliver more personalized learning to the student with better interaction through the internet. Humongous amount of digital data collected day by day increases has led to the use of big data. It helps to correlate the performance and learning pattern of individual students by analysing large amount of stored activity of the students, offering worthwhile feedback etc. The use of big data analytics in a cloud environment helps in providing an instant infrastructure with low cost, accessibility, usability etc. This paper presents an innovative means towards providing a smarter educational system in schools. It improves individual efficiency by providing a way to monitor the progress of individual student by maintaining a detailed profile. This framework has been established in a cloud environment which is an online learning system where the usage pattern of individual students are collected.

Preface

Big Data technologies have gone from the realm of hype to one of the core descriptors of the new digital age. The digital data have proliferated nine times in volume in just five years and by 2020, researchers are suggesting that its volume will increase at a rapid rate and will almost reach 35 trillion gigabytes (IDC, 2014). In this paradigm shift, a research portrays that, 90% of all the data in the world was created in this past 2 years and it is obvious that we are living a data cascade era (SINTEF, 2013). This outburst of data exploding trend embarks ample opportunities and considerable transformation in various sectors such as enterprises, healthcare, industrial manufacturing, and Transportation. Big data endows a novel technique of probability to collect, manage and analyze the vast quantities of data, which indeed offers an understanding of context towards diverse applications. In big data analytics, deep learning is a set of machine-learning techniques based on neural networking, is still evolving but shows great potential for solving business problems. Deep learning enables computers to recognize items of concern in large quantities of unstructured and binary data and to deduce relationships without needing specific models or programming instructions (Arel, Rose, & Karnowski, 2010).

Furthermore, deep learning has an integral part in the advancement in speech recognition, Computer Vision and Natural Language Processing in the last decade (Li, 2015). Using deep learning methodologies few long standing issues were sorted out in speech recognition (Hinton et al., 2012). Companies like Google and Microsoft has already deployed deep learning based speech recognition systems in their products. In computer vision, feature engineering plays a significant role which some resistance for feature learning. Further, in Natural Language Processing language model, machine translation and question answering (Domingo, 2012). Deep learning paly a predominate role in Science, it is used for a various application like protein structure prediction, analysis of genomic data, predicting chemical reactions and detecting exotic particles.

This handbook on research looks to discuss and address first in understanding on how deep analytics applied to an understanding of context provides the preconditions for a world of smart technologies. This combines with various advanced algorithms that allow systems to understand their environment, learn for themselves, and act autonomously, which offer intellectual data agility measurement as a contrast to the storage and management of key data sources, provide a concrete understanding of data management with respects to various applications.

THE CHALLENGES

In Big Data Analytics particularly in deep learning method, deep unsupervised learning requires special attention. Further, incorporating deep discriminative learning method with Bayesian models is essential. In addition, integrating neural representation with deep symbolic learning is predominant. One of the major challenges in big data analytics is with the streaming data which is used in real time processing. It is essential that big data adapts deep learning to handle fat moving or streaming data. Hence, there is a need for deep learning algorithm for fast moving data. Finally, from a computation and analytics point of view, lager scale models of Deep Learning method needs specific attention.

OBJECTIVE OF THE BOOK

The main objective of this book is to capture the state-of-the-art trends and advancements in Big Data Analytics, its technologies, and applications. The book also aims to identify potential research directions and technologies that will facilitate insight generation in various domains of science, industry, business, and consumer applications. We expect the book to serve as a reference for a larger audience, such as systems architects, practitioners, developers, new researchers and graduate level students. The book will cover fundamental to advanced concepts necessary to comprehend current Deep learning issues, challenges and possible solutions as well as future trends in big data Analytics.

ORGANIZATION OF THE BOOK

The book is organized into 11 chapters. A brief description of each of the chapters follows:

Chapter 1 is "Advanced Threat Detection Based on Big Data Technologies." Today, a constant increase in a number of cyber threats apparently shows that current countermeasures are not enough to defend it. With the help of huge generated data, big data brings the transformative potential for various sectors. While many are using it for better operations, some of them are noticing that it can also be used for security by providing a broader view of vulnerabilities and risks. Meanwhile, deep learning is coming up as a key role by providing predictive analytics solutions. Deep learning and big data analytics are becoming two high-focus of data science. Threat intelligence becoming more and more effective since it is based on how much data collected about active threats, this reason has taken many independent vendors into partnerships. In this chapter, the author explores big data and big data analytics with its benefits. And the authors provide a brief overview of deep analytics and finally we present collaborative threat Detection. Further, investigation on some aspects of standards and key functions of it is discussed and conclude by presenting benefits and challenges of collaborative threat Detection.

Chapter 2 is "A Brief Review on Deep Learning and Types of Implementation for Deep Learning." In recent years, there's been a resurgence in the field of Artificial Intelligence and deep learning which gains a lot of attention. Deep learning is a branch of machine learning based on a set of algorithms that can be used to model high-level abstractions in data by using multiple processing layers with complex structures or otherwise composed of multiple non-linear transformations. Estimation of depth in a Neural Network (NN) or Artificial Neural Network (ANN) is an integral as well as the complicated process. These methods have dramatically improved the state-of-the-art in speech recognition, visual object recognition, object detection and many other domains such as drug discovery and genomics. This chapter describes the motivations for deep architecture, the problem with large networks, the need for deep architecture and new implementation techniques for deep learning. Finally, an algorithm to implement the deep architecture using the recursive nature of functions and transforming them to get the desired output is proposed.

Chapter 3 is "Big Spectrum Data and Deep Learning Techniques for Cognitive Wireless Networks." The present world is data driven. From social sciences to frontiers of research in science and engineering, one common factor is the continuous data generation. It has started to affect our daily lives. Big data concepts are found to have a significant impact in modern wireless communication systems. The analytical tools of big data have been identified as a full scale autonomous mode of operation which necessitates a strong role to be played by learning based systems. The chapter has focused on the synergy of big data and deep learning for generating better efficiency in evolving communication frameworks. The chapter has also included discussion on machine learning and cognitive technologies w.r.t. big data and mobile communication. Cyber Physical Systems being indispensable elements of M2M communication, Wireless Sensor Networks and its role in CPS, cognitive radio networking and spectrum sensing have also been discussed. It is expected that spectrum sensing, big data and deep learning will play vital roles in enhancing the capabilities of wireless communication systems.

Chapter 4 is "Efficiently Processing Big Data in Real-Time Employing Deep Learning Algorithms." Big Data and deep computation are among the buzzwords in the present sophisticated digital world. Big Data has emerged with the expeditious growth of digital data. This chapter addresses the problem of employing deep learning algorithms in Big Data analytics. Unlike the traditional algorithms, this chapter comes up with various solutions to employ advanced deep learning mechanisms with less complexity and finally present a generic solution. The deep learning algorithms require less time to process the big amount of data based on different contexts. However, collecting the accurate feature and classifying the context into patterns using neural networks algorithms require high time and complexity. Therefore, using deep learning algorithms in integration with neural networks can bring optimize solutions. Consequently, the aim of this chapter is to provide an overview of how the advance deep learning algorithms can be used to solve various existing challenges in Big Data analytics.

Chapter 5 is "Digital Investigation of Cybercrimes Based on Big Data Analytics Using Deep Learning." Big Data Analytics has become an important paradigm that can help digital investigators to investigate cybercrimes as well as provide solutions to malware and threat prediction, detection and prevention at an early stage. Big Data Analytics techniques can use to analysis enormous amount of generated data from new technologies such as Social Networks, Cloud Computing, and Internet of Things to understand the committed crimes, in addition, to predict the new coming severe attacks and crimes in the future. This chapter introduce principles of Digital Forensics and Big Data as well as exploring Big Data Analytics and Deep Learning benefits and advantages that can help the digital investigators to develop and propose new techniques and methods based on Big Data Analytics using Deep Learning techniques that can be adapted to the unique context of Digital Forensics as well as support performing digital investigation process in forensically sound and timely fashion manner.

Chapter 6 is "Classifying Images of Drought-Affected Area Using Deep Belief Network, kNN, and Random Forest Learning Techniques." Drought is a condition of land in which the ground water faces a severe shortage. This condition affects the survival of plants and animals. Drought can impact ecosystem and agricultural productivity, severely. Hence, the economy also gets affected by this situation. This chapter proposes Deep Belief Network (DBN) learning technique, which is one of the state of the art machine learning algorithms. This proposed work uses DBN, for classification of drought and non-drought images. Also, k nearest neighbour (kNN) and random forest learning methods have been proposed for the classification of the same drought images. The performance of the Deep Belief Network(DBN) has been compared with k nearest neighbour (kNN) and random forest. The data set has been split into 80:20, 70:30 and 60:40 as train and test. Finally, the effectiveness of the three proposed models has been measured by various performance metrics.

Chapter 7 is "Big Data Deep Analytics for Geosocial Networks." Geosocial network data provides the full information on current trends in human, their behaviors, their living style, the incidents and events, the disasters, current medical infection, and much more with respect to locations. Hence, the current geosocial media can work as a data asset for facilitating the national and the government itself by analyzing the geosocial data at real-time. However, there are millions of geosocial network users, who generates terabytes of heterogeneous data with a variety of information every day with high-speed, termed as Big Data. Analyzing such big amount of data and making real-time decisions is an inspiring task. Therefore, this book chapter discusses the exploration of geosocial networks. A system architecture is discussed and implemented in a real-time environment in order to process the abundant amount of various social network data to monitor the earth events, incidents, medical diseases, user trends, and thoughts to make future real-time decisions as well as future planning.

Chapter 8 is "Data Science: Recent Developments and Future Insights." Data Science employs techniques and theories to create data products. A data product is merely a data application that acquires its value from the data itself, and creates more data as a result; it's not just an application with data. Data science involves the methodical study of digital data employing techniques of observation, development, analysis, testing and validation. It tackles the real-time challenges by adopting a holistic approach. It 'creates' knowledge about large and dynamic bases, 'develops' methods to manage data and 'optimizes' processes to improve its performance. The goal includes vital investigation and innovation in conjunction with functional exploration intended to notify decision-making for individuals, businesses, and governments. This chapter discusses the emergence of Data Science and its subsequent developments in the fields of Data Mining and Data Warehousing. The research focuses on need, challenges, impact, ethics and progress of Data Science. Finally, the insights of the subsequent phases in research and development of Data Science is provided.

Chapter 9 is "Data Science and Computational Biology." Data Science and Computational biology is an interdisciplinary program that brings together the domain specific knowledge of science and engineering with relevant areas of computing and bioinformatics. Data science has the potential to revolution the healthcare, and respond to the increasing volume and complexity of biomedical and bioinformatics data. From genomics to clinical records, from imaging to mobile health and personalized medicine, the data volume in biomedical research presents urgent challenges for computer science. This chapter elevates the researchers in what way data science play important role in Computational Biology such as Bio-molecular

Computation, Computational Photonics, Medical Imaging, Scientific Computing, Structural Biology, Bioinformatics and Bio-Computing, etc. Big data analytics of biological data bases, high performance computing in a large sequence of genome database and Scientific Visualization are also discussed in this chapter.

Chapter 10 is "After Cloud: In Hypothetical World." It is just now at the top of an aggregation point of globalization's era in terms of things and living creatures. And the communication methods including in many sorts of transfers like commodity, facility, information, system, thought, knowledge, human, etc. may cause many kinds of and many types of interactions among us. And those many kinds of and many types of interactions have been again causing many sorts of problems. Under these situations, Cloud has come out as a smart solution to these problems. However, "Cloud is the final ultimate solution to offer to these problems' solving?" On this chapter, this question is deeply concerned from various aspects. And it is studied in this regard for getting a new paradigm.

Chapter 11 is "Cloud-Based Big Data Analytics in Smart Educational System." In this modern Digital era, Technology is a key player in transforming the educational pedagogy for the benefit of students and society at large. Technology in the classroom allows the teacher to deliver more personalized learning to the student with better interaction through the internet. A humongous amount of digital data collected day by day increases has led to the use of big data. It helps to correlate the performance and learning pattern of individual students by analyzing a large amount of stored activity of the students, offering worthwhile feedback etc. The use of big data analytics in a cloud environment helps in providing an instant infrastructure with low cost, accessibility, usability, etc. This chapter presents an innovative means towards providing a smarter educational system in schools. It improves individual efficiency by providing a way to monitor the progress of individual student by maintaining a detailed profile. This framework has been established in a cloud environment which is an online learning system where the usage pattern of individual students is collected.

REFERENCES

Arel, I., Rose, D. C., & Karnowski, T. P. (2010). Deep machine learning-A new frontier in artificial intelligence research. *IEEE Comput Intell*, *5*(4), 13–18. doi:10.1109/MCI.2010.938364

Domingos, P. (2012). A few useful things to know about machine learning. *Communications of the ACM*, 55.

Hinton, G., Deng, L., Yu, D., Mohamed, A.-R., Jaitly, N., Senior, A., & Kingsbury, B. et al. (2012). Deep neural networks for acoustic modeling in speech recognition: The shared views of four research groups. *Signal Process Mag IEEE*, *29*(6), 82–97. doi:10.1109/MSP.2012.2205597

IDC. (2014). *The digital universe of opportunities: Rich data and the increasing value of the internet of things.* Retrieved from https://www.emc.com/leadership/digital-universe/2014iview/executive-summary.htm

Li, W. (2015). *Artificial intelligence laboratory.* Retrieved from https://ai.arizona.edu/sites/ai/files/resources/chen_deep_learningapril2015.pptx

SINTEF. (2013). Retrieved from https://www.sciencedaily.com/releases/3013/05/130522085217.html

Acknowledgment

The editors would like to acknowledge the help of all the individuals involved in this project and, more specifically, to the SNS Institutions for their complete support and encouragement, authors and reviewers that took part in the review process. Without their support, this book would not have become a reality.

First, the editors would like to thank each one of the authors for their contributions. Our sincere gratitude goes to the chapter's authors who contributed their time and expertise to this book.

Second, the editors wish to acknowledge the valuable contributions of the reviewers regarding the improvement of quality, coherence, and content presentation of chapters. Most of the authors also served as referees; we highly appreciate their double task.

I would like to show my warm thank to IGI Global publications who supported me at every bit and without whom it was impossible to accomplish the end task.

S. Karthik
SNS College of Technology, Anna University, India

Anand Paul
Kyungpook National University, South Korea

N. Karthikeyan
Mizan-Tepi University, Ethiopia

Chapter 1
Advanced Threat Detection Based on Big Data Technologies

Madhvaraj M. Shetty
Mangalore University, India

Manjaiah D. H.
Mangalore University, India

ABSTRACT

Today constant increase in number of cyber threats apparently shows that current countermeasures are not enough to defend it. With the help of huge generated data, big data brings transformative potential for various sectors. While many are using it for better operations, some of them are noticing that it can also be used for security by providing broader view of vulnerabilities and risks. Meanwhile, deep learning is coming up as a key role by providing predictive analytics solutions. Deep learning and big data analytics are becoming two high-focus of data science. Threat intelligence becoming more and more effective. Since it is based on how much data collected about active threats, this reason has taken many independent vendors into partnerships. In this chapter, we explore big data and big data analytics with its benefits. And we provide a brief overview of deep analytics and finally we present collaborative threat Detection. We also investigate some aspects of standards and key functions of it. We conclude by presenting benefits and challenges of collaborative threat detection.

DOI: 10.4018/978-1-5225-3015-2.ch001

INTRODUCTION

In past few years, increase in the number of network intrusions has become severe threat to the safety and privacy of computer users. Billions of malicious cyber attacks are reported in each year (Fossi et al, 2011; Wood, et al, 2012). These attacks are becoming more stealthy and advanced, driven by an "underground economy" (Fossi et al, 2008).. Today hackers not only collecting private information from the compromised nodes, but also they are using these nodes to launch attacks such as distributed denial-of-service (DDoS) attacks. As a defence to these attacks, Intrusion Detection Systems (IDS) are used widely. These systems identify intrusions by comparing observable behavior against suspicious patterns. Traditional IDSs can monitor activities on a single host or network traffic in a sub-network only. They do not have capabilities of a global view of intrusions in a network; therefore it is not effective in detecting new or unknown threats (Fung & Boutaba, 2013).

The rest of this chapter is organized as follows: firstly, provides background about cyber threats. Secondly, introduces big data with its analytics while deep learning concepts are presented thirdly. Fourthly threat detection with collaborative method explained with its benefits and challenges. Finally, the chapter conclusion is presented.

BACKGROUND

At the recent World Economic Forum (WEF) 2016, the growing number of cyber attacks was a major topic of concern. According to its 11th annual global risks report, cyber-attacks are ranked in the list of top ten threats in 140 economies ("The Global Risks" 2016). Failure in addressing and understanding these cyber attacks could affect economic sectors, national economies and global enterprises. Most of the firewall and other network-based security products provide mature and robust logging capabilities. Since the perimeter security is not enough, most of the security programs start with analyzing logs from the devices at the edge of the network. Nowadays most of the hackers of cyber conflicts are well organized with specific objectives, goals and having strong teams that are heavily funded. They are targeting information and communication systems of industrial, government, military and other private organizations. Also they are willing to use any amount of money, time to become expertise to reach their goals.

So understanding the limitations and problems of current technologies facing against advanced persistent threats (APTs) is important. APTs are significantly different from traditional attacks due to their own characteristics (Virvilis et al, 2014).

- APTs can bypass the majority of network intrusion detection systems and signature-based end points because they are using zero-day.
- The time taken by these attacks is outside the limited window of time of these detection systems due to the fact that they are generally spread over a wide period of time.
- Attackers are willing to spend significant time on focusing a particular target and explore all possible attack paths until they manage to overcome its defence.
- Attacks are highly selective. Targeted victims are selected very carefully, usually departments of an organization which are less likely to identify and report an attack and are nontechnical.
- Based on the analysis of the major APT attacks, it is observed that they are well-supported by nation-states that have significant capabilities enabled (covert physical access, manufacturing, intelligence collection) for cyber-attacks.

Due to these characteristics, present solutions of cyber security will fail to provide an effective defence against such attacks. Signature-based approach is used most widely used in intrusion detection. It is a simple testing methodology using known attack patterns where detection is based on small variations of attack patterns. But it has substantial limitations in intrusion detection systems against advanced persistent threats.

BIG DATA

Threat detection is a vision; it is the ability to discover significant action which requires immediate attention from the large number of activity across the enterprise. Today organizations are generating massive amounts of data, they can actually use those data to make intelligent security decisions and be more effective. The answers to many security questions related to user behavior, fraudulent activity, communications and security risks lie within these huge data sets (Fung & Boutaba, 2013). But multi-sources data generated from various sources such as the network, insider threats and third party vendors must be connected and correlated, then it must be analyzed to detect and mitigate threats which require high-speed analysis. The more data that is being analyzed – the more comprehensive are the results. While many companies are using big data technology to raise sales, for better operations and lower costs, at the same time many are noticing that it can also be used for security purpose by providing broader view of vulnerabilities and risks in networks (Ben-Zvi, 2016).. It can examine large amounts of data to discover hidden patterns, correlations and other insights in it.

For effective defenses against cyber-intrusions and to counter the cyber-crime wave, big data and analytics are developing more and more. With the help of big data, it is possible to identify suspicious behavior earlier by reducing the critical time between detection and remediation with faster, better, actionable security information. It provides ability to make connections between threats to create a prioritized list after analyzing massive numbers of potential security. Cyber security professionals considering proactive approach to prevent attacks with big data by connecting heterogeneous data from different sources (Wolfe, 2016).. It enables companies to preempt malicious activity on a wider and deeper scale with the help of robust risk and threat detection tools. Big data's rapid analysis capabilities on massive volume of historic information facilitate cyber-security technology to detect new threats, identify complex patterns and to develop effective responses. It provides better understanding of approaches and attack methods; in addition this analysis can be done in real time or near real-time. As a result companies able to detect new types of potential attacks before hackers succeed in committing a cyber-crime during the penetration stage. Enterprises stay ahead and respond to evolving threats by these technological developments. We can preempt tomorrow's potential cyber attack by comparing data from earlier periods to what is going on now.

So an effective big data solution able to store and analyze millions of transaction details in order to: predict/identify performance problems; detect infrastructure changes' that effect on IT reliability and performing root cause analysis.

Big Data Analytics

To improve situational awareness and information security, big data analytics can be supplemented in enterprises. For example, it can be employed to analyze log files, financial transactions and network traffic to identify suspicious activities and anomalies suspicious activities and to correlate information from multiple sources into a coherent view. Data driven information security can be used for fraud detection in banks and anomaly based intrusion detection systems. Fraud detection is one of the most visible uses for big data analytics. In forensics and intrusion detection analyzing network packets, logs and system events has been a significant problem.

Because traditional technologies fail to provide the tools to support long-term, large-scale analytics for several reasons: ("Security Intelligence with Big Data", 2016; "Big Data Working Group", 2013).

- Historical data analysis has the potential of revealing long running attack methods and identifies relapses in security over time. So organization must keep its traditional security information for longer periods of time to perform analysis.

- Since storing large amount of data was not economically feasible, as a result, most event logs and other recorded computer activity were cleared after a fixed retention period (e.g., 90 days).
- Traditional tools are inefficient in performing analytics and complex queries on large, structured data sets.
- Analyzing and managing unstructured data using traditional tools is not possible.
- Since big data system used cluster computing infrastructures, they are more reliable, and guarantees that any complex queries on the systems are processed to completion.

New technologies like stream processing and hadoop ecosystem enabled storage and analysis of large heterogeneous data sets at an unprecedented speed and scale. These big data technologies will transform security analytics by: ("Big Data Working Group", 2013).

1. Collecting data at a large scale from many external sources as well as internal sources such as vulnerability databases.
2. Conducting deeper analytics on the collected data.
3. Offering consolidated view of extracted security-related information.
4. Enabling real-time or near real-time analysis of streaming data.

Even after using predictive analytics and advanced statistical modeling, new unknown security threats still go undiscovered. Big data analytics can help to solve this problem by providing intelligence that detects potential threats and suspicious patterns by expanding the definition of security data to all parts of the business.

Benefits of Big Data Analytics

By collecting data such as network logs, DNS feed, network traffic, ip addresses big data analytics can help to wipe out cyber threats from organization, will be effective in identifying malware in earlier stages (Virvilis et al, 2014).

- Managing dynamic collection, correlation and consolidation of data from any number of data sources, such as network traffic, operating system artifacts and event data.
- Anomaly detection based on correlation of historical and recent events. For example, increase in the volume of traffic into Domain Name System (DNS) from a particular system for a small-time period can be legitimate user

actions. But, if such pattern also identified in historical traffic over a period of days, then it is a potential indication of suspicious behavior.

This ability to correlate data from a wide range of sources across significant time periods will result in a lower false-positive rate. Also allows signal of advanced persistent threat to be detected as a noise in authorized user activities. Collecting, analyzing and correlating should be completed within an acceptable time window to give the security professionals an early caution for the potential attacks against their infrastructure. Based on its capabilities, big data and its analytics can be used for following cases:

- Capturing, indexing, classifying and enriching all types of traffic data of network with threat intelligence framework.
- Continuously monitoring network for threat behaviors and suspicious activities.
- Understanding the behavior of the device in the network.
- To take immediate action against threat actor such as stopping all communications between the device and threat actor.
- Analyzing payload content.
- To detect, extract and classify suspicious or unknown files in real-time automatically.

Before big data and its analytics can be used in operational environments for the detection of advanced threats, a few obstacles need to be overcome. In particular, there is a need for new sophisticated algorithms for detection which is capable of processing massive amounts of data from multi-data sources. Additionally, there is a need to further improvement in issues related to storage and processing performance, collecting information from untrustworthy sources, meaningful visualization of information, time synchronization and ensuring the security of sensitive indicators of compromise, among others. At present, part of developments has been done that shows promising results by utilizing big data analytics for security event. To create robust solutions that can address the multidimensional problem of APT, research on this field needs to be intensified (Virvilis et al, 2014).

DEEP ANALYTICS

In all shapes and sizes, digital data is growing at incredible rates. According to National Security Agency (NSA), in each day the internet is processing 1,826 petabytes of data ("National Security Agency", 2013). Digital information has grown nine times in size in just five years in 2011 (Gantz & Reinsel, 2001) and size of the data in world will reach 35 trillion gigabytes by 2020 (Gantz & Reinsel, 2010). In the rapidly growing digital world, big data and deep learning are two hottest trends. Big data has been referred as a tool to manage and analyze digital data with exponential growth and wide availability that are impossible or difficult using conventional technologies and software tools. Deep learning refers to a set of techniques from machine learning that learn representations from deep architectures in multiple (Chen & Lin, 2014). Deep learning algorithms are one promising approach of research in automated extraction of complex data representations/features at high levels of abstraction. These algorithms develop hierarchical, layered architecture of learning and representing data, where lower-level features are used to represent higher-level features (Bengio, LeCun, 2007; Arel, Rose, Karnowski, 2010).

Deep learning has the potential to solve any challenging questions in artificial intelligence and machine learning. Deep analytics facilitate better performance and decision-making by supporting meaningful analysis of data from business events to everyday customer interactions, no matter the source. It is the application of advanced data processing methodologies that analyzes, extracts targeted information from large data sets which is multi-source data that contain not only structured data but also unstructured/semi-structured data, often with requirements for real-time or near-real-time responses. It offers complete suite of products for monitoring, analysis, web mapping, visualization and delivering an unprecedented scope of information to its users with required competitive intelligence. Deep analytics conducted by some sectors such as scientific community, financial sector and the pharmaceutical/biomedical industries for some years with good outcome. In recent years, as the amount of corporate data generated has been increased and desire to extract business value from that data the practice of analytics has become increasingly common within the enterprise.

Relative to other machine learning techniques, deep learning has four key advantages: (Amabati, 2016).

- Its ability to work with unlabeled data.
- Its ability to learn low-level features from minimally processed raw data.
- Its ability to detect complex interactions among features.
- Its ability to work with high-cardinality class memberships.

Deep learning analytics can be used in (Amabati, 2016) payment systems to identify suspicious transactions in real time and to analyze large data centers in organizations large. Also it can be used to mine log files and detect threats in any computer networks. Banks can seek better fraud protection with deep analytics.

Behavioral Analytics

Behavioral analytics (Ambati, 2016) is very important fraud detection tool which is increasingly used. For example, in banks behavioral analytics can continuously monitor activity across multiple channels to detect and suspect banking fraud and to respond more quickly by focusing on the observed characteristics of bank customers. Bank can alert the customer about the suspicious activity and block further transactions if the transaction of a customer is outside typical behavior, such as large number of transactions in a short period of time or expensive purchase, etc. Beyond examining number of transaction or frequency of transaction, behavioral analytics can also examine how users behave when using an mobile or online account. These tools can verify pattern at which users are navigating the site, entering input data and consistency in entering information, etc. It can also check for identical behavior pattern across multiple accounts. For example, a group of account holders making identical transactions could indicate a distributed attack on the system. Since fraudster uses each account only a few times, these attacks are invisible to traditional monitoring, but using analytics we can spot the related transactions across multiple accounts.

Graph Analytics

In graph analytics ("Effective Fraud" 2016) data is mapped to objects or nodes, and then the edges or a connection between these objects/nodes has been plotted. It also provides a visual representation of data from internal and external sources between any numbers of nodes. By visualizing data in this manner, it enables companies or banks to recognize relationships quickly that could indicate fraud.

COLLABORATIVE THREAT DETECTION

By its nature, threat intelligence gets more and more effective based on how much data it is able to collect about the active threats. But there is no single entity can be sure about collecting and processing all the intelligence related to cyber threats that is hidden or circulating out there on the internet. This reason has taken many independent vendors of security into partnerships, to get more value and benefit by gathering pieces of information about the malicious actors and threats that are exist in the internet. This collaboration of security vendors leads to more comprehensive and effective cyber security and can greatly benefit threat intelligence system. This is at beginning level of collaboration and it will be moved to highest level. It is a cooperative process; ability to coordinate two or more different resources to complete a goal.

Collaboration is the reasonable choice and effective control for cyber threat intelligence. Since it is a goal comprising multiple independent resources, it can greatly improve the efficiency of the implementation (Ma & Wang, 2013).. In order to counter attacks in government sectors and organizations, they must collaborate each other by sharing security intelligence. To be feasible at scale, it needs a system that allows organizations to collaborate and share threat intelligence information in a confidential, secure and timely manner. Then organizations able to respond quickly and effectively while detecting and identifying cyber threats. This research and open collaboration can help organizations to avoid falling to certain attacks which other organizations have already experienced. In addition to this, while sharing details of an attack, same platform can also be used to distribute the effort of analyzing evidence once they are developed. In some cases, better security intelligence can gathered by combining information from multiple organizations that cannot be obtained from individual organization ("Collaborative Defense, 2015).

In a distributed system, collaboration is an important method to ensure that the resource can be shared among entities and the services can accessed one another in the system. It is also an important technique for solving any complex problem. In particular to threat detection architecture, it means multiple independent detection systems can work together; they can get information as well as carry out operations that they cannot do by themselves independently. So collaboration can guide the overall situation, refine the information, and thus achieving faster and better detection results ("Collaborative Defense" 2015). Organizations belonging to the similar sectors (e.g., financial organizations) typically face from the same type of cyber crimes. Sharing and correlating such information about those could help others in detecting those crimes and mitigating the damages at early stages.

But architecture of collaboration needs certain requirements to be successful (Locasto, et al 2005):

- The exchange of information should not leak any potentially sensitive data.
- Large alert rates may hide stealthy activity; so reasonable solution required to reduce the effects of these rates.
- Centralized repositories are single points of failure and likely to fail in correlating the growing amount of alerts.
- Exchanging alerts in a complex network may increase the complexity of the problem, so it requires good management.
- Requires solution for partitioning data among nodes about threat information by disassociating evidence that considered in the same context.

Standards/Specifications for Cyber Information Sharing

Standardizing threat information is very important in this context. Defining fields, content and objects want to share when the incident occurred is bound to causes errors if it is without any standards or specifications. This is where the Cyber Observable Expression (CybOX), Trusted Automated Exchange of Indicator Information (TAXII) and Structured Threat Information Expression (STIX) come into picture ("Information Sharing" 2016; "Stix, Taxii" 2016). They are open community-driven technical specifications designed for real-time network defense, sophisticated threat analysis and to enable automated sharing for cybersecurity situational awareness. They allow cyberthreat information to be represented in a standardized format. They are standards that software can follow, not any pieces of software itself.

1. **TAXII:** It is a set of standards for exchanging cyberthreat information to help organizations share information with their partners. It does not define trust agreements and it is not an information sharing program.
2. **CybOX:** It is a standardized schema for the specification, characterization, capture, and communication of events that are observable in all system and network operations. CybOX objects can be a network connection that is established toward a specific address, email message that is received from a specific address, the MD5 hash of a file, a URI or the modification of a registry key, or a process. It can be used for threat assessment, malware characterization, log management, incident response, intrusion detection/prevention and in digital forensics.
3. **STIX:** Similar to TAXII, it is not a tool for sharing, but rather a component that supports programs or tools. It is a language for having a standardized communication for the representation of cyberthreat information. It has number of components.

Key Functions of Cyber Information Sharing and Analysis

For effective cyber information sharing and analysis, it is important to understand the various key functions required ("Health Industry" 2015). The Figure 1 identifies the key components.

1. **Collection:** In order to aggregate cyber threat information, organizations must have the ability to submit them securely and efficiently in a variety of standardized methods and formats such as STIX, TAXII, online portal, custom APIs.

Figure 1. Key functions of cyber information sharing and analysis

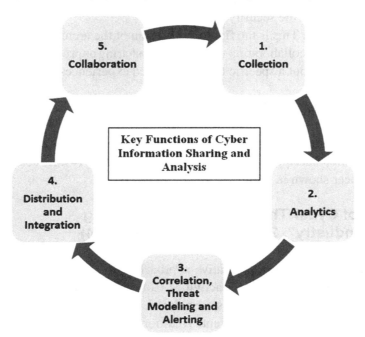

2. **Analytics:** This part takes the threat information collected and reviews them for completeness and other criteria to evaluate the probability of the threat, whereby providing highly reliable IOCs. This allows easy prioritization when it comes to assessing which threats need to be processed first and enables high quality data set to be maintained. A high false positive rate will be experienced without applying analytics to the data collected. In order to understand the magnitude of the threat, third party context and streamline analyst workflow is added to the intelligence ensuring that an analyst has enough information regarding the threat and that the IOCs are actionable.

3. **Correlation, Threat Modeling, and Alerting:** Threat modeling provides information related insights into the adversaries behind ongoing campaigns along with the general tactics they used for compromising targets. The threat correlation provides a vision on relationships between different threat model components. The alerting system assists cyber professionals with a warning that an adversary is attempting to access, is targeting the system or has already accessed organization's infrastructure.

4. **Distribution and Integration:** Organization's existing security infrastructure can be acted upon any attacks if there is timely and effective consumption of

information stored. So at minimum, TAXII, STIX and SIEM integration should be supported by the security system.

5. **Collaboration:** This is the final key function of the architecture which refers to the ability of collaborating with peers and sharing approaches, strategies and experiences about a specific threat or related experiences in secure manner.

Information Sharing Architectures

Most sharing communities exchange information using some variant of the following basic information sharing architectures (Johnson, et al, 2014): (i) centralized; and (ii) peer-to-peer shown in Figure 2.

Benefits of Cyber Threat Intelligence Sharing ("Health Industry", 2015; Johnson et al, 2014)

The main advantage of a collaborative approach in intrusion detection system is better view of global network attack activities. Collecting more and more information gathered at a single site from across the network can provide a more precise model of an attacker's behavior and his intent. Traditional IDS's are generally constrained within one domain of administrative. So in such environment, information about the global state of attack patterns is unexamined. So by collaboration, this global information can support organizations in ranking and addressing threats that they do perceive. And alerting other organizations about that threats which would not recognized before.

*   **Improved Cyber Situational Awareness:** Information sharing enables organizations to collect knowledge, experiences, and analytic capabilities from their sharing partners. Thereby enhancing the defensive capabilities

Figure 2. Information sharing architectures

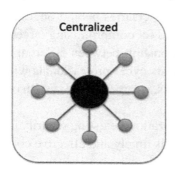
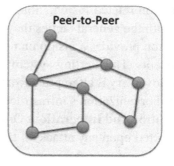

of both organizations. Each member in the community can profit from the experience and knowledge of other community members.

- **Enhanced Understanding of Cyber Threats:** By sharing threat intelligence information, organizations gain more understanding about the threat environment and are able to design and deploy countermeasures, security controls, corrective actions and detection methods, based on the changes observed in the threat environment.

- **Cyber Threat Correlation:** When raw intelligence data in the form of apparently unrelated observations is shared and analyzed, it can be correlated with other remaining data sets to build robust sets of information that are associated with a specific incident or threat.

- **Greater Defensive Agility:** As technology advances, adversaries continually adapt their TTPs to counter the protective and detective measures implemented by network defenders. So organizations that possess the ability to detect and respond to changes rapidly, can shift from reactive to proactive cyber security strategies.

- **Improved Decision Making:** In general organizations that consume and act based on shared information are able to make decisions with greater confidence and speed. When strategies of adversaries are understood better, it is possible to predict their actions and deploy defensive measures before they act.

- **Efficient Handling of Information Requests:** When investigating or reporting cyber security incidents that is criminal in nature, information sharing is essential. Because organizations that have tools, processes and trained team in place to exchange information are better trained to handle such information requests. Ensuring that artifacts and the computers involved in the incident are treated as evidence and should be handled in a proper manner.

- **Rapid Notifications:** When a cyber crime event occurs, the incident results in releasing information about another victim, so organizations are required to notify their business partners or affected customers. Organizations that understand their requirements of notification and have contact information, notification procedures and communications channels in place are able to rapidly broadcast breach notifications to business partners or affected customers.

Challenges for Collaboration

While there are many benefits of sharing information, there are also a number of challenges to effective sharing and collaboration that must be addressed. These problems must be addressed before collaborative system can safely distributed among cooperating sites (Johnson, 2014; "Collaborative Information", 2014).

- **Lack of Circles of Trust:** Everyone agrees to exchange but nobody trusts anybody. There is a clear lack of confidence, so trust building is essential, so that future systems should facilitate the exchange of data at different levels of confidence. Trust relationships form the basis for information sharing, but it can be time consuming to establish.
- **Lack of Interoperable Standards:** Standardized transport protocols and data formats can help to facilitate the secure, automated exchange of incident data between organizations, repositories and tools. But agreement on protocols and formats requires careful analysis of benefits and costs. Meanwhile each organization has tried to impose its own format which leads to lack of agility and inefficiency in the system. As far as cyber threats are concerned, the industrial community is working on the reporting format and standards like STIX, IOCs, Cybox, etc. that will solve the problem of standards.
- **Limitation of Information Sources:** When we have multiple sources, it is important to know where to look for information. It is even more important to know how to analyze and correlate it. Hence collaboration of cyber threat intelligence must facilitate the exchange of information from global and specific sources. It is essential to obtain a larger volume of first-class information (freshness), so it will be useful in battling against cybercrime.
- **Lack of Skills:** The shared information may only and specifically for a sector (industrial, financial, critical infrastructure, etc) but it should be considered by all the other agents of different industries and be able to provide analysis to learn from experience.
- **Legal and Organizational Restrictions:** In an organization, the legal terms may restrict the types of information that the organization can share with others. It may include limits on the types of information and the level of technical detail can be provided. Such restrictions are may be appropriate when they are addressing legitimate legal or privacy concerns; but same restrictions may diminish the quality and timeliness of shared information.
- **Risk of Information Leakage:** Information about the hacker's strategies is useful for a network defender but sharing this information it may put into risk by exposing the detective or protective capabilities of the organization which results in shifting threat by the hacker. Additionally, disclosure of sensitive information, such as Personally Identifiable Information (PII), trade secrets, intellectual property or other proprietary information can result in financial loss, loss of reputation, violation of sharing agreements, legal action.

- **Preserving Privacy:** Organizations can openly participate in information sharing system, but it still requires that their contributions remain anonymous and preserves its privacy.
- **Producing and Consuming Information:** Organizations looking for producing threat information must have the necessary tools, infrastructure and training to do so. It must also have the infrastructure needed to access external sources.
- **Challenges in Validating Data Quality and Reliability:** Organizations must validate data they have generated about threat intelligence before storing and sharing it with other parties, and also they must look up for the data reliability.

Some Existing Collaborative Models

IBM X-Force Exchange

The IBM X-Force Exchange ("IBM X-Force", 2016) built by IBM Security, is a new cloud-based platform that allows organizations to easily collaborate on security incidents, as well as benefit from the ongoing contributions of IBM experts and community members. This platform provides access to volumes of actionable IBM and third-party threat data from across the globe, including real-time indicators of live attacks, which can be used to defend against cybercrimes. The X-Force Exchange builds on IBM's tremendous scale in security intelligence, integrating its powerful portfolio of deep threat research data and technologies, thousands of global clients, and worldwide network of security analysts and experts from IBM managed security services. Leveraging the open and powerful infrastructure of the cloud, users can collaborate and tap into multiple data sources.

McAfee Threat Intelligence Exchange

McAfee Threat Intelligence Exchange ("McAfee Threat" 2016), which aggregates and shares file reputation intelligence across the entire security infrastructure. McAfee Threat Intelligence Exchange receives threat information from McAfee GTI, STIX file imports, threat feeds coming via McAfee Enterprise Security Manager, and information coming from endpoint, mobile devices, application control, gateway, sandboxing technologies, data centers and from both Intel Security solutions and solutions from other vendors. Collecting data from all points in infrastructure provides information on threats that may be present only in environment, as many targeted attacks tend to be. In addition, this file reputation information is instantly shared across the entire ecosystem to all products and solutions connected to McAfee

Threat Intelligence Exchange via the McAfee Data Exchange Layer. This includes data classifications, file reputations, application integrity, and user context data. Any product or solution can be integrated onto the McAfee Data Exchange Layer and after that it is configured to determine what data to publish to their system and what data to listen, subscribe from the system.

ThreatExchange

This is new collaborative threat-detection framework by Facebook ("Threat Exchange", 2016), with its participants such as Twitter, Yahoo, Tumblr, Pinterest, Box and Bitly, among others. It works like an online hub where multiple organizations can sign up and store data pertaining to the types of hacks and malicious activities they have experienced. This data includes malicious URLs, bad domains, malware and any sort of analytical data related to any type of malware. Once all information is collected, Facebook's graph-database technology can correlate all the data points together and figure out new relationships, such as which malware seems to be talking to a particular domain or if a domain happens to be hosted on a bad IP address. The aim of the project is straightforward: to allow any business or IT professional who is interested in current and potential cyber attacks to review and contribute any information they may have related to current attacks or other potential cyber threats. It can be used by subscribed users to work with the information for any legitimate purpose, including research and prevention of attacks.

These exchanges of cyber threat information can improve response time by making threat intelligence more widely available to more players. Even automating sharing processes can further quicken response times.

CONCLUSION

Undoubtedly, fraud incidents and security breaches will continue to make headlines. Even though organizations are considering steps to address APTs and other attacks, the fact remains same that traditional security has lack of advanced capabilities to detect and protect against such attacks. With the help of huge generated data, big data brings transformative potential and big opportunities for various sectors. Deep learning and big data analytics are becoming two high-focus of data science today. By utilizing big data, threat intelligence with collaboration, organizations can preempt malicious activity on a wider and deeper scale with the help of robust risk and threat detection tools. But analytics such as big data and deep analytics currently faces a number of practical limitations and further research is needed for building an operational solution. Research on deep learning needed for further exploration to incorporate specific challenges introduced by big data analytics, including high-dimensional data, streaming data, scalability of models and distributed computing.

REFERENCES

Ambati, S. (2016). Deep learning: A brief guide for practical problem solvers. *InfoWorld*. Retrieved 26 June 2016, from http://www.infoworld.com/article/3003315/big-data/deep-learning-a-brief-guide-for-practical-problem-solvers.html.html

Arel, I., Rose, D. C., & Karnowski, T. P. (2010). Deep machine learning-a new frontier in artificial intelligence research [research frontier]. *IEEE Comput Intell*, 5(4), 13–18. doi:10.1109/MCI.2010.938364

Ben-Zvi, G. (2016). Big data to the Rescue? Cyber Attacks Rank as Major Global Threat in 2016 - SQream. *SQream*. Retrieved 26 June 2016, from http://sqream.com/big-data-to-the-rescue-cyber-attacks-rank-as-major-global-threat-in-2016/

Bengio, Y., & LeCun, Y. (2007). Scaling learning algorithms towards, AI. In L. Bottou, O. Chapelle, D. DeCoste, & J. Weston (Eds.), Large Scale Kernel Machines (Vol. 34, pp. 321–360). Cambridge, MA: MIT Press. Retrieved from http://www.iro.umontreal.ca/~lisa/pointeurs/bengio+lecun_chapter2007.pdf

Big Data Working Group. (2013). *Big data analytics for security intelligence*. Cloud Security Alliance.

Chen, X. W., & Lin, X. (2014). Big data deep learning: Challenges and perspectives. *IEEE Access*, 2, 514–525. doi:10.1109/ACCESS.2014.2325029

Collaborative Defense Enriched by Dynamic Analysis. (2015). Business white paper | Collaborative Defense Enriched by Dynamic Analysis, Threat Central, developed with HP Labs.

Collaborative Information Exchange Models to Fight Cyber Threats. (2016). Retrieved 26 June 2016, from https://www.blueliv.com/corporate/the-use-of-social-media-models-in-the-fight-against-cyber-threats/

Effective fraud protection relies on deep analytics. (2016). *IBM Big data & Analytics Hub*. Retrieved 26 June 2016, from http://www.ibmbigdatahub.com/blog/effective-fraud-protection-relies-deep-analytics

Fossi, Egan, Haley, Johnson, Mack, Adams, … McKinney. (2011). *Symantec internet security threat report trends for 2010*. Symantec.

Fossi, M., Johnson, E., Turner, D., Mack, T., Blackbird, J., McKinney, D., & Gough, J. et al. (2008). *Symantec report on the underground economy: July 2007 to June 2008. Technical Report*. Symantec Corporation.

Fung, C. J., & Boutaba, R. (2013, May). Design and management of collaborative intrusion detection networks. In *2013 IFIP/IEEE International Symposium on Integrated Network Management (IM 2013)* (pp. 955-961). IEEE.

Gantz & Reinsel. (2011). *Extracting Value from Chaos*. Hopkinton, MA: EMC.

Gantz & Reinsel. (2010). *The Digital Universe Decade: Are You Ready*. Hopkinton, MA: EMC.

Health Industry Cyber Threat Information Sharing and Analysis, Annual Review of HITRUST Cyber Threat XChange (CTX) -Summary of Findings and Recommendations, Public Discussion Document. (n.d.). Retrieved from www. HITRUSTalliance.net

IBM X-Force Exchange. (2016). Retrieved 26 June 2016, from http://www-03.ibm.com/software/products/en/xforce-exchange

Information Sharing Specifications for Cybersecurity I US-CERT. (2016). Retrieved 26 June 2016, from https://www.us-cert.gov/Information-Sharing-Specifications-Cybersecurity

Johnson, C., Badger, L., & Waltermire, D. (2014). *Guide to cyber threat information sharing* (draft). NIST Special Publication 800-150 (Draft).

Locasto, M. E., Parekh, J. J., Keromytis, A. D., & Stolfo, S. J. (2005, June). Towards collaborative security and p2p intrusion detection. In *Proceedings from the Sixth Annual IEEE SMC Information Assurance Workshop* (pp. 333-339). IEEE.

Ma, D., & Wang, Y. (2013). Network Threat Behavior Detection and Trend Analysis Based on the TDLC Model. *SmartCR*, *3*(4), 285–297. doi:10.6029/smartcr.2013.04.007

McAfee Threat Intelligence Exchange I Intel Security Products. (2016). Retrieved 26 June 2016, from http://www.mcafee.com/in/products/threat-intelligence-exchange.aspx

National Security Agency. (2013). *The National Security Agency: Missions, Authorities, Oversight and Partnerships*. Available: http://www.nsa.gov/public_info/__les/speeches_testimonies/2013_08_09_the_nsa_story.pdf

Security Intelligence With Big Data: What You Need to Know. (2013). *Security Intelligence*. Retrieved 26 June 2016, from https://securityintelligence.com/security-intelligence-with-big-data-what-you-need-to-know/

STIX, TAXII and CybOX Can Help With Standardizing Threat Information. (2015). *Security Intelligence*. Retrieved 26 June 2016, from https://securityintelligence.com/how-stix-taxii-and-cybox-can-help-with-standardizing-threat-information/

The Global Risks Report 2016, 11th Edition, Insight Report. (2016). World Economic Forum, REF: 080116.

Threat Exchange | Threat Exchange - Facebook for Developers. (2016). *Facebook Developers*. Retrieved 26 June 2016, from https://developers.facebook.com/products/threat-exchange

Virvilis, N., Serrano, O., & Dandurand, L. (2014). Big data analytics for sophisticated attack detection. *ISACA Journal*, *3*, 22–25.

Wolfe, T. (2016). 6 Tips for Using Big data to Hunt Cyberthreats. *Dark Reading*. Retrieved 26 June 2016, from http://www.darkreading.com/analytics/6-tips-for-using-big-data-to-hunt-cyberthreats/a/d-id/1278970

Wood, Nisbet, Egan, Johnston, Haley, Krishnappa, … Hittel. (2012). *Symantec internet security threat report trends for 2011*. Symantec.

Chapter 2
A Brief Review on Deep Learning and Types of Implementation for Deep Learning

Uthra Kunathur Thikshaja
Kyungpook National University, South Korea

Anand Paul
Kyungpook National University, South Korea

ABSTRACT

In recent years, there's been a resurgence in the field of Artificial Intelligence and deep learning is gaining a lot of attention. Deep learning is a branch of machine learning based on a set of algorithms that can be used to model high-level abstractions in data by using multiple processing layers with complex structures, or otherwise composed of multiple non-linear transformations. Estimation of depth in a Neural Network (NN) or Artificial Neural Network (ANN) is an integral as well as complicated process. These methods have dramatically improved the state-of-the-art in speech recognition, visual object recognition, object detection and many other domains such as drug discovery and genomics. This chapter describes the motivations for deep architecture, problem with large networks, the need for deep architecture and new implementation techniques for deep learning. At the end, there is also an algorithm to implement the deep architecture using the recursive nature of functions and transforming them to get the desired output.

DOI: 10.4018/978-1-5225-3015-2.ch002

INTRODUCTION

The increase in demand for organizing the data and analyzing them is mainly due to the abundance in the raw data generated by social network users. Not all the data generated are linear and hence the single perceptron layer network or the linear classifier as it is popularly known, cannot be used for data classification. No hidden layers are required when we have a linearly separable data. In most other cases, one hidden layer is enough for a majority of problems. In few problems, two hidden layers are used for full generality in multilayer perceptrons. But lots of random initializations or other methods for global optimization are required. Local minima with two hidden layers can have extreme blades or spikes even when the number of weights is much smaller than the number of training cases (Panchal, 2011). Deep learning is a new AI trend that uses multi-layer perceptron network. Multilayer sensor containing multiple hidden layers is a deep learning structure. Deep learning architecture is a good way to extract feature, it can be used for specific issues of classification, regression, information retrieval, speech recognition, visual object recognition, object detection and many other domains such as drug discovery and genomics.

Motivation for Deep Architecture

There are three main reasons for us to have a deep network. The first one is that insufficient depth can hurt, i.e. when the depth is two, the number of nodes in the flow graph (used for representing deep architecture) may grow very large. Theoretical studies (Hastad's theorems) have shown that the order of complexity in O (n) for depth d and O (2^n) for depth d-1.

The next reason is that, the human brain itself has a deep architecture. The visual cortex is well-studied and shows a sequence of areas each of which contains a representation of the input, and signals flow from one to the next. Each level of this feature hierarchy represents the input at a different level of abstraction, with more abstract features further up in the hierarchy, defined in terms of the lower-level ones.

The last motivation for a deep architecture is that cognitive processes are deep. Humans organize their ideas and concepts hierarchically. Humans first learn simpler concepts and then compose them to build more abstract ones. Engineers break up solutions into multiple levels of abstraction and processing.

Problems With Large Networks

Increasing the depth decreases the complexity. However, there are also problems associated (Vasilev, 2015). when the number of hidden layers is increased (depth). The first one is the Vanishing Gradients. This is a problem when the transfer of data from output layer through the hidden layers to the input layer becomes more and more difficult as the number of hidden layers is increased. This concept is called back propagation. Another important concern is Over-fitting. It is the phenomenon of fitting the training data too closely. The training data may be fitted really close and good, but these will fail badly in real cases. Scientists came up with several architectures to overcome the above mentioned problems. The upcoming sections describe some of the most common deep learning methods in use.

Deep Learning Methods

Autoencoders

An autoencoder is typically a feedforward neural network which aims to learn a compressed, distributed representation (encoding) of a dataset. Conceptually, the network is trained to "recreate" the input, i.e. the input and the target data are the same. In other words, we are trying to output the same thing that was provided as the input, but compressed in some way.

Restricted Boltzmann Machines (RBM)

Restricted Boltzmann Machines is a generative stochastic neural network that can learn a probability distribution over its set of inputs. RBMs are composed of a hidden, visible, and bias layer. Unlike the feedforward networks, the connections between the visible and hidden layers are undirected (the values can be propagated in both the visible-to-hidden and hidden-to-visible directions) and fully connected.

Figure 1. Representation of a basic autoencoder

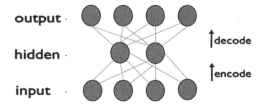

Figure 2. Restricted Boltzmann Machine

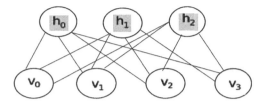

Training RBM Using Contrastive Divergence

Contrastive Divergence

Markov chain Monte Carlo methods typically take a long time to converge on unbiased estimates, but Hinton (2002) showed that if the Markov chain is only run for a few steps, the learning can still work well and it approximately minimizes a different function called "contrastive divergence" (CD). CD learning has been successfully applied to various types of random fields.

RBM and Contrastive Divergence

RBMs have connections only between the hidden and the visible layer. Boltzmann Machines (BMs) are a particular form of log-linear Markov Random Field (MRF), i.e., for which the energy function is linear in its free parameters. To make them powerful enough to represent complicated distributions (i.e., go from the limited parametric setting to a non-parametric one), we consider that some of the variables are never observed (they are called hidden). By having more hidden variables (also called hidden units), we can increase the modeling capacity of the Boltzmann Machine (BM). Restricted Boltzmann Machines further restrict BMs to those without visible-visible and hidden-hidden connections.

The energy function $E(v,h)$ of an RBM is defined as:

$$E(v,h) = -b'v - c'h - h'Wv$$

where W represents the weights connecting hidden and visible units and b, c are the offsets of the visible and hidden layers respectively.

This translates directly to the following free energy formula:

$$F(v) = -b'v - \sum_i \log \sum_{h_i} e^{h_i(c_i + W_i v)}$$

Because of the specific structure of RBMs, visible and hidden units are conditionally independent given one-another. Using this property, we can write:

$$p(h \mid v) = \prod_i p(h_i \mid v)$$
$$p(v \mid h) = \prod_j p(v_j \mid h)$$

The single step contrastive divergence algorithm works as follows (Vasilev, 2015):

1. **Positive Phase:** An input sample v is clamped to the input layer. v is propagated to the hidden layer in a similar manner to the feedforward networks. The result of the hidden layer activations is h.
2. **Negative Phase:** Propagate h back to the visible layer with result v' (the connections between the visible and hidden layers are undirected and thus allow movement in both directions). Propagate the new v' back to the hidden layer with activations result h'.
3. **Weight Update:** $w(t+1) = w(t) + a(vh^T - v'h'^T)$ where A is the learning rate and *v, v', h, h'*, and *w* are vectors. The intuition behind the algorithm is that the positive phase (*h* given *v*) reflects the network's internal representation of the *real world* data. Meanwhile, the negative phase represents an attempt to recreate the data based on this internal representation (*v'* given *h*). The main goal is for the *generated data* to be as close as possible to the *real world* and this is reflected in the weight update formula.

Figure 3. Stacked encoders

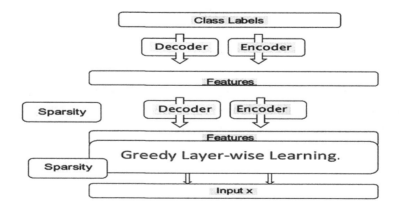

Stacked Autoencoders

This network consists of multiple stacked autoencoders. The hidden layer of autoencoder t acts as an input layer to autoencoder t + 1. The input layer of the first autoencoder is the input layer for the whole network. The greedy layer-wise training procedure works like this:

Train the first autoencoder but with an additional output layer individually using the backpropagation method with all available training data.

Train the second autoencoder t=2. Since the input layer for t=2 is the hidden layer oft=1 we are no longer interested in the output layer of t=1 and we remove it from the network. Training begins by clamping an input sample to the input layer of t=1, which is propagated forward to the output layer of t=2. Next, the weights (input-hidden and hidden-output) of t=2 are updated using backpropagation. t=2 uses all the training samples, similar to t=1.

Repeat the previous procedure for all the layers (i.e., remove the output layer of the previous autoencoder, replace it with yet another autoencoder, and train with back propagation).

Steps 1-3 are called pre-training and leave the weights properly initialized. However, there's no mapping between the input data and the output labels. For example, if the network is trained to recognize images of handwritten digits it's still not possible to map the units from the last feature detector (i.e., the hidden layer of the last autoencoder) to the digit type of the image. In that case, the most common solution is to add one or more fully connected layer(s) to the last layer. The whole network can now be viewed as a multilayer perceptron and is trained using backpropagation (this step is also called fine-tuning).

Convolution Neural Networks

A Convolutional Neural Network (CNN) is comprised of one or more convolutional layers (often with a subsampling step) and then followed by one or more fully connected layers as in a standard multilayer neural network. The architecture of a CNN is designed to take advantage of the 2D structure of an input image (or other 2D input such as a speech signal). There are four key ideas behind Convolution Nets that take advantage of the properties of natural signals: local connections, shared weights, pooling and the use of many layers (Cun et al, 2015). Another benefit of CNNs is that they are easier to train and have many fewer parameters than fully connected networks with the same number of hidden units.

Figure 4. Image classification using a Convolutional Neural Network

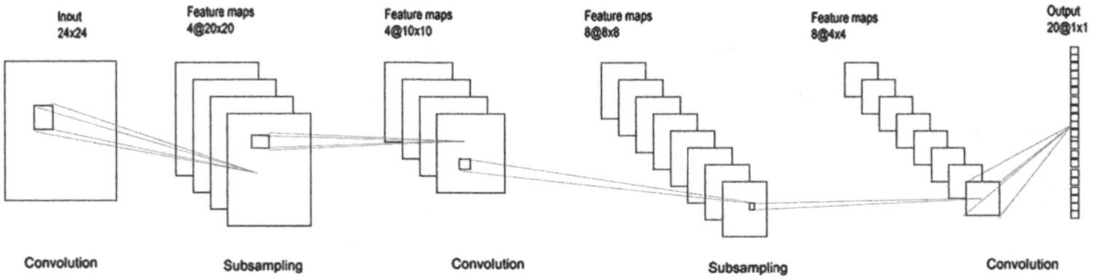

CNN Properties

Convolutional layers apply a number of filters to the input. The input to a convolutional layer is an m x m x r image where m is the height and width of the image and r is the number of channels, e.g. an RGB image has r=3. The convolutional layer will have k filters (or kernels) of size n x n x q where n is smaller than the dimension of the image and q can either be the same as the number of channels r or smaller and may vary for each kernel. Subsampling layers reduce the size of the input. The last subsampling (or convolutional) layer is usually connected to one or more fully connected layers, the last of which represents the target data. Training is performed using modified backpropagation that takes the subsampling layers into account and updates the convolutional filter weights based on all values to which that filter is applied.

Architecture

A CNN consists of a number of convolutional and subsampling layers optionally followed by fully connected layers. The convolutional and pooling layers in Convolution Nets are directly inspired by the classic notions of simple cells and complex cells in visual neuroscience (Hubel & Wiesel, 1962). The input to a convolutional layer is an m x m x r image where m is the height and width of the image and r is the number of channels, e.g. an RGB image has r=3. The convolutional layer will have k filters (or kernels) of size n x n x q where n is smaller than the dimension of the image and q can either be the same as the number of channels r or smaller and may vary for each kernel. The size of the filters gives rise to the locally connected structure which are each convolved with the image to produce k feature maps of size m−n+1. Each map is then subsampled typically with mean or max pooling over p x p contiguous regions where p ranges between 2 for small images (e.g. MNIST) and is usually not more than 5 for larger inputs. Either before or after the subsampling layer an additive bias and sigmoidal nonlinearity is applied to each feature map. The figure below illustrates a full layer in a CNN consisting of convolutional and subsampling sublayers. Units of the same color have tied weights. After the convolutional layers there may be any number of fully connected layers. The densely connected layers are identical to the layers in a standard multilayer neural network. Convolution Nets were also experimented with in the early 1990s for object detection in natural images, including faces and hands (Vaillant et al, 1994; Nowlan & Platt, 1995) and for face recognition (Lawrence et al, 1997).

Reasons for the architecture to be best suited for images:

1. In array data such as images, local groups of values are often highly correlated, forming distinctive local motifs that are easily detected.
2. Second, the local statistics of images and other signals are invariant to location. In other words, if a motif can appear in one part of the image, it could appear anywhere, hence the idea of units at different locations sharing the same weights and detecting the same pattern in different parts of the array.
3. Deep neural networks exploit the property that many natural signals are compositional hierarchies, in which higher-level features are obtained by composing lower-level ones. In images, local combinations of edges form motifs, motifs assemble into parts, and parts form objects. Similar hierarchies exist in speech and text from sounds to phones, phonemes, syllables, words and sentences (Cun et al, 2015).

Recurrent Neural Networks

The idea behind RNNs is to make use of sequential information. Thanks to advances in their architecture (Hochreiter & Schmidhuber, 1997; ElHihi & Bengio, 1995).

Figure 5. Full layer in a CNN

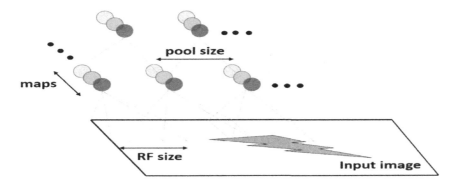

and ways of training them (Sutskever, 2012; Pascanu et al, 2013) RNNs have been found to be very good at predicting the next character in the text (Sutskever et al, 2011; Mikolov et al, 2013). or the next word in a sequence (Mikolov et al, 2013). In a traditional neural network we assume that all inputs (and outputs) are independent of each other. But for many tasks that's a very bad idea. If we want to predict the next word in a sentence it is better to know which words came before it. RNNs are called *recurrent* because they perform the same task for every element of a sequence, with the output being dependent on the previous computations. Another way to think about RNNs is that they have a "memory" which captures information about what has been calculated so far. In theory RNNs can make use of information in arbitrarily long sequences, but in practice they are limited to looking back only a few steps.

The above diagram shows a RNN being *unrolled* (or unfolded) into a full network. By unrolling we simply mean that we write out the network for the complete sequence. For example, if the sequence we care about is a sentence of 5 words, the network would be unrolled into a 5-layer neural network, one layer for each word.

Types of RNN

Bidirectional RNNs

Bidirectional RNNs are based on the idea that the output at time t may not only depend on the previous elements in the sequence, but also future elements. For example, to predict a missing word in a sequence you want to look at both the left and the right context. Bidirectional RNNs are quite simple. They are just two RNNs stacked on top of each other. The output is then computed based on the hidden state of both RNNs.

Figure 6. Representation of a RNN

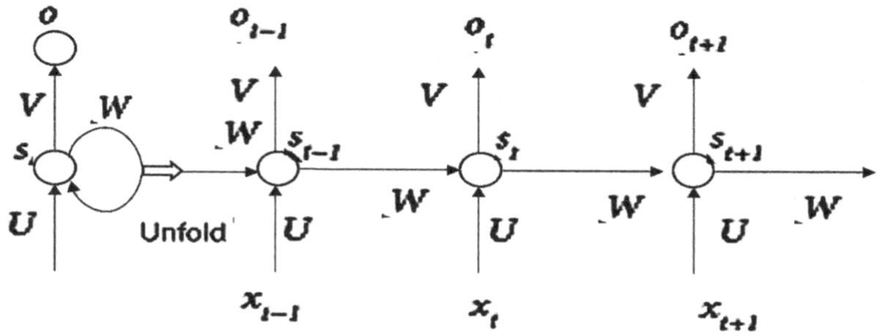

Figure 7. Bidirectional RNNs

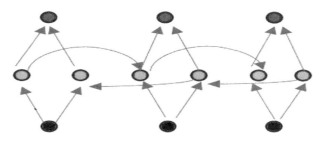

Deep (Bidirectional) RNNs

Deep (Bidirectional) RNNs are similar to Bidirectional RNNs, only that we now have multiple layers per time step. In practice this gives us a higher learning capacity (but we also need a lot of training data).

PROPOSED ALGORITHM FOR DEPTH ESTIMATION IN DEEP NETWORKS

In this section, we present a detailed overview of our proposed scheme. In our scheme, we make use of the recursive nature of the functions and transform them to implement the multiple hidden layers in a NN. Each function has a complex computation to perform and the result of one function is passed on to the next function recursively, similar in a way data is propagated in a multilayer perceptron network. The same process is repeated until the computation is complete (Sheperdson, 1963). Now, the

Figure 8. Deep RNNs

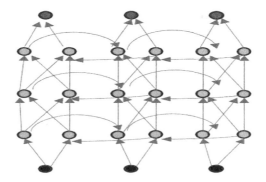

Algorithm 1. Transcursive algorithm for data propagation

```
For (every input) {
If (function1 produces desirable output) {
Pass the result of function1 to function2 }
Else {
Transform the function
Pass the result of function1 to function2}
End for
```

final output is propagated back to the main function (similar to back propagation in multilayer perceptron network). Whenever there is an undesirable output, we transform the function (similar to modifying the weights in a NN) and pass the results of this newly modified function the next layer (Thikshaja et al, 2016). This process is repeated until we get the desired output. This scheme provides an effective way of data propagation without or negligible loss in data.

RESULTS AND CONTRIBUTION

We compare the complexity of the transcursive algorithm that we have proposed with the complexity of the existing recursive algorithms (Vasilev, 2015). It is an ongoing research and the order of complexities of the transcursive algorithm will be less when compared to the existing ones as it uses the transformation function to effectively modify so that it can provide the desired output. Table 1 shows the

Figure 9. Recursive model used for data propagation

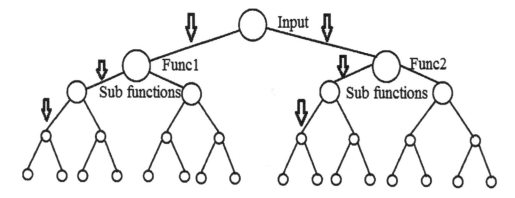

Table 1. Complexities of recursive functions

Type of Algorithms	Complexity
Binary Search	O(log n)
Sequential Search	O(n)
Tree Traversal	O(n)
Selection Sort	O(n^2)
Merge Sort	O(n log n)
Fibonacci recursion	O(2^n)
Transcursive function	T(x) O(2^n)

where T(x) is the transformation function.

complexity of different recursive functions. We can see from the table that algorithms like Selection sort and Fibonacci recursion have higher complexity, so does the transcursive function. Though the order of complexity of the transcursive function is also high, it will yield better results because of its adaptive nature and the data loss will be less as the function is transformed to produce output similar to the expected results. Figure 3 shows the graphical representation of the different time complexities of the functions listed in the table.

CONCLUSION

Deep learning has definitely got many advantages than the existing learning methods and will yield success. It is still in its initial stage of development and a lot of research has to go into it to make the fullest use of the advantages offered by deep learning. This paper illustrates the necessity of introducing deep learning by analyzing the advantages of deep learning to the shallow learning, introduces several typical deep learning models in detail, and introduces effective training methods. There is still a lot of work to be studied for deep learning, using efficient parallel algorithms to improve the training speed.

REFERENCES

ElHihi, S., & Bengio, Y. (1995). Hierarchical recurrent neural networks for long-term dependencies. *Proc. Advances in Neural Information Processing Systems*, 8. Retrieved from http://papers.nips.cc/paper/1102-hierarchical-recurrent-neural-networks-for-long-term-dependencies

Hochreiter, S., & Schmidhuber, J. (1997). Long short-term memory. *Neural Computation, 9*(8), 1735–1780. doi:10.1162/neco.1997.9.8.1735 PMID:9377276

Hubel, D. H., & Wiesel, T. N. (1962). Receptive fields, binocular interaction, and functional architecture in the cats visual cortex. *The Journal of Physiology, 160*(1), 106–154. doi:10.1113/jphysiol.1962.sp006837 PMID:14449617

Lawrence, S., Giles, C. L., Tsoi, A. C., & Back, A. D. (1997). Face recognition: A convolutional neural-network approach. *IEEE Transactions on Neural Networks, 8*(1), 98–113. doi:10.1109/72.554195 PMID:18255614

Mikolov, T., Sutskever, I., Chen, K., Corrado, G., & Dean, J. (2013). Distributed representations of words and phrases and their compositionality. Proc. Advances in Neural Information Processing Systems, 26, 3111–3119.

Panchal, Ganatra, Kosta, & Panchal. (2011). Behavioral Analysis of Multilayer Perceptrons with Multiple hidden neurons and hidden layers. *IJCTE, 3*(2).

Pascanu, R., Mikolov, T., & Bengio, Y. (2013). On the difficulty of training recurrent neural networks. *Proc. 30th International Conference on Machine Learning*, 1310–1318.

Sheperdson, J.C, & Sturgis, H.E. (1963). Computability of recursive functions. *ACM Digital Library, 10*(2).

Sutskever, I. (2012). *Training Recurrent Neural Networks* (PhD thesis). Univ. Toronto.

Sutskever, I., Martens, J., & Hinton, G. E. (2011). Generating text with recurrent neural networks. *Proc. 28th International Conference on Machine Learning*, 1017–1024.

Thikshaja, U. K., Paul, A., Rho, S., & Bhattacharjee, D. (2016). An adaptive transcursive algorithm for depth estimation in deep networks. *IEEE Conference Publications*. doi:10.1109/PlatCon.2016.7456783

Vaillant, R., Monrocq, C., & LeCun, Y. (1994). Original approach for the localisation of objects in images. Proc. Vision, Image, and Signal Processing, 141, 245–250. doi:10.1049/ip-vis:19941301

Vasilev. (2015). *An introduction to deep learning from perceptrons to deep networks.* Toptal.

Chapter 3
Big Spectrum Data and Deep Learning Techniques for Cognitive Wireless Networks

Punam Dutta Choudhury
Gauhati University, India

Ankumoni Bora
Gauhati University, India

Kandarpa Kumar Sarma
Gauhati University, India

ABSTRACT

The present world is data driven. From social sciences to frontiers of research in science and engineering, one common factor is the continuous data generation. It has started to affect our daily lives. Big data concepts are found to have significant impact in modern wireless communication systems. The analytical tools of big data have been identified as full scale autonomous mode of operation which necessitates a strong role to be played by learning based systems. The chapter has focused on the synergy of big data and deep learning for generating better efficiency in evolving communication frameworks. The chapter has also included discussion on machine learning and cognitive technologies w.r.t. big data and mobile communication. Cyber Physical Systems being indispensable elements of M2M communication, Wireless Sensor Networks and its role in CPS, cognitive radio networking and spectrum sensing have also been discussed. It is expected that spectrum sensing, big data and deep learning will play vital roles in enhancing the capabilities of wireless communication systems.

DOI: 10.4018/978-1-5225-3015-2.ch003

INTRODUCTION

The present world is data driven. From social sciences and humanities to frontiers of research in science and engineering, one common factor that is emerging is the continuous data generation (Cui, Yu and Yan, 2016). It has started to affect our daily lives. The scanned copies of old books and digital versions of recent editions in libraries, fluctuations in stock markets, daily transaction of banks, high definition movies and audio content, continuous multimedia interaction over internet, super resolution television broadcasts, diagnostic records etc are some of the major factors that are generating a significant portion of data. More importantly, some other generators are related to internet based social media services especially Facebook, Tweeter etc. which contribute (30 billion pieces of content per day for Facebook, over 90 million tweets in a day by Tweeter etc.) huge volumes of data daily. A very busy stock exchange like the one in New York generates 1 Terabytes of data daily while a single flight of the Airbus A 380 generates 640 Terabytes of data (Bi, Zhang, Ding & Cui, 2015). This voluminous expansion of data has been a decisive factor which has contributed towards the emergence of new areas of research that have significant linkages with data. In a worldwide scale, number of internet users is increasing day by day. More than 4 million users use internet daily. It is assumed that by 2020, 50 billion numbers of devices will be attached with internet and it will require separate slots for use of spectrum both in wired and wireless modes and need high end support for storage of information (Kadir, Shamsuddin, Rahman & Ismail, 2015). In Nature and another leading science and technology magazines, several special issues have been published and indicators identified to enlarge the scope of big data related research in technological domains. The most significant driving factor behind the importance being attached to big data is the fact that it is unlike the presently known forms of data blocks and along with present day technology, creates an opportunity to formulate innovative means of data driven applications. Actually big data presents a very large system which is complicated to handle using traditional data base management systems. According to popular definitions, big data has been popularized with 'five Vs'. These are volume, value, variety, velocity and veracity. Big data is a continuously expanding data base that consists of large number of data from our surroundings collected from several sources like sensors, media, videos etc. In modern wireless communication system, big data concepts are likely to have significant impact and are becoming an interesting domain of research. Communication especially wireless and mobile, are expected to be transformed due to the use of big data concepts. It is expected to be an aid to the overall quality of service (QoS) in terms of better spectrum management, call handovers, link adaptability and reliability, channel assignments, geo-location and traffic management, routing, etc. to name a few. Much of the deployment and design of emerging wireless and mobile networks are expected to go through a paradigm shift due to the use of big data concepts. The present era is also known for the evolution of smart technologies and one such development which has brought cognition in the lives of the people worldwide is Cyber Physical Systems. Around 2006, it was National Science Foundation (NSF) that coined this term. Since then, wide and deep research activities on CPS have been carried out by industries and academicians. The developments in this domain have been fuelled by the advances taken place in the genres of embedded systems, communications, sensor networks, computing and control engineering. CPS have emerged as a vital technology that can enhance human-to-human, human-to-object and object-to-object interactions. Big data,, Cyber Physical System (CPS) and deep learning are expected to contribute significantly towards the evolution of a new generation of communication technologies which will nullify most of the constrain currently encountered and improve QoS, bandwidth utilization and lower power consumption to levels previously unheard of.

This review attempts to summarize basic concepts of big data, the evolution trends, big data in communication scenario, deep learning based analytics of big data and its relevance for big data and its relevance for emerging communication scenario, CPS and it concludes with the current trends of big data and the architectural changes being formulated for use in upcoming high data rate mobile communication.

Basic Terminologies Related to Big Data

Big data, the expanding data set is defined in many ways. The big data concept with three Vs characteristics was first formulated by Doug Laney, system analyst of Gartner (earlier known as META group) in 2001 (Manyika, Chui, Brown, Bughin, Dobbs, Roxburgh and Byers, 2011). According to Laney, 'Big data is a high volume, high velocity and high variety information assets that demand cost effective, innovative forms of information processing for enhanced insight and decision making'. Gartner is known as the pioneer of big data research. Actually, these three Vs concept is not sufficient to explain big data. Later on, IBM, Microsoft etc used this concept with some extending ideas to describe big data after ten years. In 2011, International Data Corporation (IDC); an American market research, advisory and analysis firm, defined big data as 'Big data technologies designed to economically extract value from very large volumes of a wide variety of data, by enabling high-velocity capture, discovery, and/or analysis (Gantz and Reinsel, 2011). Figure 1 shows different sources of big data. The five Vs characterizing big data are discussed below:

- **Volume:** It is related to the content size, occurs naturally and represents its enormous and expanding ingredients. As the size become larger, storage and processing need to change. Data volume is related to real world. In big

Figure 1. Sources of big data

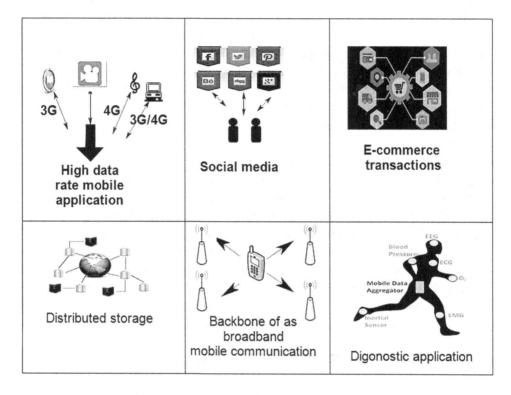

institute or in a big industry, huge amounts of data are produced every day. In Tweeter, daily almost millions of users sent text messages, videos and images daily. Similarly, in other social media like Facebook, Gmail etc. the processing mechanisms encounter huge amounts of data. Traditional database systems are not oriented to deal with such huge and expanding volumes of such data. It is assumed that the business data volume of companies all over the world may double in every 1.2 years (Chen, Mao and Liu, 2014). The presently used 3G/4G and legacy wireless/ mobile communication devices are expected to contribute significantly to this growth. With upload-download speeds varying between 10 Mbps to 60 Mbps, 4G enabled mobile systems are fast accelerating accumulation of big data. This aspect will be further accelerated with the deployment of milimetric wave (mMW) based 5G technologies when internet of thing (IoT) concepts will enhance man-machine interfaces (MMI). The increasing volume of data is to be dealt with cognitive analytics which will enable devices to use predictive approaches of processing, increasing reliability significantly.

- **Variety:** The information sources produce many types of data formats. Numeric data are structured in conventional formats. The data types like audio, email, video etc represent unstructured format. Unstructured data increases rapidly due to the rising demand of uses of mobile, internet, video calling, social media like Facebook, Twitter etc. As for example, in Facebook, 34,722 likes are registered in one minute; Twitter has 645 million users all over the world with multiple orientations and profiles (Chen, Mao and Liu, 2014). Therefore, various types of data formats are required to be handled. To manage and combine such types of data, we need big data oriented tools. A few are batch processing, real time processing, hybrid processing etc. With 4G and 5G mobile technologies data variety shall increase further. Most of the applications in communication domain will require support from machine learning (ML) tools to develop proper understanding about data variety and its handling.

- **Velocity:** Data come from various sources with varying rates of recovering, storage and demonstrate irregularity in velocities of acquisition and distribution. In real time applications, the sources like sensors, transducers etc give data streams in unpredictable speeds. To generate response appropriately and to provide quick reaction, data velocity is a challenging factor for the big data applications. Big data tools like real time processing, hybrid processing etc. is able to handle the velocity aspect of expanding data volumes (Casado and Younas, 2014).

- **Veracity:** It is also one of the parameters of big data. Data types, volume etc parameters create the complicacy issues in big data. Transformations of data, network link modification, distribution etc are difficult because of the variety of sources. Therefore, it is also a challenge to reduce this complication. The authenticity aspect places a critical role in applications. This aspect is integral to big data tools. Veracity factor is common for real time processing, batch processing and hybrid processing tools. Newly evolving coding and cryptographic aids including stenography shall be critical in enhancing reliability of such systems. The authenticity aspect of big data is being handled by currently available and evolving technologies some of which are designed to work on autonomous modes. Some of the works related to big data characteristics are as mentioned in Table 1.

Big Data: Evolving Scenario

The evolution of big data is considered according to its size and processing or storing methods. From 1980, till the present times, the sizes of big data have changed from megabyte (MB) to exabyte (XB). Similarly, processing techniques are also changing

Table 1. A few works related to big data characteristics

Sl No.	Author	Year	Contribution
1	Cui, L., Yu, F. R. & Yan, Q.	2016	Review of big data and SDN
2	Kadir, E. A., Shamsuddin, S. M., Rahman, T. H. and Ismail A. S.	2015	Explanation on big data architecture and relation with b5G communication.
3	Casado R. & Younas M.,	2014	Described the characteristics of big data and processing tools.
4	Chen, M. & Mao S. & Liu Y	2014	Review of big data and connecting technologies.
5	Manyika, J., Chui, M., Brown, B., Bughin, J., Dobbs, R., Roxburgh, C., & Byers, A. H.	2011	Work includes meaning of big data and the challenges of application.
6	Gantz, J. & Reinsel, D.	2011	Discussion about the trend of big data analysis and trend of some data base system.

day by day. Earlier in business sector, in institutions, medical or in banks, data records were manageable. As the demand of digitization is increasing, the data used in every field is changing from hard copy to soft one. So now hard copy garbage is reduced but softcopy storing problem is increasing fast. Because of this, big data concepts are getting introduced in all sectors like business, medical, education, administration, scientific research etc. In this review, the evolution is presented in terms of size and processing tools of big data. The evolving stages of big data have been shown in Figure 2.

In the late 1970's, the business data records presented the earliest form of and 'big data' the sizes started to grow from megabyte (MB) to gigabyte (GB) range. The 'database machine' concept launched in that time (Bi, Zhang, Ding & Cui, 2015). This technology could assemble hardware and software parts of a system. The aim of this assembling was to process big data at low cost. But hardware based system could not process and store efficiently as data continued to grow. In 1980s, people introduced parallel data base system (Gray & Gray, 1992) to fulfil the requirements of the big volumes of data. This is due to the fact that in the late 1980, size of big data started to turn to the terabyte (TB). This type of big data handling is impossible with normal processing in earlier generation, computing machines. To store and handle such growing data, cluster based architecture is required and the framework should have its own processor, storing device and disk. The parallel database processing have been used to increase the storage performance, data distribution and related processing tasks. A new transition was seen in 1990s. It was a transform from TB to petabyte (PB). With structured and unstructured web pages, it become difficult to handle only with parallel databases because structured data handling is quite easier than unstructured data (Jardak, Mähönen, & Riihijärvi, 2014). As the internet

Figure 2. Big data evolution with respect to its size

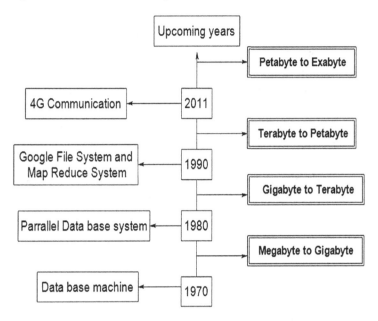

became more and more popular and available almost everywhere, the search engines like Google faced challenges to store data. Therefore, Google created Google File System (GFS) to handle big data (Hu, Wen, Chua & Li, 2014; Gantz & Reinsel, 2011) NoSQL is another database system with high storage capacity of big data, reliable and has fast operation ability. In the year 2007, database software pioneer, Jim Gray called this shifting of architecture as 'fourth paradigm' (Hey, Tansley & Tolle 2009). In coming years, as the development in big data storage and processing continued, it also saw a further increase in the data size turning from PB to XB. Though the TB data handling is simple nowadays, but for XB size, till now very few reliable methods are openly available. Major IT corporate houses like Oracle, IBM, Google etc. have started research to formulate solutions for such big data. IBM invested USD 30 billion in the research of big data (Gantz & Reinsel, 2011). Several governments such as United States have put stress on big data issues. Such efforts are likely to provide solutions and convergence mechanisms to support the enormous surge in data uses that are probable with the deployment of 4G and 5G mobile technologies all over the world. Mostly with 5G communication, huge data records will be created and it will require processing handled by big data methods. Obama government announced a USD 200 million investment in big data research. It was started on March 2012. After that, in Japan, the big data development process also started in July 2012. These are some examples of governments attaching importance to big data. In 2012, United Nations also produced a report on big data utilization for social benefits (Gantz & Reinsel, 2011).

There are some analytical tools to deal with big data. These algorithms help to design big data according to its definition. Stochastic model is a tool to estimate probability distribution of information having random variations of more than one value over time. Such random variations occur due to the fluctuation of the past values during a time period. Large scale data analysis related to big data treatment makes information more meaningful and well organized in nature. Data mining enables analysis in different perspectives including that available in compressed forms for storage and presented in uncompressed structure during retrieval. Data mining is useful to extract data from a set huge storage. Machine learning (ML) is also a tool for big data analysis which is based on pattern recognition and computational learning theory. ML solutions are preferred for retrieving data from big storages. Some related works are summarized in Table 2.

BIG DATA, MACHINE LEARNING, DEEP LEARNING, AND COGNITIVE TECHNOLOGIES FOR BETTER MAN MACHINE INTERACTION (MMI)

As mentioned earlier, big data represents a massively expanding collection of data related management with five distinct characteristics. Such data sets are expectedly difficult to handle with traditional processing and management methods and require special mechanisms. With a high volume, high velocity and increasing varieties in data, it requires new processing methods so that big data provides an increase

Table 2. A few works related to big data evolution

Sl No.	Author	Year	Contribution
1	Bi S., Zhang, R., Ding, Z. & Cui, S.	2015	Discussion on the challenges and opportunities in the designing of wireless communication networks to handle big data trouble.
2	Jardak, C., Mähönen, P. & Riihijärvi, J.	2014	Processing mechanism of big data in terms of wireless communication aspect. Hadoop and HBase are two parallel processing tools to analyze big data.
3	Hu, H., Wen, Y., Chua, T. S., & Li, X.	2014	Survey of big data analytical platforms and discussion on a systematic framework with four modules.
4	Hey, T., Tansley, S., & Tolle, K. M.	2011	Explanation of 'fourth paradigm' for scientific exploration.
5	DeWitt, D., & Gray, J.	1992	Proposed parallel data base system (first time in the computing).

in performance in decision making and enhance the processing of information in various industries, social networks like Facebook, Twitter etc. Big data with high velocity, high volume, high value, variety and veracity needs better management tools for making them beneficial for specific applications. Due to the exponential growth of data we have to train computers more than like human as part of ML methods and formulate approaches for big data handling. ML is an approach having pattern recognition, classification, prediction etc. attributes and can generate as human like decision making.

Machine Learning (ML)

ML mimics human like behaviour with training and some mathematical representation of data and the ultimate result of achieving greater efficiency and autonomy in decision making. Sources of big data are always different. Data from sensors, satellites, media etc are of different form. So it is a challenging task to organize and prepare data for storage and processing to store or process. But ML algorithms have this ability to manage it. Arthur Samuel defined machine learning as 'Field of study that gives computers the ability to learn without being explicitly programmed' (Dean and Ghemawat, 2008). ML consists of five different methods. These are Artificial Neural Network (ANN), Artificial Neuro Fuzzy System (ANFS), Genetic Algorithm (GA), combination of ANN, ANFS, GA and clustering of all these four methods.

ANNs are learning based non-parametric predictive tools that capture variations in model free data applied to them. The basic analogy is linked to the biological neural network which is based on parallel processing. Similarly, ANNs work generating parallel processing by linking layers of artificial neurons tracking variations in input data by resorting to connectionists computing. In situations, it either requires a reference (supervised learning) or may avoid references (unsupervised learning). Once configured properly and trained adequately, ANNs can be reliable tools in big data set-ups.

Fuzzy systems are known to deal with uncertainty and can handle finer variations. Their limitations are that these cannot learn or retain the learning which ANNs do. Therefore, Fuzzy systems in combination with ANNs provide advantages of both the domains which configured as neuro fuzzy systems (NFS) or fuzzy neural systems (FNS). In fuzzy based ML system, there are fuzzification or defuzzification block, a rule base and an inference system. At the end of the learning phase (which is fast), the fuzzy based systems demonstrate the abilities to track finer variations and deal with uncertainity, fast processing, adaptability, ability to handle real time data and decision support. NFS or FNS have been explored as part of big data frameworks. In Kala, Shukla and Tiwari (2009), authors discussed neuro fuzzy system for machine learning for big data system. Actually as the data size become larger, training time is also become long. Therefore traditional ANN failed to train these types of huge data. In Eibagi (2014), authors analysed big data using fuzzy classification system. This powerful system is the combination system of two methods namely, if then rules and linguistic variable. In Bharill, and Tiwari (2016), big data treatment is done using fuzzy based classification system.

Cognitive Computing

It has deep relation to big data treatment. Simply speaking, this is a method of a self learning system. In cognitive computation, data mining, pattern recognition, natural language processing (NLP) etc are used to study and mimic human brain functions. Cognitive computing enacts human and machine interaction and penetrates the complexities of big data. Actually, cognitive computing is a method which has the capability to react just like the thoughts of the human brain itself. As already mentioned, cognitive technology can be used in processing of big data in several fields. In bank sector, online payment operation, speech recognition as a response to a call at customer care and for caller identification, voice recognition etc have used cognitive computing. Among scientific domains, astronomy is one of the areas where big data has been associated from early days. The telescope named (LOFAR) produces 100TB data set per day (Garrett, 2014). Similarly another telescope named Square Kilometer Array (SKA) produce more than billions of data bytes per day (Garrett, 2014) etc. Due to the quantity, dynamic nature of data generation and variation in data types astronomical data are treated as big data. Cognitive computing is used to analyze these data. In Mane and Salian (2015), authors discussed about the application of cognitive computing and big data to optimized decision states.

Deep Learning

It is a part of ML. The traditional ANN has two prominent parts; hard craft feature extractor (in terms of hidden layer) and trainable classifier (in terms of the output layer). ANNs with many hidden layers is usually called a Deep Neural Network (DNN) and the associated learning is usually called deep learning. According to many researchers the word 'deep' in deep learning means that the ANN has more than two hidden layer. Sometimes, cascaded ANN structures are used to form deep learning architectures (Agarwalla and Sarma, 2016). For another group of researchers, the word 'deep' in deep learning is due to some unlabelled data. Some people think that this 'deep' means that there is no need for human invented features in deep learning (Kriegeskorte, 2015). The learning of a deep network is formulated in such a way that the intermediate feature extractors are also trainable. In deep learning, a trainable feature extractor stage enables learn various levels of features. Actually deep learning is a hierarchical representation of features based on conditions of learning. Huge amounts of unsupervised data are used in deep learning to extract complex representation automatically.

Deep learning has some special characteristics to make it different from other learning approaches. Two layered network cannot be considered as deep learning because there is no feature hierarchy. Kernel and SVM methods of traditional ANN are also not in the deep learning category. Deep learning has three types of architectures. These are feed forward, feed-back and bidirectional learning. DNNs perform learning without requiring external feature extractors and in certain cases labeled data to follow the patterns. Deep learning is an acceptable solution for big data handling problem. Practitioners and specialist of big data analytics are using deep learning to handle real world problems. For some useful operations, like decision making, information processing and related purposes deep learning can be considered as practical source of knowledge. In Mane and Salian (2015), some aspects of deep learning and big data are discussed. The most important nature of deep learning is that it can automatically extract data from a large volume of unsupervised data. In big data analysis, streaming and fast moving of input data is a challenging task. For these types of operations, deep learning is an essential way of handling expanding volumes of data. In Agarwalla and Sarma (2016), authors explained about the work of deep learning in big data processing is effective used to obtain efficient processing. In Chen and Lin (2014), authors reviewed the performance of deep networks on big data. Here, they discussed that deep learning can be applied in all characteristics of big data like volume, variety, veracity etc. Some related works on big data and machine learning are summarized in Table 3.

BIG DATA AND DEEP LEARNING IN EMERGING MOBILE COMMUNICATION SCENARIO

In mobile communication era, users always have the expectation of increase in the capacity and speeds of data services. Wireless communication started with the first generation techniques which evolved through each subsequent generation to offer increasing speeds and better capacity in terms of data transmission and reception. Up to 2006, the peak data rate was around 54 Mbps which during the last decade evolved at explosive rate to reach the present state where fourth generation (4G) data speeds touched 600 Mbps. At the end of 2007, 295 million users were using 3G networks (Dehuri and Sanyal, 2015) and by 2015 this figure multiplied several times with the availability of 3G/4G hand held devices, legacy systems and penetration of Wi-Fi/WiMax services. It has been predicted that by 2020, around 20 billion devices will be in connected state and a huge portion of there will be using 3G/4G/5G and Wi-Fi

Table 3. A few works related to big data and machine learning

Sl No.	Author	Year	Contribution
1	Agarwalla, S., & Sarma, K. K.	2016	Application of deep learning based technique in big data in case of speaker recognition.
2	Bharill. N. & Tiwari, A.	2016	Fuzzy based classifier to handle big data.
3	Mane D. & Salian S.	2015	Describes the benefit of combination of big data, cognitive computing and big data testing.
4	Kriegeskorte, N	2015	Explanation related to DNN.
5	Hasan. M.	2014	Explanation of application of GA to analyze big data.
6	Xu, Y., Zeng, M., Liu, Q., & Wang, X.	2014	Discussion on neuro- Fuzzy system on big data analysis.
7	Kune R., Konugurthi P.K., Agarwal, R. Rao C. & Buyya R.	2014	GA based technique for big data cloud where decoupled computational and data services are offered.
8	Yang Xu, Mingming Zeng, Quanhui Liu & Xiaofeng Wang	2014	GA based multilevel association method in case of big data analysis.
9	Chen, X. W. & Lin, X.	2014	Big data processing with focus on future trends.
10	Garrett M.A.	2014	Explanation on the treatment of big data of astronomical research.
11	Eibagi, A.	2014	Discussion on hybrid intelligent system like hybrid neuro fuzzy system to analyze big data.
12	Dean J & Ghemawat S.	2008	Discussed about ML based map reduce programming model.
13	Kala, R., Shukla, A., Tiwari, R.	2009	Mentioned a concept on FNN to deal with large data set.
14	Leung, S.T. & Gobioff, H.	2003	Mentioned Google file system

infrastructure. This expansion ensured that accumulated data continuously increased in size necessitating formulation of more reliable and efficient analytic tools. The upcoming technologies in wireless communication known as fifth generation or 5G are likely to provide data rates around 1Gbps which shall complicate matters further. Communication shall be taking place through dense networks requiring link adaptability for better QoS. In such a scenario, viable solutions and efficient analytic tools are likely to be autonomous the working of which shall be driven by deep learning based processing.

The accumulation of digital data through mobile communication set-ups has made it necessary to develop and deploy analytic tools that work with very less latency. Certain researches are going on in this domain. In Suzhi, Zhang, Ding and Cui (2015), authors proposed a framework of big data driven mobile network for 5G communication network optimization. The 5G communication is expected to be increasing data communication speeds ($\cong 1\,Gps$) and have ten times more connections with better QoS in comparison with 4G/legacy communications (Hasan, 2014). Big data with structured and unstructured content need high transmission rates. The 5G attributes (Eibagi, 2014) including network function virtualization (NFV), cloud computing (CC), machine to machine (M2M) communication, massive MIMO etc. essentially shall be closely linked to big data situations. In case of transmission rate, spectral density, delay, reliability and battery life expected etc, the 5G performance promises to be considerably better than 4G/ legacy systems (Eibagi, 2014). Similarly, big data also need better mobile communication systems to store, analyze and process data. Better communication links shall ensure smooth flow of data from various sources which will get accumulated for processing by cognitive analytic tools. In this respect, 4G/5G mobile communication and big data shall be closely linked and gelled well by deep learning techniques.

Upcoming and legacy standards of wireless networks are attached with wireless sensor networks (WSN), Wi-Fi etc. The forth coming 5G communication and milimetric wave (mMW) line of sight (LoS) Wi-Fi with the expected data speeds in gigabits per second (Gbps) range is likely to inundate presents day bases data. In such a scenario, data analysis shall be highly dependent on intelligent approaches most of which are likely to be based on deep learning. In 5G standard, WSNs are expected to play important roles in data sensing, accumulation, processing and distribution. For WSN, data management and post processing are also big tasks. Above all, the collected data volume shall be huge and continuously expanding. Exploring innovative data mining methods and deployment of appropriate infrastructure are gearing up to meet such challenges but intelligent solutions shall become indispensible. Due to the particular nature, the traditional data mining methods are not suitable for WSNs. Therefore, some modifications are required in the process of data mining. In Casado and Younas (2015), these methods are discussed. According to Casado and Younas (2015), data mining in WSN is the process of extracting information related with application and pattern and process it in new data streams. In same work, authors explain algorithms and direction of approaches of data mining for WSN with different choices of the solution. A more noticeable aspect shall be the role played by deep learning in modeling stochastic wireless channels. This aspect is discussed next. A conceptual diagram depicting 5G communication and big data is shown in Figure 3.

The emerging scenario of 5G communication shall be characterized by relentless M2M communication links. There shall be wireless communication in Personal Area Networks (PAN), Neighbourhood Area Network (NAN) and Local Area Networks (LAN) supported by 1 to 10 Gbps links based on mMW and optical fiber backbones (Peng, Li, Zhao and Wang, 2015). Banking, scientific institutions, computational clusters etc. linked to central routing and access hubs are likely to be provided by

Figure 3. 5G communication and big data

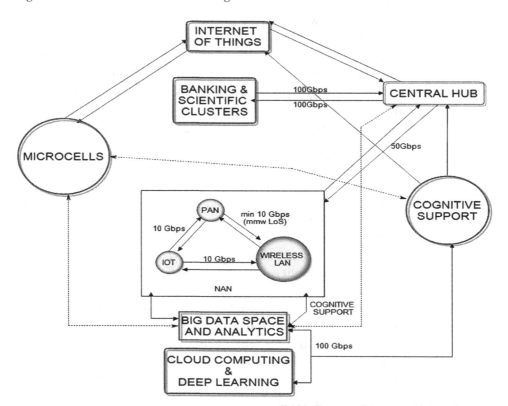

PAN- Personal Access Network
NAN- Neighbourhood Area Network
IoT- Internet of Things

10 to 100 Gbps links as per requirements. These wireless/wired connections are likely to generate huge volumes of data and the analytics shall be based on cognitive principles. In the PAN and WAN levels, there shall be multiple microcells each generating considerable data with M2M connections. Spectrum conservation shall be a sought after process and it will be driven by cognitive sensing techniques. Deep learning based methods will determine traffic loads, predict congestion and find routing paths enabling free flow of data between source and destination. Proper wireless profiling and link adoption will ensure better QoS. In each of these areas, deep learning will play significant roles by providing forecast, prediction and representative models for visualization, planning, resource utilization and provide enhanced performance.

Similarly a probable scheme of 5G communication and big data in smart city application is shown in Figure 4.

Figure 4. 5G communication and big data in smart city application

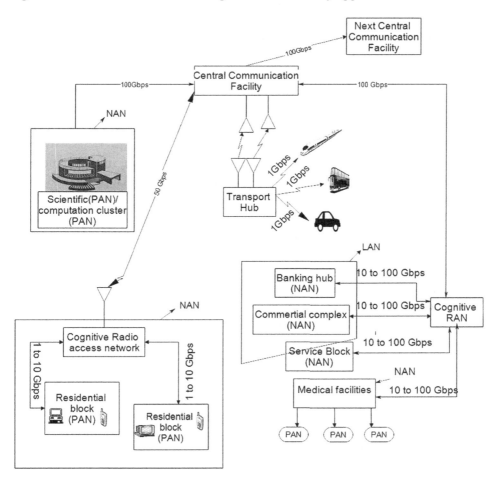

Huge data flow from several sources like small (mobile phone, personal computers etc. in residential blocks) and large (banking hub, commercial complex, medical facilities etc.) computation and communication intensive units accumulated in structured and unstructured forms shall be stacked, processed, manipulated, retrieved and distributed using cognitive principles of data mining. The complete collection shall represent big data and its analytics shall be based on deep learning principles. These data are to be maintained and deciminated using advanced techniques like deep learning and cloud computing. Deep learning will provide autonomy in data applications. For example, if fading in wireless channels are severe, deep learning based stochastic models will provide approximate representation of channels and help in better recovery of transmitted blocks without relying much on pilot carriers which is the conventional practice. It will result in spectrum conservation. This is because of the fact that the deep learning based tools will locally provide the channel state which shall be generated from continuous background training, recording and sharing of the knowledge regarding the dynamically changing wireless profile. It will have significant changes in the methods of data recovery like lowering dependence on pilot retransmissions, unblocking a channel slot for communicating with transmission for reference symbols during data recovery and reduced computational cycles while extracting required portions of data from transmitted blocks. It shall lead to significant changes in receiver architecture designs.

Rise in data flow will be commonly observed phenomena in the immediate future. Residential blocks are likely to be provided with 1-10 Gbps links to fulfil requirements. All transportation resources like trains, buses, cars etc. provided with mobile wireless communication are supposed to be covered by 1 Gbps links. Scientific and commercial clusters may have multiple cells with PAN and NAN topologies provided with high data rate mobile or wireless access using 100 Gbps links to central communication units. All data from each section are to be controlled by specially designed Cognitive Radio Access Network (CRAN) architectures. CRAN and central communication facilities are to be linked with 50-100 Gbps connections and work as relay for subsequent network links and ensure seamless data flow between neighbourhoods, cities, states and countries of all over the world. A list of probable domains in which big data and deep learning resources will be commonly observed and supported by 5G links are summarizes in Table 4.

In commercial sectors, all money transactions, buying or selling, order placing or confirmation and product details etc. constitute big data with a large area coverage which expands continuously. These data flow, based on 5G communication technique (Prasad & Aithal, 2015) shall make commercial linkages interactive. Money transaction, advanced ATM services, biometric verification, credit card scanning etc. are the upcoming technologies which are to be made further efficient using 5G communication (Prasad and Aithal, 2015). All these facilities will have big data dimensions and the analytics part shall require support of deep learning. Decision support and autonomous operation will be ensured by deep learning structures which shall enable real-time interaction between man and machine resulting in high reliability in operations.

In hospitals real time health care monitoring systems are becoming increasingly popular (Aminian and Naji, 2013). Patient health condition diagnostics etc. can be monitored and intervened using 5G communication. A significant portion of it will be WSN based and driven by IoT protocols. Processing conditions shall continuously change which will require predictive decision support. The deep learning based architectures aid by 5G links in M2M interaction mode shall prove handy. In Aminian and Naji (2013) authors report the design of Body WSN (BWSN) to

Table 4. Summary of probable applications domain of deep learning and emerging wireless or mobile communication technologies

Transport		Residential Application	Commercial Application	Medical Section	Scientific Sector	Energy Sector
Public sector	Private sector	Laptop, PC	Transactions (banking etc.)	Patient condition	Neuro science	Distribution grid.
Booking, check in/ out	Fuel position	Gaming consoles	Billing/ selling	Instrument details	Biological science and Genetic Engineering	Wind, solar and biological sources.
Location details	acceleration	SHD TV	Order placing/ confirmation	Doctor records in hospitals	Tele-communication	Nuclear
Baggage details	Environment control	Smart phone, tablets	Inventory update	CC TV coverage	Robotics and Astronomical system design	Thermal
CC TV coverage	Parking details	Toys (with Zigbee, IR links)	Quality of Service confirmation	Emergency service confirmation	Physical science	Hydro
Speed limit	Speed limit	Appliances (Fridge, AC, Washing machine, Water heater)	Product details	Medicine details	Chemical science	------------

monitor patient's blood pressure, heart beat and some critical medical conditions. This monitoring system is controlled by some coordinating mechanism with base station. Data sensing in the area of e -Health is a common practice but now huge data generated and its continuous transmission and accumulation is becoming a critical aspect. Predictive diagnostics based on ML and autonomous systems are increasingly making inroads in this regard. Further, in medical practices, data analysis and decision support can be facilitated using deep learning. In Wang, Shao, Shu, Zhu and Zhang (2016), authors proposed a three layer based architecture called 'interest based reduced variable neighbourhood search (RVNS) queue architecture (IRQA)' to handle large volume of e health big data. This is an important addition to the list of tools helpful for big data.

Smart city infrastructures include smart home terminologies (Lynggaard and Skouby, 2015). The smart home application is based on Smart Home Network (SHN) technologies (Lynggaard and Skouby, 2015). The IoT interconnection is provided by SHN technologies. According to Lynggaard and Skouby (2015), a simulated model is published regarding this smart home and it extends towards smart city. The model is simulated on a mathematical tool and run it on a normal PC. Smart home appliances with IoT like personal computers, tablets, mobiles, SHD TV, heating or cooling systems are interconnected by SHN. These network turns to the internet cloud services. All smart homes are interconnected by cloud of things (CoT) and consume big data produces by all IoT of smart home. Smart city concept is formed from these big data.

Another emerging application is in energy sector where high data rate communication, big data attributes and deep learning shall enable design and deployment of efficient smart grids. Power grid system is constituted by two types of energy producers, small and large. The small energy producers are like wind turbine and solar panels. Similarly, large energy producers are like coal hydro and nuclear plants. These energy producers need to change power production rate and have a dynamic load distribution mechanism coordinating with the requirements of the power consumers. The coordination of energy producers is possible by exchanging the data of the sources, distributors, grid state, demand forecast etc. Predictive approaches can prevent distribution mismanagement and losses which shall enable the design of efficient power grids distributed over countries and continents. Such a mechanism for predictive power management and interfacing with different relevant constituents in real time using high speed data access and decision support from deep learning shall make power generation, distribution and utilization (Gungor, Lu, & Hancke, 2010) conservation oriented and efficient.

Several scientific institutions are already using high data rate mobile/wireless links to accelerate research outcome. Big data and deep learning have become integral parts of it. National Aeronautics and Space Administration (NASA), USA uses around 100 Gbps wireless connectivity. European Council for Nuclear Research (Counsil European pour la Recherche Nucleaire) (CERN) carries out experiments using similar wireless technology. In TERENA conference, 2013 (TNC 2013), for the first time, six of the world's top most leading groups of research and education networks with other two commercial partners illustrated 100 Gbps transmission link between North America and Europe. In this demonstration, to transmit big data between Maastricht and Chicago it took a few minutes rather than a few hours over the public internet. The 100 Gbps wireless connection is also known as Advanced North Atlantic 100G Pilot Project (ANA-100G) and it has been used for emerging scientific application related to e-health, software defined monitoring etc. In all these cases, the most decisive factor linked with high data rate communication have been real time processing, interactive resource management and access to critical assets with no latency. It has enabled the growth of autonomous operation which most of time, is based on tools like deep learning. Some of the works related to big data and 5G communication are as mentioned in Table 5.

Table 5. A few works related to big data and 5G communication

Sl No.	Author	Year of Publication	Contribution
1	Wang, K., Shao, Y., Shu, L., Zhu,C. & Zhang, Y.	2016	Three layer based architecture for mobile e health network.
2	Tseng, Y. L.	2015	Vehicle to vehicle communication or vehicle to other services using LTE communication.
3	Prasad, K. K. & Aithal, P. S.	2015	Focussed on the new banking technologies using 5G communication.
4	Peng, M., Li, Y., Zhao, Z., & Wang, C.	2015	A discussion on 5G based recent technologies on high through put and low power consumption.
5	Lynggaard, P. & Skouby, K. E.	2015	A technique for smart home and later smart city application using 5G communication.
6	Aminian, M. & Naji, H. R.	2013	Discussion on the patient health care monitoring system in a hospital using WSN based system.
7	Rappaport T. S.	2012	Wireless communication and new 5 G communication.
8	Gungor, V. C., Lu, B., Hancke, G.P.	2010	Discussion on challenges and application of WSN on smart grid.

Cognitive Radio Networking and Spectrum Sensing

Cognitive networking speaks about an intelligent communication system, consisting of both the wire line and/or the wireless connections, that is aware of its transmission environment, both internal and external, and acts adaptively and autonomously to attain its intended goal(s). This implies that all the network nodes and the end devices are self-aware and context-aware all of the time. The interest in cognitive networking is mainly driven from the need to manage the increasing complexity and the efficient utilization of available resources to deliver applications and services as economically as possible. WSN is one of the areas where there is highest demand for cognitive networking. There are several reasons among which the recourse constraints (spectrum and power) are the most appealing one. Although in WSN, the nodes are constrained in resources mainly in terms of battery power but these days there is scarcity increasing in terms of spectrum availability also. Traditionally, the WSN work in ISM band (2.4 GHz), but in the same band we have many competing technologies working simultaneously like WLAN 802.11 a/b/g and ZigBee (802.15.4), Wi-Fi, Bluetooth. Hence, in an environment where all these competing technologies are working simultaneously, it becomes difficult to find free spectrum to transmit without an error. Also at the same time, the licensed mobile communication bands are almost free for 85% of the time w.r.t. spatial and temporal terms. Hence there can be two motives: either to find a free channel in the unlicensed band and do wireless transmission or to find a free channel in the licensed band and do communication. Also it will be strictly needed that whenever the licensed user comes back the cognitive user backs-off from the channel and switch to another free channel without creating any difficulty to the primary user. Another important thing is that if the cognitive user finds several free channels then it can go for the best available channel to do communication. Another important scheme is there in which both the primary and secondary exist simultaneously as long as the QoS of the primary user is not compromised. If the interference created from the power transmitted by the secondary user still remains below some threshold, then this scheme can be helpful. Adding cognition to the existing WSN infrastructure will bring about many benefits. CWSN will enable current WSN to overcome the spectrum scarcity as well as node energy problem. The cognitive technology will not only provide access to new spectrum but with better propagation characteristics too. Also by adaptively changing the systems parameters like modulation schemes, Transmit power, carrier frequency, constellation size a wide variety of data rates can be achieved. These will certainly improve the power consumption and network life time in a WSN. It will also help in coping with the fading (frequency selective/ flat) (Akyildiz, Lee, Vuran & Mohanty, 2006; Akyildiz, Lo & Balakrishnan, 2011).

Spectrum sensing and frequency agility are the two key features of Cognitive WSN. On one hand, spectrum sensing involves monitoring a spectral band for its availability without causing any interference to the primary user, while frequency agility involves switching capabilities in case the spectrum becomes unavailable due to the presence of a primary user. Over the years, a number of spectrum sensing techniques have been developed. Among all such techniques, primary transmitter detection, cooperative detection and interference detection are the conventional ones. Other signal processing approaches for performing spectrum sensing includes multi-taper spectrum sensing and estimation, filter bank based sensing, wavelet based detection, random Hough transform based detection and radio identification based detection (Fanan, Riley, Mehdawi, Ammar & Zolfaghari, 2014; Kaur & Aulakh, 2015). Some of the works related to Cognitive radio networking are as mentioned in Table 6.

Spectrum Sensing: Review of Current Research Trends

Over the years, various spectrum sensing techniques were proposed to identify the presence of primary user signal as well as to exploit the spectrum by secondary user when the primary user is absent. The most popular spectrum sensing techniques are classified under three major categories: non-cooperative detection, cooperative

Table 6. A few works related to cognitive radio networking

Sl No.	Author	Year of Publication	Contribution
1	Kaur, N. & Aulakh, I. K.	2015	A Survey of Cooperative Spectrum Sensing in Cognitive Radio Networks
2	Fanan, A. M., Riley, N. G., Mehdawi, M., Ammar, M. & Zolfaghari, M.	2014	Survey: A Comparison of Spectrum Sensing Techniques in Cognitive Radio
3	Akyildiz, I. F., Lo, B. F. & Balakrishnan, R.	2011	Cooperative spectrum sensing in cognitive radio networks: A survey
4	Akyildiz, I. F., Lee, W., Vuran, M. C. & Mohanty, S.	2006	NeXt generation/dynamic spectrum access/cognitive radio wireless networks: A survey

detection and interference based detection. This survey mainly emphasizes on the different types of non-cooperative detection, i.e., energy detection, matched filter detection and cyclostationary feature detection (Ariananda, Lakshmanan & Nikookar, 2009; Zeng, Liang, Hoang & Zhang, 2009).

The energy detection is a non coherent detection technique where the primary user detection and its statistics do not need any prior knowledge of the primary user signal to determine whether the channel is occupied or not. Consequently, it is considered the one of simplest techniques of spectrum sensing to detect primary user transmitter. In the past various literatures have reported theoretical and practical findings on energy detection. The advantages of using energy detection are low computational cost, easy implementation and less complexity. Moreover, it does not need any prior knowledge of primary user (PU) as the technique solely depends on the power of PU signal, i.e., whether the signal is present or absent, these advantages makes energy detection the simplest method to detect primary user signal. In contrast, in this technique, the signal detection depends on comparing power of the received signal to the threshold level, while, the threshold level rely on the noise floor which can be estimated. But the signal power is difficult to be estimated as it changes depending on two factors: distance between primary user and cognitive radio as well as ongoing transmission characteristics. As a consequence, the selection of an appropriate threshold level caused some drawbacks in the energy detection. If the threshold is too low then, it causes false alarm. On the other hand, when the threshold is too high, the missed detection will occur because weak primary signals will be ignored. Therefore the performance of energy detection is dependent on the suitable selection of the threshold in the frequency domain. Another disadvantage is the accuracy of signal detection which is found to be low as compared to other techniques.

Another technique of the spectrum sensing is Matched filter Detection (MFD), which is known as optimum method to detect primary users when the transmitted signal is known. This technique is commonly used in radar transmission. MFD is considered as a linear filter designed in digital signal processing (DSP) which is used to maximize the output signal to noise ratio for given input signal. However, it requires proper demodulation of the primary user signal. Consequently, this technique requires a perfect prior knowledge of a primary user such as modulation type and order, bandwidth, operating frequency, pulse shaping and frame format. The advantages of this method are that the detection process requires short sensing time and low number of samples to meet required level of false alarm or missed detection. Moreover, it has high processing gain and high accuracy compared with other techniques. Its major drawback is its power consumption which is large in different receiver algorithms that are implemented to detect primary users. Match filter requires a dedicated receiver for every signal type of primary user. The implementation complexity of sensing unit is impractically large. Thus, from its requirements, advantages and disadvantages, it can be concluded that the performance of matched filter relies on the availability of perfect prior knowledge of primary users which lead to increasing cost and more complexity. Hence, the good performance and high accuracy in MFD is achieved at the expense of increased cost and complexity.

An alternative detection method is the cyclostationary feature detection. Modulated signals are, in general, coupled with sine wave carriers, pulse trains, repeating spreading, hopping sequences, or cyclic prefixes, which result in built-in periodicity. These modulated signals are characterized as cyclostationary since their mean and autocorrelation exhibit periodicity. These features are detected by analyzing a spectral correlation function. The main advantage of the spectral correlation function is that it differentiates the noise energy from modulated signal energy, which is a result of the fact that the noise is a wide-sense stationary signal with no correlation, while modulated signals are cyclostationary with spectral correlation due to the embedded redundancy of signal periodicity. Therefore, a cyclostationary feature detector can perform better than the energy detector in discriminating against noise due to its robustness to the uncertainty in noise power. However, it is computationally complex and requires significantly long observation time. For more efficient and reliable performance, the enhanced feature detection scheme combining cyclic spectral analysis with pattern recognition based on neural networks is proposed by Fehske, Gaeddart and Reed (2005). Distinct features of the received signal are extracted using cyclic spectral analysis and represented by both spectral coherent function and spectral correlation density function. The neural network, then, classifies signals into different modulation types (Akyildiz, Lee, Vuran & Mohanty, 2008; Liang,

Zeng, Peh & Hoang, 2008; Zhang, Mallik & Lataeif, 2009; Subhedar & Birajdar, 2011; Jaiswal & Sharma, 2013). Some of the works related to spectrum sensing are as mentioned in Table 7.

CONCLUSION

In this chapter, we have discussed the background of big data and its association with deep learning and the linkages with the evolving scenario of wireless/mobile communication. Of late there has been an enormous growth in wireless/mobile devices and related applications which have aided the expansion of big data infrastructure. It has been observed that analytic tools of big data are gearing up for acquiring a full scale autonomous mode of operation which necessitates a strong role to be played by learning based systems. Of late, deep learning networks have been accepted to be useful for such scenarios. The chapter has focused in some depth on the synergy of big data and DWN for generating better efficiency in existing and evolving communication frameworks. The chapter has also included discussion on ML and cognitive technologies with respect to big data and mobile communication. As CPS are emerging as indispensible elements of M2M communication, certain discussion

Table 7. A few works related to spectrum sensing

SI No.	Author	Year of Publication	Contribution
1	Jaiswal, M. & Sharma, A. K.	2013	A Survey on Spectrum Sensing Techniques for Cognitive Radio
2	Subhedar, M. & Birajdar, G.	2011	Spectrum Sensing Techniques in Cognitive Radio Networks: A Survey
3	Ariananda, D. D., Lakshmanan, M. K. & Nikookar, H.	2009	A Survey on Spectrum Sensing Techniques for Cognitive Radio
4	Zeng, Y., Liang, Y., Hoang, A. T. & Zhang, R.	2009	A Review on Spectrum Sensing for Cognitive Radio:Challenges and Solutions
5	Zhang, W., Mallik, R. K. & Lataeif, K.B.	2009	Optimization of Cooperative Spectrum Sensing with Energy Detection in Cognitive Radio Networks
6	Akyildiz, I. F., Lee, W., Vuran, M. C. & Mohanty, S.	2008	A Survey on Spectrum Management in Cognitive Radio Networks
7	Liang, Y., Zeng, Y., Peh, E. C. Y. & Hoang, A. T. H.	2008	Sensing-Throughput Tradeoff for Cognitive Radio Networks

on this aspect as also been included. Subsequently, WSN and its convergence with CPS, cognitive radio networking and evolving scenario of spectrum sensing have also been covered. It is expected that the emerging scenario of spectrum sensing, big data and deep learning will play significant roles in enhancing the capabilities of wireless/mobile communication systems which will integrate WSNs as part of CPS set ups to facilitate the design of reliable M2M interaction frameworks.

REFERENCES

Agarwalla, S., & Sarma, K. K. (2016). Machine learning based sample extraction for automatic speech recognition using dialectal Assamese speech. *Neural Networks*, *78*, 97–111. doi:10.1016/j.neunet.2015.12.010 PMID:26783204

Akyildiz, I. F., Lee, W., Vuran, M. C., & Mohanty, S. (2006). NeXt generation/dynamic spectrum access/cognitive radio wireless networks: A survey. *Elsevier Journal on Computer Networks*, *50*(13), 2127–2159. doi:10.1016/j.comnet.2006.05.001

Akyildiz, I. F., Lee, W., Vuran, M. C., & Mohanty, S. (2008). A Survey on Spectrum Management in Cognitive Radio Networks. *IEEE Communications Magazine*, *46*(4), 40–48. doi:10.1109/MCOM.2008.4481339

Akyildiz, I. F., Lo, B. F., & Balakrishnan, R. (2011). Cooperative spectrum sensing in cognitive radio networks: A survey. *Physical Communication*, *4*(1), 40–62. doi:10.1016/j.phycom.2010.12.003

Aminian, M., & Naji, H. R. (2013). *A Hospital Healthcare Monitoring System Using Wireless Sensor Networks*, Health &. *Medical Informatics*, *4*(2).

Ariananda, D. D., Lakshmanan, M. K., & Nikookar, H. (2009). A Survey on Spectrum Sensing Techniques for Cognitive Radio. *Proceedings of second International Workshop on Cognitive Radio and Advanced Spectrum Management (CogART)*, 74-79. doi:10.1109/COGART.2009.5167237

Baheti, R., & Gill, H. (2011). Cyber-physical systems. The Impact of Control Technology, IEEE, 161-166.

Bharill, N., & Tiwari, A. (2016). *Handling Big Data with Fuzzy Based Classification Approach*. Academic Press.

Bi, S., Zhang, R., Ding, Z., & Cui, S. (2015). Wireless communications in the era of big data. *IEEE Communications Magazine*, *53*(10), 190–199. doi:10.1109/MCOM.2015.7295483

Casado, R., & Younas, M. (2015). Emerging trends and technologies in big data processing. *Concurrency and Computation, 27*(8), 2078–2091. doi:10.1002/cpe.3398

Chen, M., Mao, S., & Liu, Y. (2014). Big data: A survey. *Mobile Networks and Applications, 19*(2), 171–209. doi:10.1007/s11036-013-0489-0

Chen, X. W., & Lin, X. (2014). Big data deep learning: Challenges and perspectives. *IEEE Access, 2*, 514–525. doi:10.1109/ACCESS.2014.2325029

Cui, L., Yu, F. R., & Yan, Q. (2016). When big data meets software-defined networking: SDN for big data and big data for SDN. *IEEE Network, 30*(1), 58–65. doi:10.1109/MNET.2016.7389832

Dean, J., & Ghemawat, S. (2008). MapReduce: Simplified data processing on large clusters. *Communications of the ACM, 51*(1), 107–113. doi:10.1145/1327452.1327492

Dehuri, S., & Sanyal, S. (2015). Computational Intelligence for Big Data Analysis. Springer International Publishing.

DeWitt, D., & Gray, J. (1992). Parallel database systems: The future of high performance database systems. *Communications of the ACM, 35*(6), 85–98. doi:10.1145/129888.129894

Eibagi, A. (2014). *Big Data Analysis Using Neuro-Fuzzy System* (Thesis). San Jose State University.

Eldar, Y. C., & Kutyniok, G. (2012). *Compressed Sensing: Theory and Applications.* Cambridge, UK: Cambridge University Press. doi:10.1017/CBO9780511794308

Fanan, A. M., Riley, N. G., Mehdawi, M., Ammar, M., & Zolfaghari, M. (2014). Survey: A Comparison of Spectrum Sensing Techniques in Cognitive Radio. *Proceedings of International Conference on Image Processsing, Computers and Industrial Engineering (ICICIE)*, 65-69.

Gantz, J., & Reinsel, D. (2011). Extracting value from chaos. *IDC Review, 1142*, 1-12.

Garrett, M. A. (2014). Big Data analytics and Cognitive Computing: future opportunities for Astronomical research. *IOP Conference Series Materials Science and Engineering, 67*(1). doi:10.1088/1757-899X/67/1/012017

Gunes, V., Peter, S., Givargis, T., & Vahid, F. (2014). A Survey on Concepts, Applications, and Challenges in Cyber-Physical Systems. *Transactions on Internet and Information Systems (Seoul), 8*(12), 4242–4268.

Gungor, V. C., Lu, B., & Hancke, G. P. (2010). Opportunities and Challenges of Wireless Sensor Networks in Smart Grid. *IEEE Transactions on Industrial Electronics, 57*(10), 10. doi:10.1109/TIE.2009.2039455

Guturu, P., & Bhargava, B. (2011). Cyber-Physical Systems: A Confluence of Cutting Edge Technological Streams. *Proceedings of International Conference on Advances in Computing and Communication ICACC-11.*

Hasan, M. (2014). Genetic Algorithm and its application to Big Data Analysis. *International Journal of Scientific & Engineering Research, 5*(1).

Hey, T., Tansley, S., & Tolle, K. M. (2009). The fourth paradigm: Data-intensive scientific discovery (Vol. 1). Redmond, WA: Microsoft Research.

Hu, H., Wen, Y., Chua, T. S., & Li, X. (2014). Toward scalable systems for big data analytics: A technology tutorial. *IEEE Access, 2*, 652–687. doi:10.1109/ACCESS.2014.2332453

Jaiswal, M., & Sharma, A. K. (2013). A Survey on Spectrum Sensing Techniques for Cognitive Radio. In *Proceedings of Conference on Advances in Communication and Control Systems (CAC2S).* Atlantis Press.

Jardak, C., Mähönen, P., & Riihijärvi, J. (2014). Spatial big data and wireless networks: Experiences, applications, and research challenges. *IEEE Network, 28*(4), 26–31. doi:10.1109/MNET.2014.6863128

Kala, R., Shulkla, A., & Tiwari, R. (2009, March). *Fuzzy Neuro systems for machine learning for large data sets. Advance Computing Conference, 2009. IACC 2009. IEEE International,* 541-545. doi:10.1109/IADCC.2009.4809069

Kaur, N., & Aulakh, I. K. (2015). A Survey of Cooperative Spectrum Sensing in Cognitive Radio Networks. *International Journal on Recent and Innovation Trends in Computing and Communication, 3*(11), 6313–6316.

Kriegeskorte, N. (2015). Deep neural networks: *A new framework for modeling biological vision and brain information processing. Annual Review of Vision Science, 1*(1), 417–446. doi:10.1146/annurev-vision-082114-035447

Kune, R., Konugurthi, P. K., Agarwal, A., Rao Chillarige, R., & Buyya, R. (2014). Genetic Algorithm based Data-aware Group Scheduling for Big Data Clouds. *International Symposium on Big Data Computing,* 96-104. doi:10.1109/BDC.2014.15

Le, N. T., Martin, L., Mumme, C., & Pinkwart, N. (2012) Communication-free detection of resource conflicts in multi-agent-based cyber-physical systems. *Proceedings of the 6th IEEE International Conference on Digital Ecosystems Technologies (DEST)*, 1-6. doi:10.1109/DEST.2012.6227952

Leung, S. T., & Gobioff, H. (2003). The Google file system. *SOSP'03 Proceeding of Nineteenth ACM Symposium on Operating Systems Principles*, 29-43.

Liang, Y., Zeng, Y., Peh, E. C. Y., & Hoang, A. T. H. (2008). Sensing-Throughput Tradeoff for Cognitive Radio Networks. *IEEE Transactions on Wireless Communications*, 7(4), 1326–1337. doi:10.1109/TWC.2008.060869

Lynggaard, P., & Skouby, K. E. (2015). Deploying 5G-technologies in smart city and smart home wireless sensor networks with interferences. *Wireless Personal Communications*, 81(4), 1399–1413. doi:10.1007/s11277-015-2480-5

Mane, D., & Salian, S. (2015). Utilizing Big Data, Cognitive Computing and Big Data Testing to deduce optimized result based decisions. *International Journal of Engineering Research and General Science*, 3(3), 351–356.

Manyika, J., Chui, M., Brown, B., Bughin, J., Dobbs, R., Roxburgh, C., & Byers, A. H. (2011). *Big data: The next frontier for innovation, competition, and productivity.* San Francisco, CA: McKinsey Global Institute.

Nower, N., Tan, Y. S., & Lim, A. O. (2014). Efficient temporal and spatial data recovery scheme for stochastic and incomplete feedback data of cyber-physical systems. In *Proceedings of the 8th IEEE International Symposium on Service Oriented System Engineering (SOSE)*. Oxford, UK: IEEE. doi:10.1109/SOSE.2014.29

Peng, M., Li, Y., Zhao, Z., & Wang, C. (2015). System architecture and key technologies for 5G heterogeneous cloud radio access networks. *IEEE Network*, 29(2), 6–14. doi:10.1109/MNET.2015.7064897 PMID:26504265

Prasad, K. K., & Aithal, P. S. (2015). *Massive Growth of banking technology with the aid of 5G technologies.* International Journal of Management. *IT and Engineering*, 5(7), 616–627.

Rajkumar, R., Lee, I., Sha, L., & Stankovic, J. (2010). Cyber-Physical Systems: The Next Computing Revolution. *Proceedings of Design Automation Conference*, 731-736.

Rappaport, T. S. (2012). *Wireless Communications* (2nd ed.). New Delhi: Pearson Education.

Subhedar, M., & Birajdar, G. (2011). Spectrum Sensing Techniques in Cognitive Radio Networks: A Survey. *International Journal of Next Generation Networks*, *3*(2), 37–51. doi:10.5121/ijngn.2011.3203

Tseng, Y. L. (2015). LTE-Advanced enhancement for vehicular communication. *IEEE Wireless Communications*, *22*(6), 4–7. doi:10.1109/MWC.2015.7368815

Wang, K., Shao, Y., Shu, L., Zhu, C., & Zhang, Y. (2016). Mobile big data fault-tolerant processing for eHealth networks. *IEEE Network*, *30*(1), 36–42. doi:10.1109/MNET.2016.7389829

Xu, Y., Zeng, M., Liu, Q., & Wang, X. (2014). A Genetic Algorithm Based Multilevel Association Rules Mining for Big Datasets. *Mathematical Problems in Engineering*, 1–9.

Zeng, Y., Liang, Y., Hoang, A. T., & Zhang, R. (2009). A Review on Spectrum Sensing for Cognitive Radio: Challenges and Solutions. *EURASIP Journal on Advances in Signal Processing*, *2010*, 15.

Zhang, W., Mallik, R. K., & Lataeif, K. B. (2009). Optimization of Cooperative Spectrum Sensing with Energy Detection in Cognitive Radio Networks. *IEEE Transactions on Wireless Communications*, *8*(12), 5761–5766. doi:10.1109/TWC.2009.12.081710

Zhu, Q. Y., Bushnell, L., & Basar, T. (2013). *Resilient distributed control of multi-agent cyber-physical systems. In Control of Cyber-Physical Systems*. Springer.

Chapter 4
Efficiently Processing Big Data in Real–Time Employing Deep Learning Algorithms

Murad Khan
Sarhad University of Science and Information Technology, Pakistan

Bhagya Nathali Silva
Kyungpook National University, South Korea

Kijun Han
Kyungpook National University, South Korea

ABSTRACT

Big Data and deep computation are among the buzzwords in the present sophisticated digital world. Big Data has emerged with the expeditious growth of digital data. This chapter addresses the problem of employing deep learning algorithms in Big Data analytics. Unlike the traditional algorithms, this chapter comes up with various solutions to employ advanced deep learning mechanisms with less complexity and finally present a generic solution. The deep learning algorithms require less time to process the big amount of data based on different contexts. However, collecting the accurate feature and classifying the context into patterns using neural networks algorithms require high time and complexity. Therefore, using deep learning algorithms in integration with neural networks can bring optimize solutions. Consequently, the aim of this chapter is to provide an overview of how the advance deep learning algorithms can be used to solve various existing challenges in Big Data analytics.

DOI: 10.4018/978-1-5225-3015-2.ch004

INTRODUCTION

Big Data and deep computing have gained a smashing popularity over the past few decades. The emergence of Big Data was accompanied by the exponential growth of digital data. Big Data has been defined in multiple aspects and perspectives. In general, Big Data is a prodigious amount of digital data, which is strenuous to manage and analyze using generic software tools and techniques. According to the National Security Agency, 1826 petabytes are processing by the internet on a daily basis ("National Security Agencey: Missions Authorities, Oversight and Partnerships", 2013). Surprisingly, in 2011 it was found that the world's data volume has grown in nine times within five years. This extraordinary growth rate is estimated to reach 35 trillion gigabytes in 2020 (Gantz & Reinsel, 2011). Due to this exponential digital data generation, Big Data continues to receive an extreme attention from the industrial experts as well as from the interested researchers. In fact, Big Data requires expeditious processing over voluminous data sets with high variety and high veracity (Zhang, Yang and Chen, 2016). Therefore, it creates a compelling demand to discover and to adopt technologies capable of speedy processing on heterogeneous data. Numerous embedded devices connected to the network generates heterogeneous data. Figure 1 illustrates a classical architecture of heterogeneous devices connected over different communication technologies. Generic characteristics of Big Data is known as three V's of Big Data i.e. variety, velocity, and volume. A variety of data is referred to multiple formats of data being stored. For example, a collection of text, image, audio, video, numeric, etc. data types in structured, semi-structured, and unstructured forms are considered as data sets with variety. The size aspect of the data is the volume of data. In a modern technological era, data volume is rapidly growing with the invention of social media and popularity of embedded devices. In fact, the data generation speed is known as the velocity of Big Data. The technological advancements have influenced the dramatic increase in the velocity. Moreover, Big Data includes incomplete, redundant data as well as inaccurate and obsolete data. Thus, it is denoted that Big Data consists of high veracity data. Consequent to the rapid growth in digital data, myriads of opportunities in numerous fields i.e. educational services, enterprises, manufacturing services, social networking and much more are emerging. Consequently, these opportunities of Big Data have geared the research community towards data-driven discovery. Indeed, Big Data phenomenon has influenced all aspects of the social lifestyles in the modern world. Even though, Big Data occupies a colossal amount of data, discovering precise knowledge from the gathered data is not an easy task. Henceforth, the spotlight is focused towards the standard representation, storage, analysis, and mining of Big Data. The extreme heterogeneous nature of Big Data hinders the capability of feature learning by conventional data mining methods and algorithms. In fact, not only the advancements of the existing technologies, it is required collaboration among associative teams as well in order to extract valuable knowledge from Big Data. The advancements of the computation capabilities and enhanced machine learning mechanisms have broadened boundaries of data analytics and knowledge discovery procedures. However, the extraction of knowledge from Big Data using conventional learning algorithms is an extremely laborious task. It might be impossible in certain scenarios. The large volumes of data demand the scalability of the algorithm in order to process Big Data. Moreover, the great variety of data requires the algorithm to identify hidden relationships among heterogeneous data. The interest groups have yearned to discover novel mechanisms to accomplish the tedious task, which cannot be fulfilled by the conventional learning algorithms. Efforts in the recent past have identified that the integration of deep learning with high-performance computation offers favorable outcomes in knowledge extraction from Big Data.

The conventional learning algorithms occupy shallow learning architectures. In contrast, the deep learning algorithms incorporate deep architectures (Bengio and Bengio, 2000). The deep learning mechanisms utilize machine-learning techniques such as supervised learning and unsupervised learning to learn hierarchical relationships among heterogeneous data. Accordingly, it classifies the data autonomously (Ranzato, Boureau and Yann, 2007). Deep learning algorithms have gained a wider acceptance from the research community due to its remarkable performance in various domains i.e. speech recognition, computer vision, fraud detection, and advanced search. The deep learning algorithms classify and process natural signals based on the data processing mechanisms of the human brain. In the past few decades, leading global organizations with a massive amount of data collections i.e. Apple, Google, and Facebook has decided to take a step forward towards the deep learning to receive tremendous benefits from Big Data. Deep belief networks (DBN) and convolutional neural networks (CNN) are well established deep architectures. The conventional learning mechanisms tend to trap in local optima, which leads to performance deterioration. Even though the collection of unlabeled data is a cheap task, these data are neglected in conventional algorithms. Thus, DBN architecture is introduced to learn features from both labeled and unlabeled data, while overcoming the above-stated drawbacks. The DBN includes two folds 1) unsupervised pre-training and 2) supervised fine-tuning. DBN utilizes stack/s of restricted Boltzmann machines (RBM) to perform pre-training. This helps the DBN to avoid local optima. Concisely, DBN uses a greedy approach to learn unlabeled data and uses back propagation to fine-tune the learned variables. CNN is another deep learning architecture consists of multiple layers. In CNN, there are separate layers for feature representation and classification. The process initiates with the two altering layers. One performs the convolutional operations and the other one

Figure 1. Classical network architecture connecting heterogeneous devices and components through multiple communication technologies

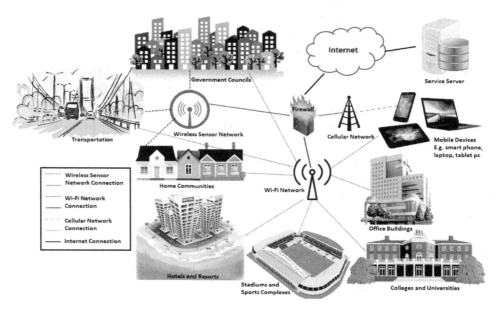

reduces the size of the next layers. The CNN follows a bio-inspired process to learn hierarchical features. Further, it automatically learns feature hierarchies and provides translational invariances to a certain extent. The performance of CNN is preserved due to the learning strategies it follows i.e. local receptive field, shared weights, and sub-sampling.

The astounding performance of deep learning in many application domains has made the experts accept deep learning as a promising technology for Big Data analysis. On one hand, training the deep learning architecture for Big Data analysis is not an easy task. On the other hand, it was found that deep learning training process can be improved significantly with the aid of great computing power. Thus, multiple attempts were made to design deep learning architectures, which performs remarkably well in the training process owing to the high-speed computation. The extensive attention of the researchers resulted in a significant improvement in large-scale deep learning mechanisms i.e. large-scale deep belief networks, large-scale convolutional neural networks, commodity off-the-shelf high-performance computing (COTS HPC) system, and parallel schemes. A large-scale DBN can train more than 100 million free parameters with millions of unlabeled data. Raina, et al. proposed a framework to parallelize DBN using graphical processing units (GPU). This large-scale DBN stores all parameters and a bigger portion of training data on the global memory. Thus, it reduces the data transfer time. The GPU based DBN performance fit for Big Data learning, since it enhances DBN performance up to 70 times (Raina, Madhavan and Ng, 2009). Similarly, CNN occupies GPU to implement large-scale CNN. The training process of large-scale CNN consists with forward and backward propagation. Moreover, it supports data parallelism. The threads perform parallel convolutional operations and store the results in global memory. Later, a software framework called DistBelief was developed to train distributed very large deep networks. It facilitates data parallelism and involves two optimization procedures. Even though DistBelief efficiently learns from very large models, the training requires 16000 central processing unit (CPU) cores. As a solution, Coates, et al. develop a deep network model, which can perform similarly with three machines (Coates, Huval, Wang, Wu, Catanzaro and Andrew, 2013). The COTS HPC is designed with CUDA kernels to manage memory and to perform computations efficiently.

The exponential growth in Big Data requires efficient deep learning methods to manage and analyze rapidly growing digital data. When applying deep computation into large-scale networks, it is essential to meet three V's characteristics of Big Data for a fruitful learning process. However, centralize processing and storing leads to inefficiencies in deep learning algorithms on massive amounts of data. Therefore, the current trend is deviating towards distributed frameworks and parallel computing to attain the training speed at no accuracy relinquish. Moreover, it is essential for deep learning to adapt the high variety of data caused due to the heterogeneity of the data generation source. Data integration is considered as the fundamental characteristic to meet a high variety of the digital data. The representational learning ability with or without supervision is used to classify or cluster Big Data. Initially, deep learning algorithms identify intermediate or abstract representations. In order to generate a natural solution, identified representations are integrated in a hierarchical manner. Another major concern is to meet the high velocity of data generation in Big Data notion. In fact, deep learning should learn timely to process data efficiently. Thus, online learning has become a prominent technique. Moreover, it is particularly applicable, since the machine cannot hold the complete dataset in the memory. In general, online learning learns a single context at a time and it will be soon after consumable to refine the model. However, the progress of this area is passive in the recent past.

OVERVIEW OF DEEP LEARNING

In general, deep learning consists of a set of learning mechanisms and techniques that learn multiple and hierarchical representations in a deep manner. Moreover, the deep learning architectures are widely divided into two main parts, i.e. 1) Deep belief networks (DBN) and convolutional neural network (CNN).

Deep Belief Networks

The performance of conventional neural networks depends on how efficiently it solves the local optimal problem for a non-convex objective function. However, most of the conventional neural networks are affected by the false local optimal problem (Rumelhart et al, 1986), Moreover, such schemes show poor performance in the case of unlabeled data. In addition, unlabeled data mainly affect the performance require extra hard work in the case of big data. In order to address the aforementioned problems, the DBN is implanted which efficiently uses a predefined deep architecture of collecting various important features both for labeled and unlabeled data (G. H., Salakhutdinov, 2006). The DBN uses a two-tier models i.e. pre-training and supervised tuning. The later one is used to perform a local search strategy for fine tuning and the former one is used to learn the distribution of data by skipping label information. The illustration of DBN based on Restricted Boltzmann machines (RBM) and an additional level of discrimination tasks is shown in Figure 2. RBMs have been widely used as a generative model for many different types of data i.e. labeled and unlabeled (Hinton, 2010). However, their main concerned is directly based on learning modules that are consisting of deep belief nets. After the initial structure of the RBM is formed, the next step is to assign weights to layers based on the training. The training module following an initial unsupervised learning. Moreover, it is very important to make decision-based on the units that are employed in the RBM system. These units also help in constructing the states at different levels. In addition, the process of learning is continuously monitored until and unless the entire training process is finished. The RBM also follows an interconnected layering architecture. The nodes in one layer are not connected to the nodes in the same layer instead, they are connected with nodes in different layers. Moreover, each node in one particular layer is completely independent of the nodes in the same layer. In addition, this phenomenon of independence helps in constructing a layer by layer architecture.

A layer-wise pre-training is performed before tuning. In pre-training phase, the output from each RBM of one layer is fed into the other layer. The process is repeated until all the layers are pre-trained. The main advantage of layer-wise training is to address the local optima and overfitting problem. The sampling probabilities of a visible and hidden layer in the case of a simple RBM and implanting Bernoulli distribution is given as follows (Wang and Shen, 2007)..

$$P\left(H_k = 1 \mid V;W\right) = \rho\left(\sum_{i=1}^{N} w_{ik}V_i + \alpha_k\right) \tag{1}$$

and

$$P\left(V_l = 1 \mid H;W\right) = \rho\left(\sum_{j=1}^{N} w_{lj}H + \alpha_k\right) \tag{2}$$

where H and V represents a K*1 hidden unit vector and J*1 represents a visible unit vector, respectively. W, α,β and η, represents the weight matrix, bias terms, and a sigmoid function respectively.

Moreover, the weights on each step are updated based on the contrastive divergence approximation (CDA) (Hinton, 2002). For instance following equation 3, shows how to update the weights at step t +1

$$\Delta W_{kl}\left(t + 1\right) = m\Delta W_{kl}\left(t\right) + \delta\left(\left\langle V_k H_l\right\rangle_{data} - \left\langle V_k H_l\right\rangle_{model}\right) \tag{3}$$

where m and δ is the momentum factor and learning rate. The expectations for data and model is represented using $\left\langle \cdot \right\rangle_{data}$ and $\left\langle \cdot \right\rangle_{model}$.

One of the important features of RBM is the sampling of data without labeling. This feature helps in processing a large amount of data in less time compared to other techniques. Thus, it can help in processing big data with reasonable computation and time. Moreover, the literature consists of several other techniques such as autoencoders spare coding instead of using RBM for unsupervised feature learning (Vincent, 2008; Larochelle, 2009, Lee, Battle, Raina, Ng, n.d.) . However, weight computation is still a challenging job in RBM instead of using above techniques. Therefore, many researchers suggest using random initial weights instead of computing predetermine weights. In particular, the DBNs uses a dual strategy of improving the performance of the network. First, it uses a greedy approach in a layerwise fashion to learn the estimated weights and then follow a propagation method for tuning.

Convolutional Neural Networks

A CNN is composed of a set of the layer in a hierarchical manner. The layers are normally of two types i.e. convolution and sub-sampling layer (LeCun, Bottou, Bengio, Haffner, 1998). In the case of convolution layer, a number of equal size filters are used to perform convolution operations. Similarly, in the case of subsampling layer,

Figure 2. A conceptual overview of the deep belief networks

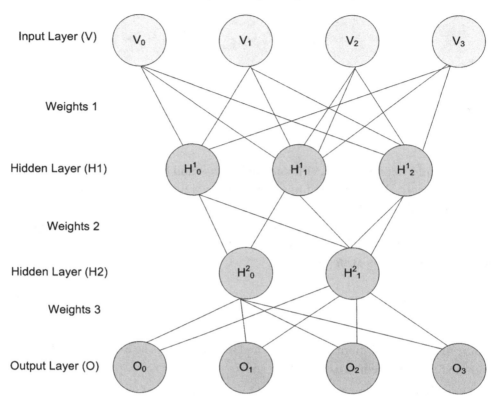

the pixels in a particular region is averaged to reduce the processing for next layers (Ciresan, Meier, Masci, Gamardella, Schmidbuber, 2011). The structure of a typical CNN concept is shown in Figure 3. The initial layer is the input layer represented by a 2d matrix of NXN images. The first convolution (C1) extract some specific visual information by applying some various filter maps. The value of each feature map depends on two factors 1i. 1) The particular receptive field of the input layer and 2) Filter used. This computation is carried out by following Equation 4.

$$O_k^l = f\left(\sum_n F_{nk} \otimes t_n^{l-1} + c_k\right) \tag{4}$$

where O is the output from Kth convolution of the previous layer "l", f represents a nonlinear functional operates over three different factors i.e. 1) a filter "F", 2) feature map "t" and 3) bias "C"

Moreover, the filter directly depends on the type of information. For example, if the filter is set to extract the information from a particular region, then it always connects that particular information from the previous layer to next layer. The researchers suggested various techniques to perform sub-sampling. However, the key functionality of sub-sampling is to reduce the spatial resolution.

Deep Belief Networks and Big Data

The DBN is used by many researchers to process big data in an efficient way. For instance, a GPU based architectural model is presented to process the massive amount of data in (Raina, 2009). The author suggested the use of stacked RBMs in a parallel fashion to incorporate a huge amount of data with less processing time. Moreover, the proposed model process and train hundred million parameters compared to the previous research work where they process 3.8 million parameters (Raina, 2009). However, implanting the proposed model for large-scale data have several problems such as transferring the data between client and global memory. One of the most efficient work has done in this regard by placing all the parameters and training solution in the global memory during the training phase. Moreover, a data parallel processing can be used to perform concurrent updates across each block of information.

However, the GPU implementation shows efficient result in the case of incorporating several million parameters in RBM. A number of 4.5 million parameters and 1 million examples is passed to RBM for testing. The speed of DBN learning is increased by a factor of 70 (Raina, 2009).

Figure 3. Deep Belief Networks based on Restricted Boltzmann machines

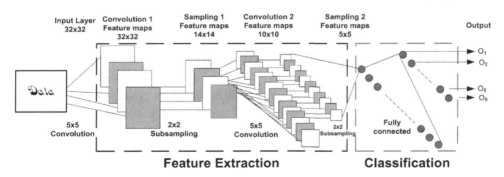

Convolutional Neural Networks and Big Data

In a CNN, a large number of deep learning methods are connected locally. Therefore, such type of networks is implemented on several hundred cores based on GPU implementation. The feature maps are assigned based on the blocks of information coming from the previous layer. However, it directly depends on the size of feature maps (Ciresan et al, 2011). A single block consists of several threads and each thread is attached to a single neuron. Similarly, the rest of the process is carried out by the convolution of neurons, activation, and summation. Finally, the output from above methods is stored in a global memory. This entire process follows a backward and propagation model for processing data efficiently. However, a single propagation doesn't generate good results, therefore, the parallelizing of propagation is carried out by pulling or pushing operations (Ciresan et al, 2011). Moreover, such process is affected by the border effects because the neurons in one layer may connect to a different number of neurons (Simard et al, 2003). The data parallelism directly depends on the global memory and feature map size. The shared memory always affect the parallelism process. However, a circular buffer concept of the limited shared memory is suggested in (Scherer, 2010). The operation of convolution is performed by a thread in a parallel fashion and the results are written back to global memory. However, in the case of big data analytics limited shared memory still exists a challenging job. Therefore, researchers suggest a method of combining the convolution and sampling process in one step (Scherer, 2010). Thus, a back propagation is applied with storing the activities and error values in one step. A similar approach of using two GPUs, five convolution, and three classification layers is suggested for high-speed processing of large data in (Krizhevsky, 2012) A layerwise processing is performed by assigning half of the layer processing to one GPU and half to another. Moreover, both the GPU transfer and communicate with each other without affecting host memory.

CHALLENGES FOR LARGE-SCALE BIG DATA

In the past few years, Big Data has been widely accepted by government bodies and public society. Though the capacity of Big Data is remarkable, achieving its full capability is still challenged in the real world. In fact, ideas and algorithms beyond the regular thinking frame help to enrich the concept of Big Data learning to overcome existing challenges. In the past, machine-learning algorithms learned patterns after loading all data into memory. However, this mode of machine learning is no longer valid and realistic for Big Data learning, since the algorithms are supposed to learn from bulky data. As previously mentioned, integrating deep learning mechanisms for Big Data learning is a worthy solution. The extreme complexity of Big Data has pulled down the evolution of large-scale deep learning. This sluggish development is mainly due to the challenges arise from three V's of Big Data. Which is commonly known as massive amounts of data (high volume), various types of data (high variety), and rapid data generation (high velocity). The rest of this section briefly explains three V's impact with respect to deep learning.

Challenges for High Volume Data

The high volume of data is considered as the greatest challenge for deep learning. Generally, Big Data includes a very large set of output classes and very large number of free parameters. Indeed, these properties immensely increase the processing time and the complexity of the deep network. Consequent to the boundless volumes of data, training of a deep learning network with a centralized architecture (processors and storage) is tedious or might be impossible. Thus, distributed architectures with parallelized machines are favored. The efforts made in the recent past became successful in alleviating certain challenges caused after high volumes. The schemed ideas occupy a collection of CPUs or GPUs to enhance the speed of training. Thus, it achieved efficiency without compromising accuracy. The two main strategies for parallelism i.e. data parallelism and model parallelism have been developed (Coates et al, 2013).

Moreover, the novel deep learning frameworks are scalable according to the number of GPUs and can handle enormous amounts samples and parameters. It expects that computational power and computer memory keep growing continuously. However, that is not enough to scale the existing deep learning frameworks. It is essential to meet the computation related features such as copying large sets of data, in order to facilitate deep learning scalability for very large data sets. Eventually, the realization of scalable deep learning frameworks for Big Data should confirm high-performance architecture along with effective parallel learning algorithms. Incomplete and noisy data included in Big Data is another major challenge. In general, the training data sets of classical machine learning are noiseless and assure completeness. However, Big Data includes noisy labels with incomplete data, as a result of vastly varied data origin and heterogeneity. The consequences are worsened with the larger portions of unlabeled data and noisy labels. Deep learning has a remarkable ability to serve unlabeled data during training. Since it learns the relationships between data without utilizing label information. In that sense, unlike the conventional learning methods, the large portions of unlabeled data are highly supported by the deep learning methods. In deep learning, it is preferable as well as beneficial to use ample data with incomplete and noisy labels instead of using a small amount of complete and carefully labeled data. However, advanced deep learning techniques are more efficient in handling noisy and cluttered data. For example, a novel training strategy with effective cost functions can create an advanced deep learning method, which can overcome the effect of noisy labels. In addition, semi-supervised learning mechanisms can be incorporated to reduce the adverse effects of noisy labels (Wang and Shen, 2007).

Challenges for High Variety Data

The variety of Big Data is another key area of concern when proposing learning mechanisms. Nowadays, all connected devices generate vast amounts of data. The invention of smartphones, social media, and the web has influenced the dramatic rise of various multimedia data i.e. audio, video, images, animation, etc. On top of the increased data volumes, the data formats vary from sensor data to satellite data. Moreover, these varieties of data can be unstructured, semi-structured, or structured data. Hence, data integration plays a major role in facilitating learning process among heterogeneous data types. Deep learning is widely known for its ability to representation learning. Certainly, this is a blessing to deal with high variety data. Moreover, representation learning supports supervised, unsupervised, and hybrid learning. Owing to the benefits of representation learning, deep learning can learn decent feature representations for classification. The representation learning follows unsupervised learning and traverse through a hierarchy. It defines one level at a time and follows bottom up approach, which uses lower-level features to define higher-level features. Consequent to the hierarchical approach, intermediate and abstracted representations can be discovered. Hence, data integration can occupy representational learning to learn about each data source. Learning data representation is supported through deep learning. All the learned features in each level are integrated to assist learning process of heterogeneous data.

Ngiam et.al. integrated audio and video data to develop an innovative application for deep learning, which learns representations of varied data (Ngiam et al, 2011). Worthy to note that deep learning is highly acknowledged for its efficiency in integrating data from different origins. Moreover, Ngiam et.al. confirm that deep learning is fruitful in two aspects 1) learning shared representations for multiple types and 2) learning single representation. The shared representations perceive interrelationships among various types of data. Meanwhile, single representation is capable of capturing single type among various unlabeled types. Srivastav and Salakhutdinov fused two contrasting data types using a multimodal deep Boltzmann machines (DBM) (Srivastava et al, 2014). They fused real-value dense image and text data to find a common representation for multi-modal data. The DBM is a generative model, which is not fine-tuned. The multi-modal DBM is formed from stacked RBMs. Each RBM represents a single modality. In order to assist collective representation of RBMs, an additional layer is added to the architecture. The additional layer of binary hidden units (BHU) resides on top of the RBMs and create DBM from RBMs. This layer of BHU learns distribution across the RBMs and allow learning from garbled modalities.

The recent works on deep learning exposed its abilities to use heterogeneous data with a high variety in order to enhance the learning performance. However, challenges in this regard still remain. One common challenge is the conflicts of information. The deep learning process can fuse and learn the common representations, but it cannot resolve the conflicts of data from multiple sources. Moreover, the benefit of deep learning to enhance the performance of multiple types is still questionable. Since existing learning mechanisms are experimented on bi-modals (two types). Further, the required number of layers in deep learning architecture for feature fusion of heterogeneous data remains as another challenge.

Challenges for High-Velocity Data

Big Data learning is further challenged by high-velocity data. An infinite number of connected devices and people generate data at a very high speed. The expeditious data generation requires timely processing of data. Online learning approach is an excellent fit for high-speed learning. Online learning learns a single instance at a time and exposes the true label of the instance soon after learning (Shalev-Shwartz, 2012). Thus, the labels can be used to improve the model. Consequent to the larger data sets, current machines are unable to hold the complete data set. Thus, the sequential processing of online approach is a promising learning method for Big Data. Online learning has been tested for classical neural networks. However, the work done on deep learning networks for online learning is minimal. Usually, deep learning approaches use a training example with a defined label to refine the model parameters. This training method is known as stochastic gradient descent approach (Shalev-Shwartz, Singer, Cotter, 2011). This learning approach is feasible extendable for online learning approach. The processing speed can be upgraded by allowing mini batch processing instead of single instance processing. Moreover, mini batch processing maintains the balance between computer memory and execution time.

The data distribution of high-velocity data shows an extremely changeable (non-stationary) nature, which is another primary challenge for Big Data learning. Non-stationary data are divided into portions, to hold data belongs to a narrow time interval. The division takes place with the assumption that proximal time scales hold approximately stationary data (Chien, Heieh, 2013). Moreover, they represent a correlation among data to a certain extent and follow a similar distribution pattern. Hence, the ability of learning data as a stream considered to be an important feature of deep learning for Big Data. The area to experiment further is deep online learning.

In general, online learning is memory bound and capable of parallel processing. Essentially, Big Data learning algorithms should be capable of learning non-independent and identically distributed (non-iid) data.

Certainly, deep learning can transfer learning or follow domain adaption to influence high variety and high velocity of Big Data. These mechanisms sample training data and test data of different distributions. Glorot, et al. developed a deep architecture based on stacked de-noising auto-encoder. It trains a large set of unlabeled data using unsupervised representation (Glorot, Bordes, Bengio, 2011). It classifies unlabeled data into a set of identified domains using few labeled data from each domain. The labeled examples determine domains of the model. The experimental data revealed the ability of deep learning to elicit valid high-level representations, which are shared across disparate domains. Recently, Benjio experimented on transfer learning by applying deep learning of multiple level representations (Bengio, 2012). The finding revealed that many abstract features identified in deep learning are common in training and test data. Therefore, deep learning is a well-fitting approach for transfer learning as it is capable of identifying common features of presented data. However, the practical application of transfer learning based on deep learning is still in its infancy. Finally, the biggest question mark is to determine the potential of transfer learning to benefit Big Data with deep networks.

MOBILE BIG DATA ANALYTICS

Mobile devices became a convenient and trustworthy platform to facilitate ubiquitous computing. The evolution of mobile device i.e. smart phones, tablet pcs, and Internet of Things (IoT) gadgets have resulted in an exponential growth in mobile data generation. The dramatic rise in the volume of mobile data coined the concept of Mobile Big Data (MBD).

MBD Overview

MBD can be defined as the colossal amount of mobile data. MBD includes valuable information to handle fraud detection, marketing, context-aware computing, etc. However, the massive amounts of MBD cannot be processed using a single machine. The benefits of MBD have drawn the attention of experts towards extracting useful information from unprocessed mobile data. This area of interest is known as MBD analytics. Deep learning is a reliable candidate for MBD analytics. Deep learning offers highly accurate results utilizing unlabeled mobile data. It occupies unsupervised feature extraction to learn the relationships among heterogeneous mobile data. However, the efficiency of deep model MBD analytics is diminished due to a large number of dimensions and high data volume. In contrast, mobile data systems tend to act real-time, since quicker decisions ensure higher user satisfaction.

MBD collects data from various mobile devices i.e. smart phones, wearable computers, laptops, IoT gadgets, etc. connected to a mobile network. Various mobile applications have come into existence thanks to the deployment of multiple sensors i.e. accelerometers, compasses, and GPS sensors. The mobile devices use stateless data interchange structures like JavaScript object notation (JSON) to wrap the service requests and sensor data, in order to share across the network. The importance of stateless structure is it supports mobile devices operates on different operating systems such as iOS, Android, and Windows. The service server finds hidden structures and patterns of collected MBD with the aid of MBD analytics. MBD analytics play an important role in building complex mobile systems. The flexibility of MBD analytics is comparatively higher than the classical MBD problems since the sources are mobile and data traffic is crowd-sourced. The large amounts of data collected from innumerable mobile devices complicate the learning process. Thus, MBD analytics become harder compared to the analysis of small datasets of mobile data.

Challenges for MDB Analytics

The generic features of MBD introduce challenges to MBD analytics. MBD is a large-scale mobile network, which generates data at a high speed. Mobile networks support mobility and allow distributed sensing via the mobile devices. This section briefly explains impacts of large-scale mobile data, mobility, and crowd sensing on MBD analytics.

The mobile data traffic is continuously increasing due to the proliferation of mobile devices and expansion high-speed mobile networks. The large-scale mobile networks have the adverse effects of high volume and high-velocity data. Importantly, MBD data flows rapidly (high velocity), which may increase the latency due to traffic. Consequently, it results in diminished user satisfaction and incremented cost as a result of delayed decisions. MBD collects data from portable devices. The mobility of the devices leads to the creation of non-stationary MBD. The mobility aspect can significantly reduce the available time duration for decision-making. Since the validity of collected data depends on the nature of mobility. Crowdsensing is another important feature of MBD that can be a challenge at the same time. In crowd sensing, the sensing devices are not of the same type and belongs to multiple users at different places. Due to the fact, MBD analytics face issues arising from the high variety and high veracity. The quality of sensed MBD is not guaranteed since the mobile system does not manipulate the mobile sensing process. Moreover, there are various reasons that increase the amount of incomplete and low-quality MBD. Noise is the most prominent reason for futile MBD. In addition, malfunctioning sensors and intruders can result in incomplete data. Indeed, less quality data leads to less accuracy in MBD analytics. The heterogeneity is another concerning factor for MBD analytics. Various types of mobile devices generate MBD traffic and analyzing high variety mobile data is an issue that is worth to address to realize MBD analytics in real world context.

In summary, MBD analytics is all about discovering new patterns and knowledge from collected MBD. Thus, MBD is beneficial to uplift the service provision, while achieving lucrative business goals. However, challenges are existing in the area of MBD analytics, which needs to be addressed to further the evolution of MBD analytics.

CONCLUSION

Big Data notion has developed along with the dramatic rise of the digital data creation consequent to smart devices, social networks, and the web. In generic terms, Big Data large volumes of data generated at a high speed by heterogeneous devices. Big Data analytics is a trending topic in the modern world due to its advantages. The deep learning phenomena such as DBN and CNN is widely used to process the data in real-time. However, the capability of conventional machine learning techniques in Big Data analytics is limited by the volume, variety, and velocity of Big Data. Thus, the experts foresaw deep learning as a potential candidate for Big Data analytics. As mentioned in the previous sections, Big Data learning facilitated through deep learning mechanisms exhibit significantly better performance. However, the applications of deep learning for Big Data should be further extended in order to overcome unresolved challenges. MBD comes under Big Data, which concern about large amounts of mobile data. MBD has become the spotlight among mobile service providers due to its benefits in achieving business goals.

REFERENCES

Bengio, Y. (2012). Deep Learning of Representations for Unsupervised and Transfer Learning. *Journal of Machine Learning Research*, 27, 17–37.

Bengio, Y., & Bengio, S. (2000). *Modeling High-Dimensional Discrete Data*. Adv. Neural Inf. Process. Syst.

Chien, J.-T., & Hsieh, H.-L. (2013). Nonstationary Source Separation Using Sequential and Variational Bayesian Learning. *IEEE Transactions on Neural Networks and Learning Systems*, 24(5), 681–694. doi:10.1109/TNNLS.2013.2242090 PMID:24808420

Ciresan, D. C., Meier, U., Masci, J., Gambardella, L. M., & Schmidhuber, J. (2011). Flexible, high performance convolutional neural networks for image classification. *Proc. 22nd Int. Conf. Artif. Intell.*

Coates, A., Huval, B., Wang, T., Wu, D., Catanzaro, B., & Andrew, N. (2013). Deep learning with COTS HPC systems. *Journal of Machine Learning Research, 28*(3), 1337–1345.

Gantz, J., & Reinsel, D. (2011). *Extracting Value from Chaos*. Available: https://www.emc.com/collateral/analyst-reports/idc-extracting-value-from-chaos-ar.pdf

Glorot, X., Bordes, A., & Bengio, Y. (2011). Domain adaptation for large-scale sentiment classification: A deep learning approach. *28th International Conference on Machine Learning*.

Hinton, G. (2002). Training products of experts by minimizing contrastive divergence. *Neural Computation, 14*(8), 1771–1800. doi:10.1162/089976602760128018 PMID:12180402

Hinton, G. (2010). *Apractical guide to training restricted Boltzmann machines*. Toronto, Canada: Dept. Comput. Sci., Univ.

Krizhevsky, I. S. G. H. A. (2012). *ImageNet classification with deep convolutional neural networks*. Proc. Adv. NIPS.

Larochelle, Y. B. J. L. P. L. H. (2009). Exploring strategies for training deep neural networks. *Journal of Machine Learning Research, 10*, 1–40.

LeCun, Y., Bottou, L., Bengio, Y., & Haffner, P. (1998). Gradient-based learning applied to document recognition. *Proceedings of the IEEE, 86*(11), 2278–2324. doi:10.1109/5.726791

Lee, H., Battle, A., Raina, R., & Ng, A. (n.d.). Efficient sparse coding algorithms. Proc. Neural Inf. Procees. Syst.

National Security Agency. (2013). *The National Security Agency: Missions, Authorities, Oversight and Partnerships*. Available: https://www.nsa.gov/public_info/_files/speeches_testimonies/2013_08_09_the_nsa_story.pdf

Ngiam, J., Khosla, A., Kim, M., Nam, J., Lee, H., & Ng, A. Y. (2011). Multimodal Deep Learning. *28th International Conference on Machine Learning*.

Raina, A. M. A. N. R. (2009). Large-scale deep unsupervised learning using graphics processors. *Proc. 26th Int. Conf. Mach. Learn.* doi:10.1145/1553374.1553486

Raina, R., Madhavan, A., & Ng, A. Y. (2009). Large-scale deep unsupervised learning using graphics processors. *26th Annual International Conference on Machine Learning*. doi:10.1145/1553374.1553486

Ranzato, M., Boureau, Y.-L., & Yann, L. (2007). *Sparse Feature Learning for Deep Belief Networks*. Adv. Neural Inf. Process. Syst.

Rumelhart, D., Hinton, G., & Williams, R. (1986). Learning representations by back-propagating errors. *Nature*, *323*(6088), 533–536. doi:10.1038/323533a0

Salakhutdinov, G. H. R. (2006). Reducing the dimensionality of data with neural networks. *Science*, *313*(5786), 504–507. doi:10.1126/science.1127647 PMID:16873662

Scherer, A. M. S. B. D. (2010). Evaluation of pooling operations in convolutional architectures for object recognition. *Proc. Int. Conf. Artif. Neural Netw.* doi:10.1007/978-3-642-15825-4_10

Shalev-Shwartz, S. (2012). Online learning and online convex optimization. *Foundations and Trends in Machine Learning*, *4*(2), 107–194. doi:10.1561/2200000018

Shalev-Shwartz, S., Singer, Y., Srebro, N., & Cotter, A. (2011). Pegasos: Primal estimated sub-gradient solver for SVM. *Mathematical Programming*, *127*(1), 3–30. doi:10.1007/s10107-010-0420-4

Simard, P., Steinkraus, D., & Platt, J. (2003). Best practices for convolutional neural networks applied to visual document analysis. *Proc. 7th ICDAR*. doi:10.1109/ICDAR.2003.1227801

Srivastava, N., & Salakhutdinov, R. (2014). Multimodal Learning with Deep Boltzmann Machines. *Journal of Machine Learning Research*, *15*(1), 2949–2980.

Vincent, H. L. Y. B. P.-A. M. P. (2008). Extracting and composing robust features with denoising autoencoders. *Proc. 25th Int. Conf. Mach. Learn.* doi:10.1145/1390156.1390294

Wang, J., & Shen, X. (2007). Large Margin Semi-supervised Learning. *Journal of Machine Learning Research*, *8*(8), 1867–1891.

Zhang, Q., Yang, L. T., & Chen, Z. (2016). Deep Computation Model for Unsupervised Feature Learning on Big Data. *IEEE Transactions on Services Computing*, *9*(1), 161–171.

Chapter 5

Digital Investigation of Cybercrimes Based on Big Data Analytics Using Deep Learning

Ezz El-Din Hemdan
Managlore University, India

Manjaiah D. H.
Mangalore University, India

ABSTRACT

Big Data Analytics has become an important paradigm that can help digital investigators to investigate cybercrimes as well as provide solutions to malware and threat prediction, detection and prevention at an early stage. Big Data Analytics techniques can use to analysis enormous amount of generated data from new technologies such as Social Networks, Cloud Computing and Internet of Things to understand the committed crimes in addition to predict the new coming severe attacks and crimes in the future. This chapter introduce principles of Digital Forensics and Big Data as well as exploring Big Data Analytics and Deep Learning benefits and advantages that can help the digital investigators to develop and propose new techniques and methods based on Big Data Analytics using Deep Learning techniques that can be adapted to the unique context of Digital Forensics as well as support performing digital investigation process in forensically sound and timely fashion manner.

DOI: 10.4018/978-1-5225-3015-2.ch005

INTRODUCTION

Big Data Analytics and Deep Learning are two important topics in data science. Big Data has become important for several organizations and companies because they have been collecting huge amounts of data, which can contain useful and vital information about certain problems in many areas like banks, cyber security, fraud detection, marketing, and medical and healthcare. Many companies such as Google and Microsoft are analyzing massive volumes of data for business analysis and making decisions for future plans. Deep Learning is a set of machine-learning techniques based on neural networking, is still developing gradually but shows great potential for solving several problems. Deep Learning enables computers to recognize items of interest in large quantities of unstructured and binary data, and to deduce relationships without needing specific models or programming instructions. A key benefit of deep learning for big data analytics is the analysis and learning of massive amounts of unsupervised data, making it a valuable tool for big data analytics where raw data is largely unlabeled and un-categorized.

Cyber criminals and terrorists are highly trained persons and experts in computer, network, digital systems and new technologies. Massive amounts of data is gathered about criminals and their behavior from different data sources in the Internet for monitoring and tracing them in real-time and online using analytics techniques. These enormous amount of data need new fast and efficient processing tools and techniques for extracting and analyzing in less period of time. Big Data can be used to leverage predictive analytics. Digital investigators and experts can use various innovative data visualization analysis and mining technologies to identify data patterns from the massive collected data to find any digital evidence about attackers or detect and trace them through their activities by identifying suspicious behavior patterns to identify threats that are likely to happen. One important benefit of Big Data Mining for large set of data to look for key information that can be used in forensics investigation and help refute or support a claim or put together a missing piece, this has seen rapid increase in the field of digital investigation. Big Data Analytics using Deep Learning algorithms can support and improve the process of digital investigation in forensically sound and timely fashion manner.

Researchers and scientists can contribute by harnessing the power of Big Data Analytics with digital investigation to provide more effective ways to obtain useful and vital information from available digital evidence about attackers. By apprehending data thieves and disrupting attacks, digital investigations and data science can help reinforce privacy, safety, and financial security in modern society. Employing Big Data Analytics techniques to help digital investigation has various benefits and advantages such as:

- Reduce system and human processing time for huge amount of data.
- Improve the analysis of evidential data which extracting from crime scene.
- Reduce costs of digital investigation.
- Better utilization of available computing, processing and storage resources.

This chapter introduces a study based on using of Big Data Analytics using Deep Learning in the digital forensics domain to help digital practitioners and experts to design and develop new techniques and methods to cope with new technologies such as Cloud Computing and Internet of Things that generating huge and massive amount of data.

The rest of this chapter is organized as follows: firstly, provides digital forensic definition and digital forensic investigation process. Secondly, introduces cybercrime definition and categories while Big Data concepts, techniques and tools are presented thirdly. Fourthly, describes Deep Learning concepts, techniques and applications while Digital Investigation based on Big Data Analytics using Deep Learning is discussed fifthly. Finally, the chapter conclusion is presented.

DIGITAL FORENSICS

Digital forensics is a branch of forensic science that concern with finding and collecting digital evidence then analysis and examine them to find any traces related to crimes against digital systems. Digital forensics has many directions like Computer Forensics, Mobile Forensics, Network Forensics and Cloud Forensics. This sections discusses digital forensics definition as well as digital forensics investigation process that digital investigators follow it during investigation of crimes to reconstruct the crime events that occurred.

Digital Forensics Definition

The process of collecting, identifying, preserving and examining digital evidence from crime scene is known as Digital Forensics. One of the popular definition for the digital forensics is introduced by first Digital Forensic Research Workshop (DFRWS). The DFRWS defined the digital forensics as:

The use of scientifically derived and proven methods toward the preservation, collection, validation, identification, analysis, interpretation, documentation, and presentation of digital evidence derived from digital sources for the purpose of facilitating or furthering the reconstruction of events found to be criminal, or helping to anticipate unauthorized actions shown to be disruptive to planned operations (Gray, 2001).

Digital Forensic Investigation Process

Criminals and attackers after committing their cybercrimes some trails leaves behind them. Collecting, extracting and preserving digital evidences from the crime scene need careful strategies to handle and manage them to become ready for presenting in the court of law. From the digital forensics definition, the digital forensic investigation process involves many stages as shown in figure 1 as follows:

- **Identification:** Identification process is the identification of an incident and the evidence, which will be required to prove the incident.
- **Collection:** In the collection process, an examiner and digital investigator collect the digital evidence from crime scene.
- **Extraction:** In the extraction stage, digital investigator extracts digital evidence from different types of media e.g., hard disk, cell phone, e-mail, and many more.
- **Analysis:** In the analysis stage, digital investigator interprets and correlates data to come to a conclusion, which can prove or disprove an incident.

Figure 1. Digital forensics investigation process

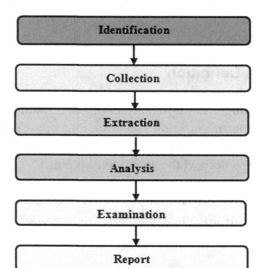

- **Examination:** In the examination stage, an investigator extracts and inspects the data and their characteristics.
- **Report:** In this process, the digital investigators make an organized report to state his findings about the incident which have to be appropriate enough to present in the jury.

CYBERCRIME

Recently, cybercrimes become a rapid-growing area of crimes that breaching system security due to innovative ideas that attackers and criminals pose in addition to new ideas and ways to commits the cybercrimes. The criminals are exploiting the convenience of the Internet to commit a range of illegal activities and severe crimes that cause big harm and pose very real threats to victims worldwide. Also, the criminals exploit vulnerabilities of new technologies to commit their crimes in a way that prevent or make it difficult to discover and trace them back.

Cybercrime Definition

Cybercrime means any illegal or criminal activity that cause crimes through the use the Internet to commit it. Cybercrime also defined as:

Offences that are committed against individuals or groups of individuals with a criminal motive to intentionally harm the reputation of the victim or cause physical or mental harm to the victim directly or indirectly, using modern computing devices and telecommunication networks. (Kamal, 2012)

Cybercrime Categories

Cybercrime is categorized as the following (Kamal, 2012):

- **The Computer as a Target:** The criminal seeks to deny the legitimate users or owners of the system access to their data or computers such as Denial of Service (DOS) attacks.
- **The Computer as a Tool of the Crime:** The computer is used to gain some other criminal objective. For example, a thief may use a computer to steal personal information.
- **The Computer as Incidental to a Crime:** It used the computer to facilitate the crime where the computer is not the main instrument of the crime.

- **Crimes Associated with the Prevalence of Computers:** This means the crimes against the computer industry, such as software copyright and piracy.

BIG DATA

Big Data topic is full of interest and promise masses of large data set. Big Data describes the tools and techniques used to manage and process data that classical and traditional means cannot easily accomplish. There are many benefits from using Big Data for example in business to make better decisions and plan for future. In the last years, several Big Data solutions are used to solve and handle complex problems in timely fashion manner.

Big Data Concept

Recently, Big Data has become popular and future research confines. Big Data is the description for large amount of data sets that traditional techniques and tools are inadequate or cannot manage and process this data. Big Data can be in multitude forms like structured, unstructured, and semi-structured data. Big Data pose various challenges which include analysis, search, manage, process, store, visualize and transfer in secure manner. To solve these challenges, there is a serious need for Big Data solutions such as enormous storage and rapid processing engines that can work in distributing and parallel way. Big Data providing benefits and advantages through using analytics tools and techniques to help make better decision, save costs, best utilization of available resources, high performance, provide high quality services and reduce business risk. Big Data has three main attributes and characteristics called 3Vs which are widely accepted to define the Big Data. The 3Vs of data are Volume, Velocity, and Variety. Volume means large or complex data sets. Velocity means the speed and rate of massive data generation and transmission. Variety means different types of data such as structured, unstructured and semi-structured. Big Data is not just 3Vs, but rather 3^2 Vs (or 9Vs). These additional attributes of Big Data reflect the real motivation behind Big Data Analytics. There are different attributes of Big Data which are discussed in (Wu et al, 2016) as illustrated in Figure 2 as follows:

- **Douglas Laney - 3Vs Definition:** There are many attributes are added to Big Data connotation such as 3Vs which are the most popular and it called Gartner's interpretation or 3Vs. This term was casted by Douglas Laney (Laney, 2001). Data has grown along three dimensions, namely:
  - **Volume:** It means incoming data stream and Cumulative volume of data.

- ○ **Velocity:** It represents the pace data used to support interaction and generated by interactions.
- ○ **Variety:** It signifies the variety of incompatible and inconsistent data formats and data structures.
- **IBM - 4Vs Definition:** IBM added another attribute called "Veracity" on the top of Douglas Laney's 3Vs notation, which is so called as 4Vs of Big Data ("The Four V's" 2016). It defines each "V" as follows:
  - ○ **Volume:** It stands for scale of data.
  - ○ **Velocity:** This denotes to analyze data.
  - ○ **Variety:** Which indicates different forms of data.
  - ○ **Veracity:** implies uncertainty of data.
- **Yuri Demchenko - 5Vs Definition:** Yuri Demchenko (Demchenko, 2014) added new attribute to the IBM 4Vs' definition. This attribute called Value. The Yuri Demchenko's 5Vs are Volume, Velocity, Variety, Veracity and Value.
- **Microsoft - 6Vs Definition:** Microsoft added three attributes to Douglas Laney's 3Vs attributes to become 6Vs. These new three attributes are Variability, Veracity and Visibility. The Microsoft's 6 Vs are:
  - ○ **Volume:** Stands for scale of data.
  - ○ **Velocity:** Refers to analyse data.
  - ○ **Variety:** Means different forms of data.
  - ○ **Veracity:** Focuses on trustworthiness of data sources.
  - ○ **Variability:** It refers to the complexity of data set. In comparison with "Variety", it refers to the variables number in data sets.
  - ○ **Visibility:** Emphasise that you need have a full picture of data in order to make informative decision.

Big Data Techniques

Big Data techniques includes a several of disciplines such as optimization methods, statistics, data mining, machine learning and visualization approaches as follows (Chen, Pillip, Zhang, 2014):

- **Optimization Methods:** Optimization methods are very important for solving complex problems in several fields such as economics, chemistry, physics, engineering and biology. There are many methods and strategies that are computational for dealing with optimization problems as simulated annealing, adaptive simulated annealing and quantum annealing. One of

Figure 2. Different attributes of big data connotation
Source: Wu et al, 2016

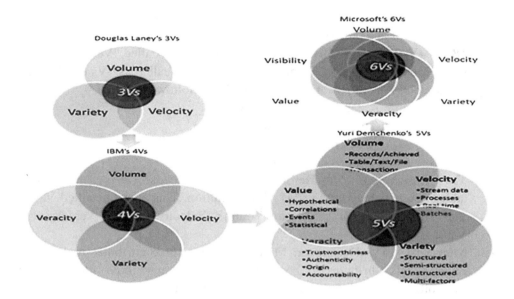

popular method is genetic algorithm that can give highly efficient in solving problems.

- **Statistics:** Statistics is the topic that concerns on collecting, organizing and interpreting data. The main task of Statistical techniques for exploiting causal relationships between different objectives. These Classical techniques will not be suitable to handle and manage Big Data.
- **Data Mining:** Data Mining is the science that concern with extracting patterns from data. Data mining includes many techniques like clustering analysis, classification, regression and association rule learning. Now, the trend for data mining changed and become Big Data mining. Big Data mining techniques is more challenging compared with classical data mining techniques. This make researchers and scientists to design and develop new techniques in addition to improve the existing techniques to cope with Big Data.
- **Machine Learning (ML):** Machine learning is the topic that is considered as subjection of Artificial Intelligence (AI). The ML aimed to design algorithms that enable computer to evolve behaviors based on empirical data. Machine Learning techniques interesting in extracting and discover knowledge to make automatically intelligent decisions for many fields such as business.

With the appearance of Big Data, there is a need to scale up new machine learning techniques to cope with it. These techniques includes supervised and unsupervised learning. Recently, there is new research topic called Deep Leering that will improve of classical machine learning techniques performance.in addition to this, there are many frameworks, like Map/ Reduce, DryadLINQ, and IBM parallel machine learning toolbox, that have capabilities to scale up machine learning techniques.

- **Visualization Approaches:** these means the approaches that used to visualize data through creating tables, diagrams and figures to enable and allow understanding of data. Big Data requires new visualization approaches in addition to extension the existing approaches to visualize Big Data in efficient and effective manner.

Big Data Tools

Big Data tools are the tools that help to sense, manage and analysis of Big Data. In recent times, there are three types of Big Data tools which are batch processing, stream processing, and interactive analysis (Chen, Phillip, Zhang, 2014). The batch processing which are analytics on data at rest and the batch processing tools are based on the Apache Hadoop infrastructure such as Mahout. The second type is stream processing which are analytics on data in motion and the stream processing is used for stream data applications for real-time analytics. There are many tools for large scale streaming data analytic such as Storm and S4. Possess the data in interactive environment using interactive analysis tools and platforms like Google's Dremel and Apache Drill that allow users to undertake their own analysis of information through interact with the computer in real time. Table 1 shows types of Big Data tools.

Table 1. Big data tools

Tools Based on Batch Processing	Tools Based on Stream Processing	Tools Based on Interactive Analysis
• Apache Hadoop • Dryad • Apache Mahout • Jaspersoft BI Suite • Pentaho Business Analytics • Skytree Server • Tableau • Karmasphere Studio and Analyst • Talend Open Studio	• Storm • S4 • SQLstream sServer • Splunk • Apache Kafka • SAP Hana	• Google's Dremel • Apache drill

Big Data Systems Design Principles

Big Data analytic systems pose complex challenges than classical data analysis systems. To carry out complex data-intensive tasks in effective manner for real-time applications so that there is a need to enormous capabilities of resources like that in Cloud Computing for handling and managing massive amount of data through performing processing of them entirely in memory with linearly scale up and down per on request. In (Chen, Phillip, Zhang, 2014), they summarized seven important principles for designing Big Data Analytic systems as follows:

1.   Good architectures and frameworks are necessary and on the top priority.
2.   Support a several of analytical methods.
3.   No size fits all.
4.   Bring the analysis to data.
5.   Processing must be distributable for in-memory computation.
6.   Data storage must be distributable for in-memory storage.
7.   Coordination is needed between processing and data units.

DEEP LEARNING

Deep Learning is an attractive research topic that belong to Artificial Intelligence (AI). Deep Learning refers to machine learning techniques that based on supervised and unsupervised methods to automatically learn hierarchical representations in deep architectures (Sudha, Kowsalya, 2015). It tries to mimic the human brain, which is capable of processing complex input data and learning different knowledge intellectually to solve complicated problems. Deep Learning comes from the human brain concept which have multiple types of representation with simpler features at the lower and higher level abstractions built on top of that. The ideas can be arrange hierarchically by humans where the humans first learn simple concepts and then shape them to represent more abstract ones. The human brain is like deep neural network, consisting of several neurons layers that act as feature detectors, detecting more abstract features as the levels go up. The most objective of Deep Learning is to extract more abstract features in the higher levels of the representation using Artificial Neural Networks (ANN) where the ANN separates various explanatory factors in the data in easily manner. Deep Learning can be applied to several fields such as computer vision, speech recognition, and Natural Language Processing (NLP).

In last decades, deep architecture is motivated by biological and circuit complexity theories. The deep architecture has been considered to be more efficient than shallow architectures with the problems that have complex behaviors with highly varying mathematical functions. They are usually presented with multiple hidden layers. The hidden layer is which contains internal abstract representation of the training data. When compared to traditional neural networks with Deep Learning, there is different where computing the hidden layers be entirely different fashion. In deep network, each layer is pre-trained with an unsupervised learning algorithms, resulting in a nonlinear transformation of its input or the output of the previous layer and extract more abstracted features from its input. Finally, the deep architecture is fine-tuned with regard to a supervised training criterion at the last training stage. There are three major classes for deep networks architectures as follows (Deng, Yu, 2014; Deng, 2012):

1. **Deep Networks for Unsupervised Learning:** The objective of this network is to extract high-order correlation of the observed data for pattern analysis when no information about target class labels is available. Unsupervised feature or representation learning when used in the generative mode, may also be intended to characterize joint statistical distributions of the visible data and their associated classes when available and being treated as part of the visible data.
2. **Deep Networks for Supervised Learning:** This type of learning also called discriminative deep networks which intended to provide discriminative power for pattern classification directly. This occurs often by characterizing the posterior distributions of classes conditioned on the visible data. Target label data are always available in direct or indirect forms for such supervised learning.
3. **Hybrid Deep Networks:** Where the goal is discrimination which is assisted, often in a significant way, with the results of unsupervised deep networks. This can be achieved by better optimization or/and regularization of the deep networks in deep networks for supervised learning. The target can also be achieved when discriminative criteria for supervised learning are used to estimate the parameters in any of the unsupervised deep networks.

There are challenges (Sudha, Kowslya, 2015) when using deep networks that require enough examples to fit the parameters of a complex model, which is difficult task. Training on insufficient data would also result in overfitting, due to the high degree of expressive power of deep networks. Training a shallow network with 1 hidden layer using supervised learning usually resulted in the parameters converging to reasonable values, but when training a deep network, this turns out with bad local optima. When using back propagation to compute the derivatives, the gradients that are propagated backwards from the output layer to the earlier layers of the network rapidly diminish in magnitude as the depth of the network increases. The weights of the earlier layers change slowly when using gradient descent and the earlier layers fail to learn much leading to "diffusion of gradients."

Deep Learning Techniques

This part explains Restricted Boltzmann Machine (RBM), Autoencoders, Convolutional Neural Network (CNN), Deep Belief Network (DBN) and Deep Neural Network (DNN) that can help to understand Deep Learning architecture as follows (Sudha, Kowsalya, 2015; Deng, 2012):

- **Deep Neural Network (DNN):** Which is a multilayer network with many hidden layers, whose weights are fully connected and are often pre-trained using stacked Restricted Boltzmann Machine.
- **Restricted Boltzmann Machine (RBM):** Restricted Boltzmann Machine a special Boltzmann machine (BM) consisting of a layer of visible and hidden units with no visible-visible or hidden-hidden connections. RBM is a two layer undirected neural network that consisting of visible and hidden layers. It is trained to maximize the expected log probability of data. The inputs are binary vectors as it learns Bernoulli distributions over each input. The activation function is calculated the same manner like in a regular neural network and the logistic function used is in range 0-1. The output is handled like a probability and each neuron is activated if the activation is greater than random variable. The hidden layer neurons take visible units as inputs. Visible neurons take binary input vectors as initial input and then hidden layer probabilities.
- **Autoencoder:** Refers to deep neural network whose output target is the data input itself, often pre-trained with Deep belief network or using distorted training data to regularize the learning. An auto-encoder is three layer neural network, which is trained to reconstruct its inputs by using them as the output. It needs to learn features that take the variance in the data so it can be reproduced. It is classically a feedforward neural network that intent to learn representation of data.
- **Convolutional Neural Network (CNN):** It consists of many layers of hierarchy with some layers for feature representations and others as a type of conventional neural networks for classification. There are two altering types of layers called convolutional and subsampling layers. The convolutional layers carry out operations of convolution with many filter maps of equal size, while subsampling layers reduce the sizes of proceeding layers by averaging pixels within a small neighborhood.

- **Deep Belief Network (DBN):** It is probabilistic generative models composed of multiple layers of stochastic, hidden variables. The top two layers have symmetric and undirected connections between them. The lower layers receive top-down, directed connections from the layer above.

Deep Learning Applications

One of the emerging area of Deep Learning application is Natural Language Processing (NLP) because the possibility of understanding the meaning of the text that people type or say is very important for providing better user interfaces, advertisements, and posts. Learning from text, audio, and video is evolving into a new frontier of deep learning, beginning to be accepted by research communities including speech processing, natural language processing, computer vision, machine learning, information retrieval, cognitive science, artificial intelligence and knowledge management. Here, will discuss some applications for deep learning as follows:

1. **Automatic Speech Recognition (ASR):** in last years, Automatic Speech Recognition become attractive research area that help humans to interact with machines in efficient manner. The ASR can be used in many fields such as mobiles domain in new applications like Short Message Dictation (SMD) and Voice Search (VS). Using Deep Learning in Speech Recognition can add more benefits and significant through utilizing Big Data Analytics solutions.
2. **Image Recognition:** Image recognition process involves two basics steps which are image classification and object detection. Using Deep learning in the image recognition area can speeds the deep-learning classification and object-detection system rather than traditional techniques and methods.
3. **Natural Language Processing (NLP):** Natural Language Processing become an important research area that help to solve problems related to natural language that has many applications where people communicate such as emails. Chats, social networks, web search, language translation and advertisement. Recurrent neural networks, especially LSTM, are most appropriate for sequential data such as language. The LSTM helped to enhance machine translation and language modeling. Deep learning techniques can improve the process of natural language through using techniques like Deep Belief Network (DBN) and Convolutional Neural Network (CNN).
4. **Bioinformatics:** There are many problems in bioinformatics such as predict Gene Ontology annotations and gene-function relationships. Deep-learning techniques based on an autoencoder neural network can be used to solve this problem.

5. **Drug Discovery:** The pharmaceutical industry faces the problem that a large percentage of candidate drugs fail to reach the market. These failures of chemical compounds are caused by insufficient efficacy on the biomolecular target (on-target effect), undetected and undesired interactions with other biomolecules (off-target effects), or unanticipated toxic effects. Drug discovery though medical imaging-based diagnosis using deep learning.

6. **Recommendation systems:** Recommendation systems have used deep learning to extract meaningful deep features for latent factor model for content-based recommendation for music. Recently, a more general approach for learning user preferences from multiple domains using multiview deep learning has been introduced. The model uses a hybrid collaborative and content-based approach and enhances recommendations in multiple tasks.

DIGITAL INVESTIGATION BASED ON BIG DATA ANALYTICS USING DEEP LEARNING

In recent times, Current forensics techniques cannot cope with Big Data that generated from variety sources such as Cloud Computing, Social Networks and Internet of Things. This led to think about new techniques that have ability to extract patterns and knowledge from the data that generated from these sources. One of the important topic that can be used recently in digital forensics is Big Data Analytics. Also machine learning can use in digital forensic for analysis of digital evidence. An extension technique from machine learning is Deep Learning. Big Data Analytics using deep learning can use to capture and extract complex representation and features of data that help analysis enormous amount of data sets in timely fashion way. This section discusses the use of Deep Learning with Big Data Analytics in digital forensic area to help digital investigators and practitioners for performing the digital investigation in efficient and effective manner.

Mining Terabytes of Data for Digital Investigation

Knowledge discovery and mining for terabytes of data is an important topic that can use in digital investigation area for analyzing of digital evidence to extract patterns from data in efficient manner. It is not common for law enforcement agencies to face digital investigation with massive volume of data sets (i.e. Big Data). Current digital forensic tools cannot do the extraction and analysis activities for terabyte of data in efficient way so that there is need to scale up these tools to be suitable to Big Data. There are many benefits of using data mining in digital forensics such as (Beebe, Nicole, Clark, 2005):

- Reduced system and human processing time associated with data analysis.
- Improved information quality associated with data analysis.
- Reduced monetary costs associated with digital investigations.

Data mining is a topic that used to find, extract and retrieval information. With data mining various discipline like computer science, statistics and mathematics can corporate to provide efficient models through using techniques and methods such as machine learning and pattern recognition. Data mining can be categorized into three classes as follows (Beebe, Nicole, Clark, 2005):

1. **Descriptive Modeling:** It is used to summarize or discriminate data through mining past data to report, visualize, and understand WHAT has already happened after the fact or in real-time
2. **Predictive Modeling:** It can used to identify characteristics that can predict future observations. Leverage past data to understand the underlying relationship between data inputs and outputs to understand WHY something happened or to predict WHAT will happen in the future across various scenarios.
3. **Content Retrieval:** It can used to extract feature from complex semi-structure and unstructured data sets.

Data mining techniques such as classification and clustering can be useful for crime detection and investigation for analysis of digital evidence in effective and efficient manner.

Big Data Analytics Using Deep Learning

Big Data Analytics and Deep Learning are two important topics of data science. Big Data generally refers to data that exceeds the classical storage and computing systems like databases. In addition to this, data analysis tools, methods and techniques cannot cope with new trend of data that requires new type of tools and methods that can analyze and extract patterns from this data. Big Data analytics (BDA) is a process of analyzing Big Data. This can extract knowledge from data to better decision making. Many organizations are interesting in developing products based on Big Data Analytics to addressing complex problems like data analysis of massive amount of data. There are several factors that advance in storage, processing, and analysis of Big Data as:

- Less cost of storage and CPU power.
- Cloud computing that providing cost-effectiveness services like processing and storage.

- The advanced development of new platforms and frameworks such as Hadoop and Mahout.

Big Data Analytics workflow consists of several phases as shown in Figure 3. Data from various sources, including databases, streams, marts, and data warehouses, are used to build models. The large volume and different types of the data can demand pre-processing tasks for integrating the data, cleaning it, and filtering it. The prepared data is used to train a model and to estimate its parameters. Once the model is estimated, it should be validated before its consumption. Normally this phase requires the use of the original input data and specific methods to validate the created model. Finally, the model is consumed and applied to data as it arrives. This phase, called model scoring, is used to generate predictions, prescriptions, and recommendations. The results are interpreted and evaluated, used to generate new models or calibrate existing ones, or are integrated to pre-processed data.

The main task of Big Data Analytics is to extract meaningful and knowledge patterns from huge volume of input data for much purpose like decision making and prediction. There various challenges facing Big Data Analytics such as fast moving streaming data, highly distributed input sources, noisy and poor quality data, high dimensionality, scalability of algorithms, unsupervised and un-categorized data, limited supervised/labeled data and format variation of the raw data (Beebe, Nicole, Clark, 2005) so that there is a need to solve these challenges through using extension of machine learning techniques such as Deep Learning.

Machine learning is an important domain in artificial intelligence that aims to representation of data to generate machine learnt patterns that captured from the data

Figure 3. Big data analytics workflow
Source: Assuncao et al, 2015

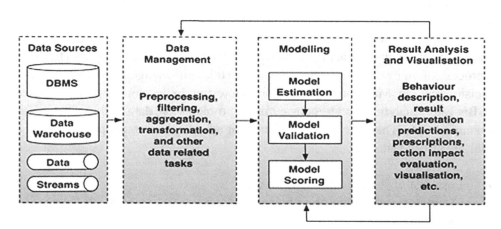

to be used in future for unseen data. The performance of machine learnt depends on the quality of data representation so that if the data representation good the performance of the machine learnt will be high else the performance will be low. Feature engineering is an essential element of machine learning that concern with constructing features and data representations from raw data. In Machine learning task a large effort is consuming in feature engineering that allow to extract features automatically without direct human input. There are many feature engineering such as Scale Invariant Feature Transform (SIFT) and Histogram of Oriented Gradients (HOG) which are used in computer vision area.

Deep learning is a branch of machine learning techniques based on automated extraction of complex data representations or features at high levels of abstraction using multiple processing layers, with complex structures or otherwise, composed of multiple non-linear transformations. Deep Learning algorithms are beneficial when dealing with learning from large amounts of unsupervised data. Using Deep Learning to obtain data representations and features can achieve many benefits such as improved classification modelling, better quality of generated samples by generative probabilistic models and the invariant property of data representations (Najafabadi et al., 2015) at based on supervised and unsupervised methods to automatically learn hierarchical representations in deep architectures. Deep Learning algorithms can extract high-level and complex abstractions as data representations through a hierarchical learning process. Complex abstractions are learnt at a given level based on relatively simpler abstractions formulated in the preceding level in the hierarchy. A key benefit of Deep Learning is the analysis and learning of enormous amounts of unsupervised data, making it a valuable tool for Big Data Analytics where raw data is largely unlabeled and un-categorized. Recently, there are some problems in Big Data Analytics that includes extracting complex patterns from enormous volumes of data, semantic indexing, data tagging, fast information retrieval, and simplifying discriminative tasks. There are several useful characteristics of the learnt abstract representations using Deep Learning as follows (Najafabadi et al., 2015):

- Relatively simple linear models can work effectively with the knowledge obtained from the more complex and more abstract data representations.
- Relational and semantic knowledge can be obtained at the higher levels of abstraction and representation of the raw data. While there are other useful aspects of Deep Learning based representations of data, the specific characteristics mentioned above are particularly important for Big Data Analytics.
- Increased automation of data representation extraction from unsupervised data enables its broad application to different data types, such as image, textural and audio.

Digital Forensics Based on Big Data Analytics using Deep learning

Digital Forensics is a topic that is becoming increasingly important in computing and often requires the intelligent analysis of large amounts of complex data extracted from crime scene. Digital forensics investigation is the process of extracting, analysis digital evidence for use as admissible proof about committed crimes. This process can help to reconstruct the crime events. Big Data analytics (BDA) is a process of analyzing Big Data. The objective of Big Data Analytics is to extract knowledge patterns from massive volume of input data. Recently, there are several challenges led to use Big Data Analytics for digital forensics investigations. Some of these challenges are (Mohan, Salisu, 2015):

- **Storing and Backups of Large Volume of Data:** Traditional data storage not suitable for large amount of data that created as a result of big data concept. These large amount of data that generated from different data sources need high size storage capacity to store for the digital investigation purpose.
- **Faster Indexing of Enormous Amounts of Data:** In recent time, data become big so faster indexing of the data is a challenge for digital investigators. In order to rapid indexing to analysis of large size of data there is a need to faster methods and devices that have the ability analysis data within a given time frame.
- **Presentation and Visualization of Large Amounts of Data to the Court of Law:** Presentation and visualization of finding from analysis of digital evidence is an important for presenting the results in a court of law. Presentation and visualization of large of data is a problem faced digital practitioners and examiners in the digital forensics area so that there is a need for new techniques and methods to deal with massive size of data that generated from crime scene in forensically and timely fashion way.

Machine learning can considered as an ideal approach to deal with many problems that currently exist in various areas such as multimedia processing, pattern recognition and computer security. Machine learning techniques also can use in digital forensics to solve complex problems in extracting and analysis digital evidence from crime scene. There are several areas in digital forensics where machine learning techniques can be used as follows:

- **Authorship Identification:** Attackers and criminals can use fake E-mails for performing activities without tracing them through hiding their identity. Authorship Identification is an important technique which used to solve this problem by identifying the authors of these fake E-mails that can help digital investigators and examiners to perform investigation process in timely fashion manner. The authorship identification process involves many sub-process as authorship attribution, authorship characterization and similarity detection (Nirkhi, Smita, Dharaskar, 2015). Authorship attribution is known as Authorship identification that determine the probability that a piece of writing produced by a particular person by examining the other writings from that the same person. Authorship characterization method is used to determine the personal attributes of author like age, gender and other personal attributes by using existing writings from that author. Similarity detection is a popular technique that used in plagiarism detection. This technique can use to compare different pieces of writing and determines if they were produced by the same person or not.

- **File Fragments:** Detection of data from disks is challenging faced by digital investigators to recover the data from disk. The data when deleting from disk is not permanent where they simply mark each block of the file as unallocated and available for use. The process of recovering unallocated data known as 'file carving'. Machine learning provide a methods to recognizing the file types of file fragments for the purpose of file carving for the reconstruction of partially erased files on disk into whole files. In (Duffy, 2014) they used different type of classification techniques such as Support Vector Machine, Multinomial Naive Bayes, and Linear Discriminant Analysis models to apply them for file fragments. They used 257 calculated features of an input fragment then applied the three above techniques to choose the most accurate method of classification where was Support Vector Machine with accuracy 75.03%.

- **Pattern Recognition:** Pattern recognition is an important domain in machine learning that working on extracting patterns from input data. Supervised data that trained from labeled data and unsupervised learning that discover unknown patterns. Both of them can used in the Pattern recognition. It is used to identify pattern or feature in data through determine and specify types or clusters of data. The pattern recognition can help in digital forensics for performing detecting a pattern in an e-mail message which indicates malicious code like spam or virus. Also can be used to discover identities in digital evidence that are extracting from crime scene. In (Henseler, Hans, Hofste, Keulen, 2013), they proposed an algorithm to extract, merge and rank identities that are encountered in the electronic evidence during processing. This algorithm can assist with the identification of frequently occurring identities so that investigators can prioritize the investigation of evidence units accordingly.

Using techniques that can automatic extraction of complex data representations or features in digital forensics can improve and enhance the process of analysis large amount of digital evidence in short time with high quality and accuracy of results. These techniques motivated by digital investigators and examiners to use in the forensic analysis phase. One of recently become popular as extension of machine learning is Deep learning. The Deep Learning algorithms are beneficial when dealing with learning from large amounts of unsupervised data to automatically learn hierarchical representations in deep architectures. The combination of Deep Learning with Big Data Analytics can use for many areas inside digital forensics as follows:

- **Image Region Forgery Detection:** In recent time, the number of tampered images is increased incredible way due to the use of social networks like Facebook and Flicker, Instagram and Twitter. These tampered images can be shared easily by the users that may lead serious consequences so the authenticity of digital images is urgently needed. The presence of tampered images is an important topic in digital forensics. There are many work done to cover this area but to identify certain tampered image using tampering methods. In (Zhang, Ying et al, 2016), they proposed a two stage deep learning approach to learn features in order to detect tampered images in different image formats. In the first stage, they utilized a Stacked Autoencoder model to learn the complex feature for each individual patch while in the second stage; they integrated the contextual information of each patch so that the detection can be conducted more accurately. This work utilized deep learning approach for feature learning in the field of tampered region localization. The experiment results of the proposed method detect tampered regions well with an overall accuracy of 91.09%.

- **Data Indexing:** Large-scale volume of data such as text, image, video, and audio are being extracted and collected from different sources that can make investigation process harder especially when crimes related to environment like social networks and cloud computing. These massive amounts of data needs semantic indexing rather than being stored as data bit strings. Semantic indexing presents the data in a more efficient manner and makes it useful as a source for knowledge discovery and understanding. Deep Learning can be used to generate high-level abstract data representations which will be used for semantic indexing of data rather than using raw data for indexing. An example for using Deep Learning for indexing is document representation that increase the process of retrieval information in a given frame time that can useful for digital investigators during the investigation process.

- **Data Tagging:** Data tagging task can be performed through Big Data Analytics using Deep Learning algorithms for help in performing the search process. Data tagging is another method to semantically index of data. The difference between data tagging with semantic data indexing where semantic indexing, the focus is on using the Deep Learning abstract representations directly for data indexing purposes while the abstract data representations are considered as features for performing the discriminative task of data tagging. Here it possible to tag massive amounts of data using simple linear modeling methods on complicated features which extracted by Deep Learning algorithms. For example, Microsoft Research Audio Video Indexing System (MAVIS) that uses Deep Learning with aids of Artificial Neural Networks (ANN) to enable search of audio and video files speech (Najafabadi, Maryam et al, 2015).

CONCLUSION

Fighting cybercrimes has become an important topic for individuals, organizations and governments for protecting them from severe attacks. Nowadays, massive amount of generated data from Social Media, Cloud Computing and Internet of Things which contain vital and valuable information that can help to detect, prevent and predict cybercrimes in a given time frame. Managing and analyzing these data cannot be done using traditional tools and techniques so that there is a serious need for new tools and solutions. Big Data solutions will be the best for handling these type of data. Digital investigators, practitioners and experts are leveraging big data tools to identify the potential threats and prevent cybercrime incidents. One of important area in information security is Digital Forensics. Digital forensics is the process of collecting, extracting and analysis digital evidence about committed crimes and incidents. Using machine learning techniques such as deep learning with Big Data Analytics can help to improve the existing Big Data Analytics techniques and tools to fight different type of crimes. A key benefit of Deep Learning for Big Data Analytics is the analysis and learning of massive amounts of unsupervised data, making it a useful tool for Big Data Analytics where data is largely un-categorized or un-labeled. This chapter introduce a study on the use of Big Data Analytics in the digital investigation field to help digital practitioners and experts to design and develop new techniques and methods to cope with new technologies like Internet of Things that generated enormous amount of data. The chapter contents includes Big Data attributes, digital forensics definition and process, cybercrimes definition and categories, Big Data Analytics classifications and workflow, Deep Learning techniques and applications, Big Data Analytics using Deep Learning and finally the use of Big Data Analytics using Deep Learning in the digital forensic area to perform the investigation process in efficient and timely fashion manner.

REFERENCES

Assunção, M. D., Calheiros, R. N., Bianchi, S., Netto, M. A. S., & Buyya, R. (2015). Big Data computing and clouds: Trends and future directions. *Journal of Parallel and Distributed Computing*, *79*, 3–15. doi:10.1016/j.jpdc.2014.08.003

Beebe, N., & Clark, J. (2005). *Dealing with terabyte data sets in digital investigations*. Springer.

Chen, C. L. (2014). Data-intensive applications, challenges, techniques and technologies: A survey on Big Data. *Information Sciences*, *275*, 314–347. doi:10.1016/j.ins.2014.01.015

Demchenko, Y., De Laat, C., & Membrey, P. (2014). Defining architecture components of the Big Data Ecosystem. *IEEE International Conference on Collaboration Technologies and Systems*. doi:10.1109/CTS.2014.6867550

Duffy, A. (2014). *CarveML: Application of machine learning to file fragment classification*.

Henseler, H., Hofste, J., & van Keulen, M. (2013). Digital-forensics based pattern recognition for discovering identities in electronic evidence. European. *IEEE Intelligence and Security Informatics Conference (EISIC)*. doi:10.1109/EISIC.2013.24

Kamal, M. (2012). Digital investigation concepts. *Security Kaizen Magazine*, *2*(6), 6–10.

Laney. (2001). *3D Data Management: Controlling Data Volume, Velocity and Variety*. Application Delivery Strategies, Meta Group, 1-4.

Li. (2012). Three classes of deep learning architectures and their applications: a tutorial survey. *APSIPA Transactions on Signal and Information Processing*.

Mohan, U., & Salisu, S. (2015). The use of big data in the field of digital forensics investigations (comparative study between digital forensics in UK and Nigeria). *International Journal of New Technologies in Science and Engineering*, *2*(4).

Najafabadi, M. M., Villanustre, F., Khoshgoftaar, T. M., Seliya, N., Wald, R., & Muharemagic, E. (2015). Deep learning applications and challenges in big data analytics. *Journal of Big Data*, *2*(1), 1–21. doi:10.1186/s40537-014-0007-7

Nirkhi, S., & Dharaskar, R. V. (2015). Authorship Identification in Digital Forensics using Machine Learning Approach. *International Journal of Latest Trends in Engineering and Technology*, *5*(1).

Palmer, G. (2001). A road map for digital forensic research. *First Digital Forensic Research Workshop*, Utica, NY.

Pream Sudha, V., & Kowsalya, R. (2015). a survey on deep learning techniques, applications and challenges. *International Journal of Advance Research in Science and Engineering*, 4(3).

The Four V's of Big Data. (n.d.). Retrieved May 08, 2016 from http://www.ibmbigdatahub.com/infographic/four-vs-big-data/

Wu, C., Buyya, R., & Ramamohanarao, K. (2016). *Big Data Analytics= Machine Learning+ Cloud Computing*. arXiv preprint arXiv:+1601.03115

Li & Yu. (2014). *Deep Learning: Methods and Applications*. Now Publishers.

Zhanga, Y. (2016). Image Region Forgery Detection: A Deep Learning Approach. *Proceedings of the Singapore Cyber-Security Conference (SG-CRC) Cyber-Security by Design*, 14.

Chapter 6
Classifying Images of Drought–Affected Area Using Deep Belief Network, kNN, and Random Forest Learning Techniques

Sanjiban Sekhar Roy
VIT University, India

Pulkit Kulshrestha
VIT University, India

Pijush Samui
NIT Patna, India

ABSTRACT

Drought is a condition of land in which the ground water faces a severe shortage. This condition affects the survival of plants and animals. Drought can impact ecosystem and agricultural productivity, severely. Hence, the economy also gets affected by this situation. This paper proposes Deep Belief Network (DBN) learning technique, which is one of the state of the art machine learning algorithms. This proposed work uses DBN, for classification of drought and non-drought images. Also, k nearest neighbour (kNN) and random forest learning methods have been proposed for the classification of the same drought images. The performance of the Deep Belief Network(DBN) has been compared with k nearest neighbour (kNN) and random forest. The data set has been split into 80:20, 70:30 and 60:40 as train and test. Finally, the effectiveness of the three proposed models have been measured by various performance metrics.

DOI: 10.4018/978-1-5225-3015-2.ch006

1. INTRODUCTION

Drought is a condition of a land where the rainfall in less than average. This situation thus reduces the groundwater level of the drought affected area. The condition of drought develops cracks in the soil which then lowers the agriculture productivity of the land to zero. It's a life-fighting situation for human and animals due to lack of water resources which results in poor agricultural output. The general trend is to move away from the drought affected places to some water efficient places. Drought is a natural disaster as it occurs due to climatic conditions which wipes out living beings. Most of the drought comes in the category of temporary droughts rather than the permanent one. Causes of drought include less precipitation which means precipitation methods includes convective, strait-form (Anagnostou, Emmanouil, 2004).and orographic rainfall (Dore et al, 2006). The convective method is the one in which vertical motions are induced that further helps in precipitating in the particular region in no time. On the other hand, while strait-form induces weak upward motion, helps in the long run (Pearce, Penrose, 2002)..These factors are very important for precipitation else the result will be a severe drought. Another reason of drought can be due to the intense reflection of sunlight, high-pressure system, winds with continental air masses which refrain the area from rainfall and the low evapotranspiration worsen the conditions (Paepe, Roland, Rhodes, Jelgersma, 2012). The dry season is also a cause for drought (Wang, Bin, 2006; Boken et al, 2005). If the dry weather occurs in excess it will reduce groundwater and water bodies starts drying up so the living organisms leave that place and go to nearby place. These situations reduce the resources of that place such as plants etc. These plants and living organisms evaporate at a high rate which results in a high amount of loss of water. Even deforestation, over farming (H, excessive irrigation and erosion reduce the ability of the land to hold water. These above reasons result in a shortage of water and hence drought occurs. These activities flow off the top layer of the soil which is the most fertile and the most absorption takes place on that layer of soil which gets prevented. Hence it lowers the groundwater level (Richthofen, Baron, 1882). Due to global warming, the temperature (Smith, B, Katz, 2013) of the planet earth is on the rise, which affects the world temperature. Therefore, the ice caps are melting and the average surface temperature is increasing gradually. This affects the environment and causes uneven effects (Brahic, 2007) across the globe. Some places have heavy rainfall causing a flood and on the other side, some places receive very less rainfall and hence causing drought.

Types of drought are as below,

1. Meteorological drought occurs, when the primary condition that is precipitation is less than average, for a long time. Regular short duration drought gives birth to this kind. (Palmer, C, 1965).
2. Agricultural droughts are the one that defers the production of the crop. This occurs due to the human activities and natural soil erosion. (Wang, et al, 2015)
3. Hydrological drought is the one in which the water bodies starts to get shrink due to less refueling and probably higher usage. This usually brings the condition of low water levels in the nearby areas (Tallaksen, M, Lamen, 2004).

Drought is not a new calamity, it's a problem faced from decades. Over the period of time some tree and plants have tried to oppose the effects of drought and hence during the process of evolution some plants developed tendency to degrade their growth rate or turn brown in a way to save water while some trees start to get off with their leaves in a way to utilize the minimal amount of water. However, if the condition exists for a longer period they began getting die.Some plants also developed a tendency to overcome the effect of long period drought such as yuccas plant which has deep roots that can absorb water with high efficiency. Cacti got spines all over the body and on leaves which minimize the transpiration effect. Moses can even grow in almost less water environment. Juniper tree has the ability to only supply the water to the branches which are in need of the water in order to survive. Some plants have seeds which can 1989) lie under the soil in a healthy way till they get the perfect condition for the germination. However, many plants and animals are not able to cope up with the condition of drought. Thus, drought results in damaging habitats, loss of biodiversity, soil erosion, and fires in the forest. Drought not only affects the living organisms, it also creates social and economic problems. Due to less (Keddy, Paul, 2007) rainfall, the production of crops will be less than the normal production. If the land becomes barren then the prices of the land will go down unemployment decreases due to less production. The shrinkage of water bodies can create the shortage of water to the nearby residences, other issues include poor nutrition and famine. There are even chances of conflicts over water usage and food, and forcing migration to go away from drought affected area (Glantz, H, 1988; Falkenmark, Malin, Lundqvist, Widstand, 1989) Drought is a natural calamity which is a part of weather cycle and is not preventable but human activities can have an impact on the effect of drought. New techniques of irrigation increase the chances of drought by developing water scarcity in that region. The techniques indeed increase the production and the area under cultivation but also increased the abuse of water ("Productivity Commission" 2009). The over farming and overgrazing leads to exploitation of soil, in which soil particle compacts and hence their tendency to hold water reduces. As the soil becomes drier, it is vulnerable

Table 1. Drought situation in India after independence

Serial No.	Year	Percentage Affected Area in India	Category
1	1951	33.2	moderate
2	1952	25.8	slight
3	1965	42.9	Moderate
4	1966	32.3	Moderate
5	1968	20.6	Slight
6	1969	19.9	Slight
7	1971	13.3	Slight
8	1972	44.4	severe
9	1974	29.3	Moderate
10	1979	39.4	Moderate
11	1982	33.1	Moderate
12	1985	30.1	Moderate
13	1986	1.0	Slight
14	1987	49.2	Severe
15	2002	Areas in 14 states	severe

Source: http://www.nih.ernet.in/rbis/india_information/draught.htm.

to erosion. This process can lead to fertile land becoming desert-like, a process known as desertification (West, O, Post, 2002).

This paper adopts Deep Belief Network(DBN) for drought classification. DBN has been adopted for classification of drought and non-drought images. Besides, k nearest neighbor (kNN) and random forest methods have been proposed for the classification of the same drought images. The performance of the Deep Belief Network(DBN) has been compared with k nearest neighbor (kNN) and random forest. The drought images have been captured from Google. The collected images have been split in train and test iamges. Experimental outcomes of the proposed methods produce good results.

2. THEORETICAL BACKGROUND

2.1 Deep Belief Network (DBN)

Deep Learning is the upcoming trend in the field of Machine Learning. It has the potential for a powerful and fast processing of data which takes us one step closer

Table 2. Probability of occurrence of drought in different meteorological sub division

Meteorological Sub Division	Frequency of Deficient Rainfall (75% of Normal or Less)
Assam	Very rare, once in 15 years
West Bengal, Madhya Pradesh, Konkan, Bihar and Orissa	Once in 5 years
South interior Karnataka, eastern Uttar Pradesh and vidarbha	Once in 4 years
East Rajasthan, Gujarat, and western Uttar Pradesh	Once in 3 years
West Rajasthan, Tamilnadu, Jammu & Kashmir and Telangana	Once in 2.5 years

Source: http://www.nih.ernet.in/rbis/india_information/draught.htm.

to Artificial Intelligence. Inefficiency in human interpretation of small objects in this vast line of sight motivated the use of the machine learning to interpret data with more accuracy than that of human (Hinton, et al, 2006).Recently, classification of the high-dimensional image is done using the concept of Deep Learning . Deep Learning models high-level abstraction of data using multiple layers with processing complex structures. The Deep Belief Network an alternative type of deep neural network, consists of multiple layers connected to each other. In this work, DBN has been trained first on the available training set, which then takes drought images as an input and based on that it classifies test drought images (Bengio et al, 2007; Bengio et al, 2009).Deep Belief Network machine behaves as a pseudo-human with most of the thinking capabilities. It produces high accuracy and efficiency on any image classification. This study will also provide an interaction with the essence of theoretical aspects of Deep Learning. The visualization of drought is done by the software according to the input training set. The Classification process includes matching of the probability of each pixel density and the relationship between nearby pixels so as to determine the feature of the image.

2.1.1 System Architecture of Deep Belief Network

The DBN structure consists of three layers namely, an Input layer, Hidden Layer, and an Output layer. Each layer consists of a net of neurons (Restricted Boltzmann Machine namely RBM).

1.   **Input Layer:** The image interacts with the software via input layer.
2.   **Hidden Layer:** This consists of several layers which are trained over each iteration. The dataset passes sequentially through these Hidden layers. Each neuron of the each layer gets trained. Learning rate increases with each layer but can make the system slow if excess layers are used.

3.   **Output Layer:** When the input image passes through the Hidden layers the probability is calculated at each layer and the neuron with the highest probability classifies the image and displays the predicted one.

In this work the each drought image consists of pixel values in the range 0-255, so first the image has been translated to a greyscale image and then scaling happens i.e. 0-255 to 0-1 where 0 (total absence) depicts black and 1 (total presence) depicts white. Now image data is passed to the hidden layer and the process of finding the highest probability takes place. DBN works on the data ranging between 0 and 1.

Deep Belief Network has various qualities i.e. it's composed of multiple layers with the connection between the layers but not between the neurons of each layer. Deep Belief Network requires restricted Boltzmann machine. Each Hidden layer is visible for the next layer which further increases the training procedure. Deep Belief Networks can be trained greedily i.e. one layer at a time .

$$p \equiv p\left(s_i = 1\right) \frac{1}{1 + \exp\left(-\Sigma_j s_j w_{ji}\right)} \tag{1}$$

$$\Delta w_{ji} = \varepsilon sj\left(s_i - p_i\right) \tag{2}$$

where ε is the learning rate.

Figure 1. Deep Belief Network

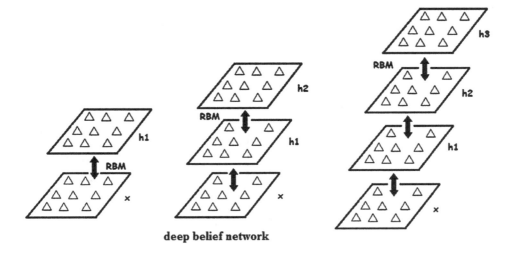

deep belief network

The learning method used here is supervised learning. This learning process involves the use of drought image labels which helps in the recognition of pattern with the true value. The image dataset is used to train the hidden layer and then the DBN algorithm works to check the accuracy. Afterwards, we can give the custom image or test image whose pixel pattern is to be identified and then the label will be given to that image .

Restricted Boltzmann machine helps in getting the learning process in a way to achieve the high accuracy. These layers contains neurons which gets trained and develops the tendency to acquire knowledge from the testing images with the distribution of the probability over a binary state vectors via energy function. The energy of the joint configuration (v, h) is given by,

$$\backslash E\left(v, h; \theta\right) = \sum_{i=0}^{v} \sum_{j=1}^{H} w_{ij} v_i h_j - \sum_{i=0}^{v} b_i v_i - \sum_{j=0}^{H} a_j h_j \tag{3}$$

where $\theta = (w, b, a)$ and w_{ij} describes the symmetric interaction of unit i of visible layer and unit j of hidden layer. The terms a_i and b_i are the bias terms while V is the number of visible units and H is the number of hidden units. Therefore the probability assigned to the vector v is (Roy et al, 2017).

Figure 2. Overall flow of the work

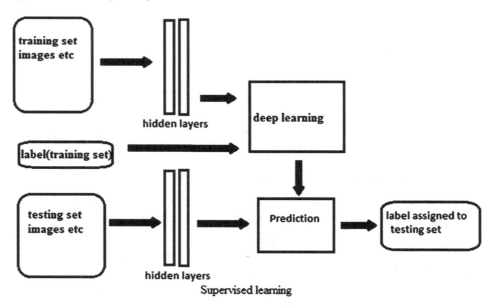

$$p(v;\theta) = \frac{\sum_h e^{-E(v,h)}}{\sum_u \sum_h e^{-E(u,h)}} \tag{4}$$

The conditional distributions p(v|h) and p(h|v) are given by:

$$p(h_j = 1 \mid v;0) = \sigma\left(\sum_{i=0}^{v} w_{ij} v_i + a_j\right) \tag{5}$$

$$p(v_j = 1 \mid h;0) = \sigma\left(\sum_{i=0}^{H} w_{ij} h_i + b_i\right) \tag{6}$$

Here $\sigma(x) = (1 + e^{-x})^{-1}$ the training of the RBM takes place by the joint distribution of data as well as of respective labels. Energy is concatenation of visible vector with label vector so the energy function will be

$$E(v,l,h;0) = \sum_{i=1}^{v}\sum_{j=1}^{H} w_{ij} h_j v_i - \sum_{y=1}^{L}\sum_{j=1}^{H} w_{yj} h_j l_y - \sum_{j=1}^{H} a_j h_i - \sum_{y=1}^{L} c_y l_y - \sum_{i=1}^{v} b_i v_i \tag{7}$$

Therefore

$$p(l \mid v) = \frac{\sum_h e^{-E(v,l,h)}}{\sum_l \sum_h e^{-E(v,l,h)}} \tag{8}$$

2.2 k Nearest Neighbor(kNN)

The kNN is a popular classifier and in this work this helps in classifying the drought images. The process of giving labels is done by the k nearest neighbors which are placed as input during the training process. If the trainer has some training with labels then it will use distance metrics else it will go for Euclidean distance to measure the common or difference between the images.

In this work the training phase consists of drought images from which the features has been be extracted. While in the testing phase image is rated by the nearest neighbours. In this process the value of k is defined by the user and hence the method is called k nearest neighbors. (Jaskowiak et al, 2011).

Parameter selection is a tedious work while working with k-NN. Several things should be kept in mind while selecting the parameters. Choosing high parameter will result in low noise but it also deteriorates the boundary of the objects. Therefore, several techniques can be used to choose the value of k. If k=1 then the method will be called as nearest neighbor method (Coomans et al, 1982). The drought images were converted to numbers which then define the vector values and hence the word feature vector comes in existence. PCA randomizer is the commonly used feature extracting technique, and in this work also PCA extracts the features of the images.

2.2.1 Proposed Model of kNN

The analysis of kNN application consists of labeled drought images. These images have been passed into numpy arrays for training .Let the training set be {Xi,Y$_i$} where i=0 to n be the set of n input images which will train the system and let the y$_i$ be the corresponding label of these images. A linear transformation by which the squared distances will be computed is (Weinberger et al, 2009).

$$D\left(x_i, x_j\right) = \left\| L\left(x - x_j\right) \right\|^2 \tag{9}$$

Next part is to choose the value of k which will be specified manually. K neighbors are basically total k inputs with the same label that have minimal distance to Xi by applying the distance formula of above(equation 9).If prior knowledge is not present then the identification of target neighbors is computed by using Euclidean distance formula of Xi with same Yi. The cost function consists of two parts: first is the large distance between each input and its target neighbor and the second term is the small distance between each input.All other input never share the same label. Therefore, the cost is given by (Weinberger et al, 2005).

$$\varepsilon\left(L\right) = \sum \eta_{ij} \left\| L\left(x_i - x_j\right) \right\|^2 + c \sum \eta_{ij} \left(1 - y_{il}\right) \left[1 + \left\| L\left(x_i - x_j\right) \right\|^2 - \left\| Lx_i - x_l \right\|^2 \right] \tag{10}$$

2.3 Predictive Model of Random Forest for Drought Images

Random forest is a classification algorithm developed by Leo Breiman (Breiman, 1998) and extended by Adele cutler (Kam, 1995; Kam, 1998). The idea is to use the combination of bagging method proposed by Breiman and the function to use the randomly selected features independently which was poposed byHO, Amit, and

German (Amit, Yali, Geman, 1997). The combination will construct the forest of decision trees will control variance. Random selection of features is done by random subset method (Breiman, 2001; Amit, Yali, Geman, 1997) .Decision trees that are grown deep get the ability to learn the high amount of data which not regular and the overfitting takes place as they have low bias and high variance. When there are multiple deep decision trees which are trained produces the result, the average of those result is helpful in reducing the variance.But, it might cost small increase in the bias (Friedman et al, 2001).

2.3.1 Tree Bagging Technique

It is the bootstrap aggregating technique which is applied on a training set X .with labels Y.

For b= 1,......,B

1. Sample with replacement, n training examples from X,Y call these Xb,Yb
2. Train a decision tree Fb on Xb,Yb.

The prediction process includes the testing sample lets say X and then the similar process of averaging is done on individual predictions

$$\hat{F} = \frac{1}{B} \sum_{b=1}^{B} \hat{f}b\left(x'\right) \tag{11}$$

This process reduces the variance and it is better than nearest k as the biases never increase. Forest of trees, that is a number of decision trees is helpful in a way as it is not a single prediction, rather it's a pool of predictions and then its average value. The only condition is that the decision trees must be correlated (Roy et al, "Spam Detection"; 2016; Roy et al. "Spam Emails" 2016; Roy et al, 2015). The sample training and testing images haven been shown below.

3. EXPERIMENTAL OUTCOME OF PROPOSED PREDICTIVE MODELS

3.1 DBN Classification Results

DBN classification results are shown in Tables 3-8.

Table 3. DBN classification report when the dataset is split in 60:40

	Precision	Recall	F1- Score	Support
0	0.48	0.73	0.58	91
1	0.56	0.31	0.40	103
Avg/total	0.52	0.51	0.48	194

Table 4. DBN confusion matrix report when the dataset is split in 60:40

Drought	Non Drought	Accuracy
66	25	0.5051
71	32	

Table 5. DBN classification report when the dataset is split in 70:30

	Precision	Recall	F1-Score	Support
0	1.00	0.05	0.10	78
1	0.53	1.00	0.69	83
Avg/total	0.76	0.54	0.40	161

Table 6. DBN confusion matrix report when the dataset is split in 70:30

Drought	Non Drought	Accuracy
4	74	0.540372
0	83	

Table 7. DBN classification report when the dataset is split in 80:20

	Precision	Recall	F1-Score	Support
0	1.00	0.03	0.05	72
1	0.44	1.00	0.61	54
Avg/total	0.76	0.44	0.29	126

Table 8. DBN confusion matrix report when the dataset is split in 80:20

Drought	Non Drought	Accuracy
2	70	0.4444
0	54	

3.2 kNN Classification Result

kNN classification result shown in Tables 9-14.

Table 9. kNN classification report when the dataset is split in 60:40

	Precision	Recall	F1-Score	Support
0	0.55	0.49	0.52	117
1	0.55	0.61	0.58	118
Avg/total	0.55	0.55	0.55	235

Table 10. kNN confusion matrix report when the dataset is split in 60:40

Drought	Non drought	Accuracy
57	60	0.5489
46	72	

Table 11. kNN classification report when the dataset is split in 70:30

	Precision	Recall	F1-Score	Support
0	0.49	0.40	0.44	102
1	0.41	0.51	0.46	85
Avg/total	0.46	0.45	0.45	187

Table 12. kNN confusion matrix report when the dataset is split in 70:30

Drought	Non Drought	Accuracy
41	61	0.4491
42	43	

Table 13. kNN classification report when the dataset is split in 80:20

	Precision	Recall	F1-Score	Support
0	0.66	0.64	0.65	61
1	0.59	0.62	0.60	52
Avg/total	0.63	0.63	0.63	113

Table 14. kNN confusion matrix report when the dataset is split in 80:20

Drought	Non Drought	Accuracy
39	22	0.6283
20	32	

3.3 Random Forest Classification Method

Random forest classification method shown in Tables 15-20.

Table 15. RF classification report when the dataset is split in 60:40

	Precision	Recall	F1-Score	Support
0	0.54	0.65	0.59	20
1	0.61	0.50	0.55	22
Avg/total	0.58	0.57	0.57	42

Table 16. RF confusion matrix report when the dataset is split in 60:40

Drought	Non Drought	Accuracy
13	7	0.5714
11	11	

Table 17. RF classification report when the dataset is split in 70:30

	Precision	Recall	F1-score	Support
0	0.67	0.53	0.59	15
1	0.63	0.75	0.69	16
Avg/total	0.65	0.65	0.64	31

Table 18. RF confusion matrix report when the dataset is split in 70:30

Drought	Non Drought	Accuracy
8	7	0.6451
4	12	

Table 19. RF classification report when the dataset is split in 80:20

	Precision	Recall	F1-Score	Support
0	0.78	0.50	0.61	14
1	0.59	0.83	0.69	12
Avg/total	0.69	0.65	0.65	26

Table 20. RF confusion matrix report when the dataset is split in 80:20

Drought	Non Drought	Accuracy
7	7	0.65384
2	10	

4. CONCLUSION

Drought is a natural calamity which affects the living beings due to the extreme shortage of water. This paper proposes Deep Belief Network(DBN) learning technique, which is one of the most recent machine learning methods, for classification of drought and non-drought images. The performance of the Deep Belief Network (DBN) has been compared with k nearest neighbor (kNN) and random forest. The data set has been split 80:20, 70:30 and 60:40 as train and test. The comparatively studies show the difference between the results of the three different classification algorithms on three difference instance of the dataset.

REFERENCES

Amit, Y., & Geman, D. (1997). Shape quantization and recognition with randomized trees. *Neural Computation*, *9*(7), 1545–1588. doi:10.1162/neco.1997.9.7.1545

Anagnostou, E. N. (2004). A convective/stratiform precipitation classification algorithm for volume scanning weather radar observations. *Meteorological Applications*, *11*(4), 291–300. doi:10.1017/S1350482704001409

Bengio, Y. (2007). Greedy layer-wise training of deep networks. *Advances in Neural Information Processing Systems*, *19*, 153.

Bengio, Y. (2009). Learning deep architectures for AI. *Foundations and Trends® in Machine Learning*, *2*(1), 1-127.

Boken, V. K., Cracknell, A. P., & Heathcote, R. L. (2005). *Monitoring and predicting agricultural drought: a global study*. Oxford University Press.

Brahic, C. (2007). Sunshade "for global warming could cause drought". *New Scientist*.

Breiman, L. (2001). Random forests. *Machine Learning*, *45*(1), 5–32. doi:10.1023/A:1010933404324

Coomans, D., & Massart, D. L. (1982). Alternative k-nearest neighbour rules in supervised pattern recognition: Part 1. k-Nearest neighbour classification by using alternative voting rules. *Analytica Chimica Acta*, *136*, 15–27. doi:10.1016/S0003-2670(01)95359-0

Dietterich, T. G. (2000). An experimental comparison of three methods for constructing ensembles of decision trees: Bagging, boosting, and randomization. *Machine Learning*, *40*(2), 139–157. doi:10.1023/A:1007607513941

Dore, A. J., Mousavi-Baygi, M., Smith, R. I., Hall, J., Fowler, D., & Choularton, T. W. (2006). A model of annual orographic precipitation and acid deposition and its application to Snowdonia. *Atmospheric Environment*, *40*(18), 3316–3326. doi:10.1016/j.atmosenv.2006.01.043

Falkenmark, M., Lundqvist, J., & Widstrand, C. (1989). Macro-scale water scarcity requires micro-scale approaches. Natural Resources Forum, 13(4).

Friedman, J., Hastie, T., & Tibshirani, R. (2001). The elements of statistical learning (Vol. 1). Springer.

Glantz, M. H. (1988). *Drought and hunger in Africa*. CUP Archive.

Hinton, G. E., Osindero, S., & Teh, Y.-W. (2006). A fast learning algorithm for deep belief nets. *Neural Computation*, *18*(7), 1527–1554. doi:10.1162/neco.2006.18.7.1527 PMID:16764513

Ho, T. K. (1998). The random subspace method for constructing decision forests. *Pattern Analysis and Machine Intelligence, IEEE Transactions on, 20*(8), 832–844. doi:10.1109/34.709601

Ho, T. K. (1995). Random decision forests. *Document Analysis and Recognition, 1995, Proceedings of the Third International Conference on, 1.*

Hofman, V., & Franzen, D. (1997). Emergency tillage to control wind erosion. North Dakota State University.

Jaskowiak, P. A., & Campello, R. J. G. B. (2011). Comparing correlation coefficients as dissimilarity measures for cancer classification in gene expression data. *Proceedings of the Brazilian Symposium on Bioinformatics.*

Keddy, P. (2007). *Plants and vegetation: origins, processes, consequences.* Cambridge University Press. doi:10.1017/CBO9780511812989

Paepe, R., Fairbridge, R. W., & Jelgersma, S. (Eds.). (2012). *Greenhouse effect, sea level and drought* (Vol. 325). Springer Science & Business Media.

Palmer, W. C. (1965). *Meteorological drought* (Vol. 30). Washington, DC: US Department of Commerce, Weather Bureau.

Pearce, R. P. (2002). *Meteorology at the Millennium* (Vol. 83). Academic Press. doi:10.1016/S0074-6142(02)80150-4

Productivity Commission. (2009). *Government drought support.* Inquiry Reports.

Richthofen, B. F. (1882). II.—On the Mode of Origin of the Loess. *Geological Magazine, 9*(07), 293–305. doi:10.1017/S001675680017164X

Roy, Abhinav, Rishab, Obaidat, & Krishna. (2017). *A Deep Learning Based Artificial Neural Network Approach for Intrusion Detection.* Springer. DOI: 10.1007/978-981-10-4642-1_5

Roy & Madhu Viswanatham. (2016). Classifying Spam Emails Using Artificial Intelligent Techniques. *International Journal of Engineering Research in Africa, 22.*

Roy, S. S., Biba, M., Kumar, R., Kumar, R., & Samui, P. (2017). A New SVM Method for Recognizing Polarity of Sentiments in Twitter. In *Handbook of Research on Soft Computing and Nature-Inspired Algorithms* (pp. 281–291). IGI Global. doi:10.4018/978-1-5225-2128-0.ch009

Roy, S. S., Mittal, D., Basu, A., & Abraham, A. (2015). Stock market forecasting using lasso linear regression model. In *Afro-European Conference for Industrial Advancement* (pp. 371–381). Springer International Publishing. doi:10.1007/978-3-319-13572-4_31

Roy, S. S., Viswanatham, V. M., & Krishna, P. V. (2016). Spam detection using hybrid model of rough set and decorate ensemble. *International Journal of Computational Systems Engineering*, *2*(3), 139–147. doi:10.1504/IJCSYSE.2016.079000

Smith, A. B., & Katz, R. W. (2013). US billion-dollar weather and climate disasters: Data sources, trends, accuracy and biases. *Natural Hazards*, *67*(2), 387–410. doi:10.1007/s11069-013-0566-5

Tallaksen, L. M., & Van Lanen, H. A. J. (2004). Hydrological drought: processes and estimation methods for streamflow and groundwater. Elsevier.

Wang, B. (2006). *The Asian monsoon*. Springer Science & Business Media.

Wang, Q., Shi, P., Lei, T., Geng, G., Liu, J., Mo, X., & Wu, J. et al. (2015). The alleviating trend of drought in the Huang-Huai-Hai Plain of China based on the daily SPEI. *International Journal of Climatology*, *35*(13), 3760–3769. doi:10.1002/joc.4244

Weinberger, K. Q., Blitzer, J., & Saul, L. K. (2005). Distance metric learning for large margin nearest neighbor classification. *Advances in Neural Information Processing Systems*.

Weinberger, K. Q., & Saul, L. K. (2009). Distance metric learning for large margin nearest neighbor classification. *Journal of Machine Learning Research*, *10*, 207–244.

West, T. O., & Post, W. M. (2002). Soil organic carbon sequestration rates by tillage and crop rotation. *Soil Science Society of America Journal*, *66*(6), 1930–1946. doi:10.2136/sssaj2002.1930

APPENDIX: ABBREVIATIONS

DBN: Deep Belief Network.
kNN: k Nearest Neighbour.

Chapter 7
Big Data Deep Analytics for Geosocial Networks

Muhammad Mazhar Ullah Rathore
Kyungpook National University, South Korea

Awais Ahmad
Yeungnam University, South Korea

Anand Paul
Kyungpook National University, South Korea

ABSTRACT

Geosocial network data provides the full information on current trends in human, their behaviors, their living style, the incidents and events, the disasters, current medical infection, and much more with respect to locations. Hence, the current geosocial media can work as a data asset for facilitating the national and the government itself by analyzing the geosocial data at real-time. However, there are millions of geosocial network users, who generates terabytes of heterogeneous data with a variety of information every day with high-speed, termed as Big Data. Analyzing such big amount of data and making real-time decisions is an inspiring task. Therefore, this book chapter discusses the exploration of geosocial networks. A system architecture is discussed and implemented in a real-time environment in order to process the abundant amount of various social network data to monitor the earth events, incidents, medical diseases, user trends and thoughts to make future real-time decisions as well as future planning.

DOI: 10.4018/978-1-5225-3015-2.ch007

INTRODUCTION

Social media is drastically advancing their features day by day while altering themselves from social networks to geosocial networks. It enables people to create their contents publically related to any social events with the geographic location information. This results in the rise of the usage of geosocial media users by empowering them to be voice opinions, to reports events, transfer thoughts, show anger and love while connecting with each other. Such intercommunication from people to people was unconceivable in pre-Internet age. Now, the information shared by most of the social media becomes geosocial as: 1) with the posts from users with extensive contents, the geographical information are also attached. The geolocation information can either be explicitly entered (by checking-in) or implicitly added (by earth coordinates, like latitude, altitude), and 2) the users thoughts shared on social media reveals social knowledge and also strengthen the relationship and communication among communities.

The technology advancement enables the use of GPS system in smart phone, which marks the location data to be very easy to get. The location of any person, who comments on any status, posts on any social media wall, or unloading a picture regarding any event, is recorded. Thus, gathering such type of location data, from all social network users, produces warehouses of geosocial data. There is another way generating geosocial data by crowd-sourcing while providing self-developed application for various purposes or a cause, such as disease or infection control. By this way, the geosocial data is harvested by from volunteer or paid user, who are willing to provide information for that cause. For Example, In Haiyan typhoon at Philippine in 2013, virtually community of huge number of supporters, volunteers, IT professionals created online street maps for emergency reliefs (Hern, 2013). Such type of online information gathered by crowed-sourcing was given a new name as 'volunteer geographic information' (VGI) (Haklay, 2010). These days many platforms and softwares have been developed that are using crow-sourcing for geosocial data harvesting in order to promote businesses, promote any cause, or other commercial purposes. One of such software platform example is Ushahidi. It provides the reports by matching the specific keyword on the geosocial network at the given locations. That report is then used for social awareness and help in case of any emergency or disaster (Zook, Graham, 2010). There are also some other applications with limited functionalities like Hootsuite ("Hootsuite" n.d.) and 140kit ("140kit" n.d.)

Now these days, researchers are more concerned in geosocial networks by considering it as new data asset (Stefanids et al, 2012; Cheng et al, 2011). Crooks et al. (2012), in their work, used Twitter data to map the earthquake in United States using geolocated tweets. Among 21,362 geolocated tweets, the first tweet announcing about the earthquake appeared after 1 minute of the earthquake on Twitter (Crooks et al, 2012). Similarly, Chow (Chow et al, 2010) and Papadimitriou (Papadimitriou et al, 2011). proposed architectures using geo-tagged recommendation while creating new social network. GeoLife 2.0 in (Zheng et al, 2009) does similar detection, trajectory analysis, and recommendation selection. There are also few other systems that perform analysis on text and contents of the tweets e.g. (O'Connor et al, 2010)., some uses locations. Some research works are also done in the detection of hotspots and hyper-local events in a city using Twitter's data (Ferrari et al, 2011; Xia et al, 2014). In addition, Ahmad et al. (Ahmad et al, 2016). introduced the use of social data with other parameters for predicting the human behavior being a part of a smart society. There are a lot of other works that have been done using geosocial networks using geolocated information. However, all of the work is done at a limited level, ignoring the size and velocity of data generated.

Using Geosocial network data not only beneficial to the government, but it also have major impact on the human life. It provides befits from an ordinary citizen to an entrepreneur. However, when we talk about the harvesting of geosocial data, such as, from Twitter or Facebook, these networks have millions of users who are posting millions of tweets and statuses within an hour. So you can imagine how much data is generated by all of the users of various social networks. The data generated might be in terabytes within a minute. So, this is very challenging task to process this high volume and high velocity geosocial data. We need special computational environment and advanced computing techniques with intelligent management in order to provide in-time/real-time analysis. All the existing techniques discussed above don't consider more than 1 social network at the same time. These techniques gave much attention to the size and speed of data generation, therefore, analysis are not scalable... On the other hand, many big data processing technologies has been introduced, such as big data processing using data fusion approach (Ahmad, Paul, Rathore, Chang, 2016), remotely sensed big satellite data processing (Rathore, Paul, Ahmad, Chen, Haung, Ji, 2015; Mazhar, Rathore, Ahmad, Paul, Wu, 2016), and illegal activity detection in high speed big data environment (Rathore, Mazhar, Ahmad, Paul, 2016). However, all of these approaches cannot be deployed for geosocial data analysis.

Therefore, in order to meet these computational challenges, this chapter is discussing an advanced geosocial data analytics system, which not only processes offline data within a time limit but also provides the real-time data analysis of various social networks including Twitter, Flickr, Facebook, YouTube, etc. The system uses the deployment of Hadoop ecosystem for the analysis with the Spark at 3rd party tool for real-time analysis. The analysis are performed by taking two social network, i.e., Twitter and Flickr. The rest of the section describes all about the mentioned system including the system details, data analysis, the implementation and evaluation.

THE SYSTEM COMPUTING MODEL

This section describes the computing model including the system overview, the architecture, its application, and it limitation.

System Overview

Humans are the most reliable source to report events, activities and important issues. Geosocial network can use humans as sensors by building a Human Sensor Network (HSN) to monitor the activities in the world.

When a user of the geosocial network posts any activity relating to some events or sharing thoughts for anything, he is acting as sensor that sends data to its station i.e. Geosocial network. Afterwards, the main station performs some analysis on the data in order to find what is going on in the particular area of the world. These geosocial networks works as HSN as shown in Figure 1. In other words, we can say the system uses HSN to generate and harvest the data in order to monitor the various areas of the earth. The system analyzes all the tweets generated from the Twitter users, Facebook statuses, images and other geosocial networks, such as YouTube, Foursquare, etc. corresponding to the users' locations to provide the real time monitoring in case of any disaster, fatal diseases, and accidents. Moreover, the

Figure 1. How human works as sensors in Geosocial networks

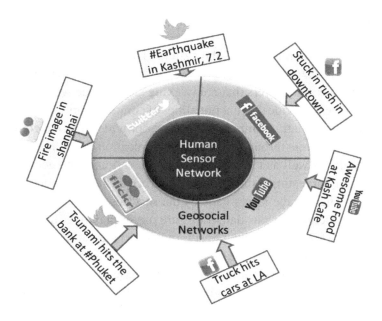

users' data with their location information can also be used to recommend various systems based on user's current location such as useful products, restaurants, hotels, transport, etc.

Our system harvests the data of users from Geosocial networks as a tuple (L, T, U) of location L, time T and user U. It describes what the distinguished user 'U' posted on the geosocial network at time T from location L. This was a challenging task to get the location of a user, which become easier due to the advanced remote smart devices and GPS system. The smart devices, by default send the location coordinates to the network when any user posts any activity or event. The IP based technique uses the 'at' tag of Facebook, check-in, and friends tag to determine the location of the user when the location information is missing within the post. The posts, texts, tweets, comments, statuses, smiley are analyzed using text analytics, statistical analytics, complex machine learning and data mining techniques to monitor and find out what is going on, where and why. It happens that such type of data can be used to predict the future events depending on current user trends corresponding to various areas. So businessmen, entrepreneurs, government agencies, and citizens as well, can make future plans based on current trends. But the major challenge is how to analyses to such huge amount of data generated by many social networks. The discussed system uses advanced technologies of computing in order to meet the challenges. The detail description of the system including the system architecture, implementation model, its applications, issues and challenges are given in the upcoming sections.

The System Architecture

Figure 2 shows the architecture of the system. The system has three basic top to bottom layers i.e. data collection, data processing, and services and application layers plus two auxiliary layers that are working side by side with the basic layers. The auxiliary layers provide the functionalities of communication and storage of raw as well as structured data. Communication layer provides internal communication between various servers through various communication technologies such as Wi-Fi, Ethernet, etc. as well as the external communication to the geosocial network servers for data harvesting using any fast internet technology such as, WiMAX, 3G, LTE, etc. The storage layers handles the services of storing data that can be structured, unstructured or raw data for future use or planning. Instead of working with all the three basic layers like the communication layer, the storage layer only works side by side with last two basic layers i.e. Data processing layer and services and application layer. The data is stored at database after classification and the results are stored after analysis and decision making. As the data sources are geosocial networks such as Twitter, Facebook and YouTube, Flickr, Foursquare, etc. the data collection layer works for data harvesting, which takes data or contents from Geosocial network servers distinguished by tuples (L, T, u) with location l, posting time t and user u. The main thing to harvest the data is the central software plus hardware platform that works like switch/hub. This central platform is called data harvesting server which provides the intermediate point between the geosocial network and the analysis building.

Data harvesting is one of the main and challenging task of the system because of capturing and harvesting high speed data at real time. There are two possible ways to get data from social networks. Firstly, the data can easily be taken from friend's walls, joined groups, liked pages and from your account. However, by this method, you are required to have many friends, like pages, groups, etc. with diverse location in order to get huge amount of heterogeneous data with diverse topics. Secondly, we can harvest data that is publicly available for all the people by the social networks. But in such way, we are not sure to get all real time data of that particular social network. In either way, the data is harvested by using two types of APIs, such as 1. Steaming APIs and 2. State transfer API. The streaming APIs used to get real time data with minimum delay while the state transfer API allows you to get data with static time slots like after 5 minutes, one hour, one day, etc.

In any geosocial network, the data is harvested by query method sent as http request. The response of the query might be either in XML or JASON format. The

Figure 2. The system architecture

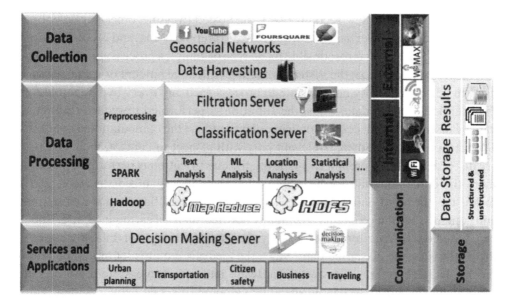

query is always sent and the data is received based on the given location, time, particular user ID, or contents. In case of Twitter, Two APIs are provided to get the tweeters data i.e., 1) 'Streaming', which is used to get the real-time data continuously without any delay by giving the topic/contents, location, and maximum size limit, 2) RESTful, which can works as state transfer API, used to get data in discrete delays like after 5 minutes, 1 hour, 1 data, etc., (Fielding, n.d.). The received data is in any case contains the actual data and the Metadata itself. In case of Flickr images, the response received contains the User information, the time, and the location with the attached image. Twitter's response is also contains the metadata with the tweet or comment.

In any of the geosocial network data analysis. The location, and time are two most important things with the contents. As time is used to find out the relevancy and authenticity of the post, while the location tells the area where the various things are happening and activities are performed. However, how to gain and extract the metadata is also have technical aspects. The location can be identified by various IP techniques (Poese, et al, n.d.; Erikson et al, n.d.). Moreover, these days with the advancement of GPs technology, every smart device send the geo-located information such as, the earth co-ordinates with the data to the geosocial networks. In case of Flickr, location is given as metadata is either precise or descriptive. Actual location can be obtain from EXIF record of the image. Flickr image contains two type of time attached with the image post. i.e., 1) time taken, which is the actual time the image is taken from camera, and 2) the update time, which is the time the image is uploaded on Flickr or updated on Flickr. The time information are encapsulated in EXIF record. In case of Twitter, the tweet posting time is also attached as a metadata with the tweets. After few seconds (2-5), the posted tweet becomes public/online.

Data processing layer has two sub parts i.e., 1) preprocessing, and 2) computations and analysis. This layer is responsible for all type of complex processing, analysis and results generation. Since, the system is dealing with huge amount of social network data, therefore, it is very not possible to process each and every byte regardless of the usefulness of the data. Thus, the filtration is performed to reduce the size of data by discarding unnecessary data in order to reduce the computational overhead. The unnecessary metadata, irrelevant post with respect to content, area, and time are discarded. Next at preprocessing level, the classification is performed to reduce more the computational overhead by giving the data organized structure, which makes the access of data very fast. The data is classified based on location, time, and contents. Various contents are already notified such as, earthquake, fire, Ebola, etc., based on the requirement to classify the data. Next phase of data processing is the analysis on the classified data. Since the analysis requires lot of computations on the data. Therefore, a powerful hardware and a software system are needed, which have the ability to handle such huge amount of social networks data. Thus, the Hadoop ecosystem is deployed that have strong distributed file system HDFS with the ability of storing data across multiple nodes with higher security, reliability, and fast access. Hadoop ecosystem have the ability to perform parallel processing on the same data stored on HDFS nodes by using its parallel programing paradigm i.e., Map Reduce. As, Hadoop is initially developed for batch processing, but, here a real-time processing is needed to efficiently process continuously coming geosocial data. Therefore, in order to perform real-time analysis and getting the benefit of Hadoop at the same time. Apache SPARK is deployed on the Top of Hadoop system that can provide the efficient processing on real-time data. Various machine learning algorithms, statistical analysis, text analytics, content based analysis are performed on processing layer to generate results for decision making. In This chapter, we just provide basic analysis to find out various disaster events such as earthquake, fire, diseases, etc.

Finally, we have service and application layer, which is responsible for decision making and using results for various application depending on the needs. E.g., in case of earthquake detection in various areas, the Hadoop provided all the computation and statistical analysis of the tweets containing earthquake information at time t. Hadoop can just provide the results, which can be manipulated by the decision server. Decision server identify the location based on the results generated, such as time, how much tweets received, authenticity of results etc. Then Decision server decides whether there is earthquake or other event at a particular location or not. Later these analysis results can be used for many application such as urban planning, transportation, citizen safety, business, travelling, etc. the details of the system's application in

the market will come in next section. Figure 3 shows the details flow by flow implementation model of the system.

Applications

The geosocial network analysis have lot of application especially, when we are talking about the system, which are unique among others in many aspects. Here we are giving some of the system's application in various scenarios.

- **Disaster Management:** Our system can work well in order to detect any disaster in any area and broadcast it to the people in order to manage it and save lives. Such as fire, earthquake, flood, etc. Moreover, it can also provide the deep insight into the causes of the disaster and people opinion. Based on the results the planning can be done to control and properly manage the future events.

Figure 3. The system implementation model

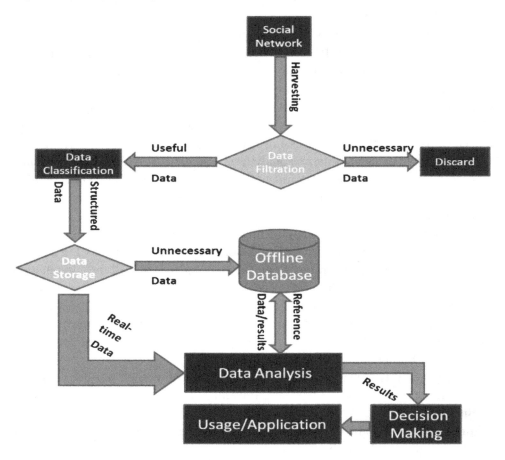

- **Recommended System:** The system provides the analysis architecture, which can be used for analyzing social behaviors of the public or specific class around a particular area. The results can be used to provide the recommended system to the people. Like shopping, hotels, cheap markets and goods, banking systems, advertisements etc., and recommended systems works on people likings and theirs constrains (Babadilla et al, 2013). Firstly they does filtering and profile matching then recommend some system based on the people profile and class.
- **Traffic Monitoring and Urban Planning:** the system can also be used for detected in any traffic incidents like blockage, accidents, damaged by geosocial network tweets, photos, status, comments, etc., the historical data related to such incidents or activity is useful for urban planning regarding the

construction of roads, buildings, parking, amusement and relaxation parks, etc., based on public reactions. Moreover, due to geosocial tweets harvesting, the system gets the user mobility patterns, what's the trends of people movement etc. Therefore based on the people movement, the authorities can make better planes. Some of the work is already done in (Becker et al, 2011; Kanza et al, 2014; Ratti et al, 2006) at a limited level that only consider limited aspects of urban planning.

- **Monitoring Traffic:** Real-time geosocial network data with people's location can be used for monitoring the traffic. Therefore, by continuous analysis, the people can be recommended the suitable routes related the current circumstances as in (Hefez et al, 2011; Levin et al, 2014).

- **Health Care:** One major advantage of the geosocial network analysis is healthcare. Like Twitter is used in many healthcare applications like (Lan et al, 2014; Lan et al, 2012, Waller et al, 2004) to monitor and control the fatal diseases and infections. It can also be used for future planning in order to control the infection. The system alerts and guide the people based on their current behaviors and trends against infection.

In additions to all of these application, the discussed system can be used for many other application, such as tourism, business in order to maximize profit by launching new products based on current human trends, public safety in case of any accidents, mishap, any war situation, or any crime.

LIMITATIONS AND SOLUTIONS

The geosocial network have lot of applications, but still there are some issues and challenges raised due to user location information that is available as public while analyzing user data. The public user mobility allows other people to track their daily routine, to know their thoughts, to know where you are moving, to know his house and workplace, etc. This makes the major damage to the privacy of the person. Therefore he can easily be traced and can be spoiled by anyone.

Similarly, when we see in other aspect of the geosocial networks, we came across lot of benefits to the society as well as government authorities. However, as people know that this will definitely spoil their privacy, they are hesitated to make their data public. On the other hand, the social networks also don't allow their user data to be used for business or for commercial purpose. Some of the networks don't make their data public to anyone. The makes the harvesting of such data as challenging task. Useful analysis can only be performed when you have all type of full-fledged data.

Business and economy can grow if the data is public to the business and entrepreneur, even commercially, so that it can be used for profit maximization and economy growth. However, no social network open their data for commercial purposes. Similarly, there are few other issue that makes the use of geosocial data analysis impractical in open environment. These limitations can be catered by building an attractive social media application for users, which also harvest user's data by taking user permissions. Moreover, users can also be paid for giving their personal data through any application. Moreover, geosocial media can sell their data on users' permission to the commercial organizations for profit maximization or new product launching. They can also provide data to the social NGOs for specific cause that serves the humanity. In addition, the data harvesting can also be achieved by any android or other mobile application, such as VGI (Haklay, 2010) However, building such applications for data harvesting is out of the scope of this chapter. The data is harvested through publicly available datasets.

ANALYSIS AND DISCUSSION

In this section, we provide the geosocial data analysis details aiming at detecting various events and disasters. Firstly, the datasets details are given and later, the analysis discussion is made.

Dataset Description

We have taken the data from Twitter stream grab ("Archive Team" n.d.) for analysis containing the tweets from 2010 to 2015. Each of the dataset has the size more than 40 GB with more than a month tweets, classified by the date. We also took the data from MAPD ("MAPD Twitter" n.d.) for simple analysis that contains tweets from November 1, 2014 to March 01, 2015 with more than 60000000 tweets. The data can be classifier with respect to popular # tags. The tweet are of heterogeneous types with multiple languages.

Discussion

The analysis are done on Twitter's data considering November 2014 to march 2015. The overall tweet map is shown in Figure 4. The color of tweets show the language in which the tweet is posted. English is the most popular language on Twitter as near as 40% tweets are in English as shown in Figures 5. Therefore, we give more focus to English by analyzing the English keywords rather than other language. However, we cannot ignore the importance of other languages such as Spanish

Figure 4. Overall tweets' map from November 2014 to March 2015

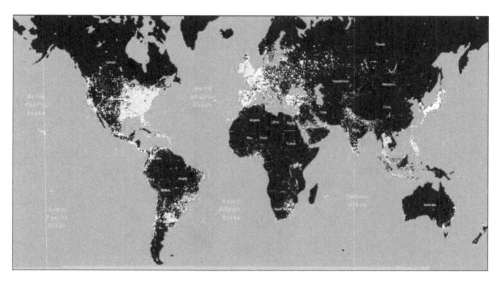

Figure 5. The majority of languages used for all tweets

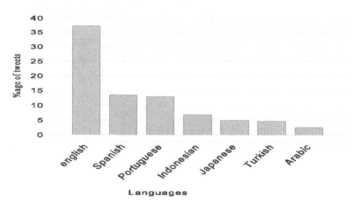

and Portuguese that are used in more than 10% tweets and other languages such as Indonesian, Japanese, Turkish and Arabic which are used for almost in 5% tweets individually. Therefore, while analyzing social network data, we should also give more focus to other popular languages as well. Similarly map also reflects this situation by showing more tweets in USA, UK and other European countries and then Indonesia, Japan and other Asian countries.

We also analyze all the tweets by considering various events and disasters such as fire, earthquake, snow, Ebola virus on various regions of the earth by analyzing the corresponding hashtags as well as contents. The Figure 6 shows the number

Figure 6. Various events in the world and number of tweets

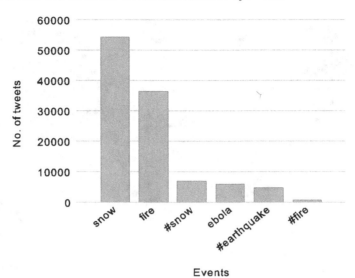

of tweets for each of the event/disaster. The tweets containing #snow, #Ebola and #earthquake are almost near to 5000 which the number of five and snow is quite higher. Since in most of the countries it is snowing in winter, the number is quite high. Similarly the keyword fire cannot only be used for actual fire event. It can also be used for hot topics, anger, etc. Therefore the number of tweets in case of fire is also higher. We also have to do the content analysis for such type of keywords that can be used for multipurpose.

In case of earthquake analysis, we found that majority of the tweets are form USA and Japan. The overall tweet map with #earthquake tag is shown in Figure 7 while the Figure 8 map shows the earthquake tweets in various area of Japan including its ocean area. Figure 9 also shows the countries which tweets maximum with #earthquake tag. Moreover, we also found that most of the tweets are posted within few minutes after the earthquake and also contains the magnitude of the earthquake. Similarly the fire and #fire tweet map for the whole world is shown in Figure 10 where it is obvious that mostly the fire event occurred in the USA and UK. The locations of fire and #fire tweets with USA are shown in Figure 11 which shows most of the tweets are from east coast and west coasts. The number of countries where most of the fire event occurs are depicted in Figure 12.

Snow event is also important in order to monitor the floods and water resources. Therefore, we also consider snow keyword in Twitter to find out the snow event. Figures 13 and 14 depicts the snow event analysis in which again USA is on the

Figure 7. Tweets found with #earthquake tag in various areas of the world

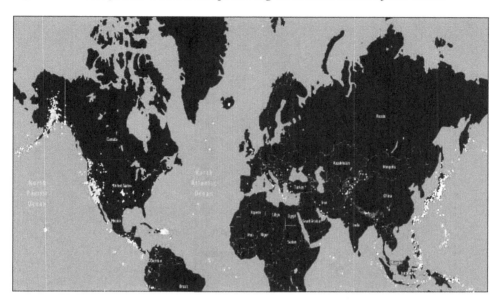

Figure 8. Tweets found with #earthquake tag in Japan

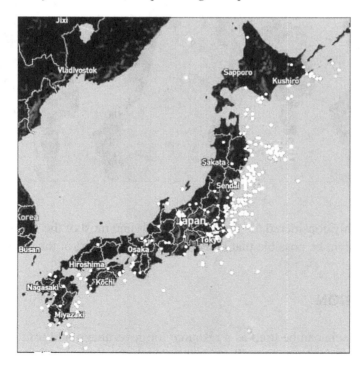

Figure 9. Countries with maximum number of #earthquake tag

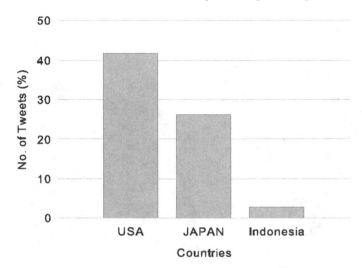

Figure 10. Tweets found with #fire tag and 'fire' keyword respectively in various areas of the world

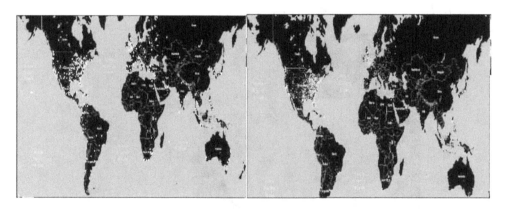

top. As we only considered the English keywords and most of the Twitter users are in USA, it might be possible that USA is on the top in most of the cases.

CONCLUSION

Geosocial media can be used as a resource for government authorities in order to facilitate their population by facilitating them while providing safety from disastrous

Figure 11. Tweets found with #fire tag and 'fire' keyword respectively in USA

Figure 12. Countries with maximum number of #fire tag

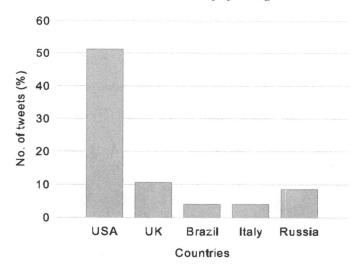

event by suitable management, reducing the fright of the spread infection. Similarly, Geosocial media might also assist the public citizens by providing health care, transport safety, suitable recommended systems, etc., as well as entrepreneur while providing guidance to start new product in difference areas depending upon the current trends in the area by observing the geosocial data of that specific area. All these facilitations can only be provided by better analytics of huge volume and diverse nature of geosocial data. Such analytics on big geospatial data can only be achieved

Figure 13. Countries with maximum number of 'fire' keywords in the tweets tag

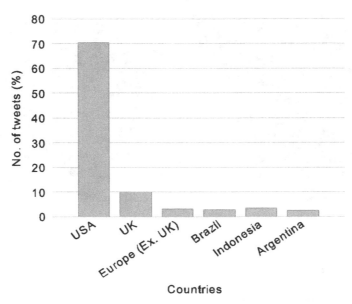

Figure 14. Tweets found with #snow tag in various areas of the world

with advanced technology, better analytics and fast system with parallel computing. Therefore, this chapter is recommending a system architecture to use geosocial data for better planning, proper management, safety from disasters, social awareness, etc., corresponding to several geo-locations. The system harvest the high-speed and high

Figure 15. Countries with maximum number of 'snow' keywords in the tweets tag

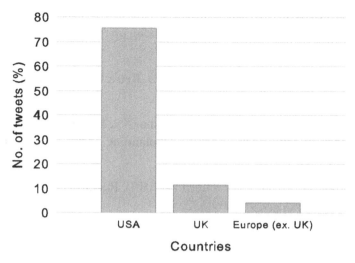

volume data from various geosocial networks and then efficiently process the data by analyzing and making in-time decision based on the scenario. The Twitter data is taken as exploration for several events using the discussed system. The system is developed using Spark over Hadoop (HDFS and Map Reduce) system.

ACKNOWLEDGMENT

This work was supported by Institute for Information & communications Technology Promotion (IITP) grant funded by the Korea government (MSIP). [No. 10041145, Self-Organized Software platform (SoSp) for Welfare Devices]. This work is also supported by the National Research Foundation of Korea (NRF) grant funded by the Korea government (MSIP) (NRF- 2013R1A2A1A01014020).

REFERENCES

Ahmad, Paul, Rathore, & Chang. (2016). An Efficient Multidimensional Big Data Fusion Approach in Machine-to-Machine Communication. *ACM Trans. Embed. Comput. Syst., 15*(2).

Ahmad, A., Rathore, M. M., Paul, A., & Rho, S. (2016). Defining Human Behaviors Using Big Data Analytics in Social Internet of Things. *2016 IEEE 30th International Conference on Advanced Information Networking and Applications (AINA)*, 1101-1107.

Archive Team. (n.d.). *The Twitter Stream Grab*. Retrieved from https://archive.org/details/twitterstream

Becker, Caceres, Hanson, Loh, Urbanek, Varshavsky, & Volinsky. (2011). A tale of one city: Using cellular network data for urban planning. *IEEE Pervasive Computing*, *10*(4), 18-26.

Bobadilla, Ortega, Hernando, & Gutierrez. (2013). Recommender systems survey. *Knowledge-Based Systems*, *46*, 109-132.

Cheng, Z., Caverlee, J., Lee, K., & Sui, D. Z. (2011). Exploring millions of footprints in location sharing services. *ICWSM*, *2011*, 81–88.

Chow, J. (2010). Towards location-based social networking services. *Proceedings of the 2nd ACM SIGSPATIAL International Workshop on Location Based Social Networks*, 31-38. doi:10.1145/1867699.1867706

Crooks, A. (2012). #Earthquake: Twitter as a distributed sensor system. *Transactions in GIS*.

Eriksson, B., Barford, P., Sommers, J., & Nowak, R. A learning-based approach for IP geolocation. In A. Krishnamurthy & B. Plattner (Eds.), *Passive and Active Measurement* (Vol. 6032, pp. 171–180). Berlin: Springer Lecture Notes in Computer Science. doi:10.1007/978-3-642-12334-4_18

Ferrari, L., Rosi, A., Mamei, M., & Zambonelli, F. (2011). Extracting urban patterns from location-based social networks. *Proc. of the 3rd ACM LBSN*. doi:10.1145/2063212.2063226

Fielding, R. T. (n.d.). *Architectural styles and the design of network-based software architectures*. (PhD Thesis). University of California, Irvine, CA.

Haklay, M. (2010). How good is volunteered geographical information? A comparative study of OpenStreetMap and Ordnance Survey datasets. *Environment and Planning. B, Planning & Design*, *37*(4), 682–703. doi:10.1068/b35097

Hefez, Kanza, & Levin. (2011). Tarsius: A system for traffic-aware route search under conditions of uncertainty. SIGSPATIAL'11, 517-520.

Hern. (2013). Online volunteers map Philippines after typhoon Haiyan. *The Guardian*. Retrieved from http://www.theguardian.com/technology/ 2013/nov/15/ online-volunteers-mapphilippines-after-typhoon-haiyan

Hootsuite. (n.d.). Retrieved from hootsuite.com

Kanza, Y., Kravi, E., & Motchan, U. (2014). City nexus: Discovering pairs of jointly-visited locations based on geo-tagged posts in social networks. SIGSPATIAL'14, 597-600.

140. kit. (n.d.). Retrieved from https://github.com/WebEcologyProject/140kit

Lan, R. (2014). Spatio-temporal disease tracking using news articles. HealthGIS'14, 31-38.

Lan, R., Lieberman, M. D., & Samet, H. (2012). The picture of health: map-based, collaborative spatio-temporal disease tracking. HealthGIS'12, 27-35.

Levin, R., & Kanza, Y. (2014). Tars: Traffic-aware route search. *GeoInformatica*, *18*(3), 461–500. doi:10.1007/s10707-013-0185-z

O'Connor, Krieger, & Ahn. (2010). Tweetmotif: Exploratory search and topic summarization for twitter. ICWSM.

Papadimitriou, P. (2011). Geo-social recommendations. *ACM Recommender Systems 2011 (RecSys) Workshop on Personalization in Mobile Applications*.

Poese, I., Uhlig, S., Kaafar, M. A., Donnet, B., & Gueye, B. (n.d.). IP Geolocation databases: Unreliable. *Computer Communication Review*, *4*(2), 53–56.

Rathore, M. (2016). Real time intrusion detection system for ultra-high-speed big data environments. *The Journal of Supercomputing*, 1–22.

Rathore, M. M. U., Paul, A., Ahmad, A., Chen, B. W., Huang, B., & Ji, W. (2015, October). Real-Time Big Data Analytical Architecture for Remote Sensing Application. *IEEE Journal of Selected Topics in Applied Earth Observations and Remote Sensing*, *8*(10), 4610–4621. doi:10.1109/JSTARS.2015.2424683

Ratti, S., Frenchman, D., Pulselli, R. M., & Williams, S. (2006). Mobile landscapes: Using location data from cell phones for urban analysis. *Environment and Planning. B, Planning & Design*, *33*(5), 727–748. doi:10.1068/b32047

Mazhar, Rathore, Ahmad, Paul, & Wu. (2016). Real-time continuous feature extraction in large size satellite images. *Journal of Systems Architecture*, *64*(March), 122–132.

Stefanidis, A. (2012). Harvesting ambient geospatial information from social media feeds. *GeoJournal*, 1–20.

TwitterMAPD. (n.d.). Retrieved from http://tweetmap.mapd.com/

Waller, L. A., & Gotway, C. A. (2004). *Applied Spatial Statistics for Public Health Data* (Vol. 368). Hoboken, NJ: John Wiley & Sons. doi:10.1002/0471662682

Xia, R. CityBeat: real-time social media visualization of hyper-local city data. *Proc. of WWW Conference*.

Zheng, Y., Chen, Y., Xie, X., & Ma, W. (2009). GeoLife 2.0: A location-based social networking service. *Mobile Data Management: Systems, Services and Middleware 2009, MDM'09, Tenth International Conference on*, 357-358.

Zook, M., Graham, M., Shelton, T., & Gorman, S. (2010). Volunteered geographic information and crowdsourcing disaster relief: A case study of the Haitian earthquake. *World Medical & Health Policy.*, 2(2), 7–33. doi:10.2202/1948-4682.1069

Chapter 8

Data Science:
Recent Developments and Future Insights:

Sabitha Rajagopal
SNS College of Technology, Anna University, India

ABSTRACT

Data Science employs techniques and theories to create data products. Data product is merely a data application that acquires its value from the data itself, and creates more data as a result; it's not just an application with data. Data science involves the methodical study of digital data employing techniques of observation, development, analysis, testing and validation. It tackles the real time challenges by adopting a holistic approach. It 'creates' knowledge about large and dynamic bases, 'develops' methods to manage data and 'optimizes' processes to improve its performance. The goal includes vital investigation and innovation in conjunction with functional exploration intended to notify decision-making for individuals, businesses, and governments. This paper discusses the emergence of Data Science and its subsequent developments in the fields of Data Mining and Data Warehousing. The research focuses on need, challenges, impact, ethics and progress of Data Science. Finally the insights of the subsequent phases in research and development of Data Science is provided.

1. INTRODUCTION

Data science employs techniques and theories drawn from many fields within the broad areas of mathematics, statistics, operations research, information science, and computer science, including signal processing, probability models, machine learning, statistical learning, data mining, database, data engineering, pattern

DOI: 10.4018/978-1-5225-3015-2.ch008

recognition and learning, visualization, predictive analytics, uncertainty modeling, data warehousing, data compression, computer programming, artificial intelligence, and high performance computing. Methods that scale to big data are of particular interest in data science, although the discipline is not generally considered to be restricted to such big data, and big data solutions are often focused on organizing and preprocessing the data instead of analysis. The development of machine learning has enhanced the growth and importance of data science (Davenport and Patil, 2012; "Wikipedia Data Science" n.d.) Data science affects academic and applied research in many domains, including machine translation, speech recognition, robotics, search engines, digital economy, but also the biological sciences, medical informatics, health care, social sciences and the humanities. It heavily influences economics, business and finance. From the business perspective, data science is an integral part of competitive intelligence, a newly emerging field that encompasses a number of activities, such as data mining and data analysis (Hays, 2004). This paper discusses the emergence of Data Science and its subsequent developments in the fields of Data Mining and Data Warehousing. The research focuses on need, challenges, impact, ethics and progress of Data Science. Finally the insights of the subsequent phases in research and development of Data Science is provided.

Chapter 9

2. DATA SCIENCE AND ITS EMERGENCE

The term "data science" has existed for over thirty years and was used initially as a substitute for computer science by Peter Naur in 1960. In 1974, Naur published *a Concise Survey of Computer Methods*, which freely used the term data science in its survey of the contemporary data processing methods that are used in a wide range of applications. In 1996, members of the International Federation of Classification Societies (IFCS) met in Kobe for their biennial conference. Here, for the first time, the term data science is included in the title of the conference ("Data Science, classification, and related methods").

In November 1997, C.F. Jeff Wu gave the inaugural lecture entitled "Statistics = Data Science?" for his appointment to the H. C. Carver Professorship at the University of Michigan. In this lecture, he characterized the statistical work as a trilogy of data collection, data modeling and analysis, and decision making. In his conclusion, he initiated the modern, non-computer science, usage of the term "data science" and advocated that statistics be renamed data science and statistician data scientists. Later, he presented his lecture entitled "Statistics = Data Science?" as the first of his 1998 P.C. Mahalanobis Memorial Lectures. These lectures honor Prasanta Chandra Mahalanobis, an Indian scientist and statistician and founder of the Indian Statistical Institute.

In 2001, William S. Cleveland introduced data science as an independent discipline, extending the field of statistics to incorporate "advances in computing with data" in his article "Data Science: An Action Plan for Expanding the Technical Areas of the Field of Statistics," which was published in Volume 69, No. 1, of the April 2001 edition of the International Statistical Review / Revue Internationale de Statistique. In his report, Cleveland establishes six technical areas which he believed to encompass the field of data science: multidisciplinary investigations, models and methods for data, computing with data, pedagogy, tool evaluation, and theory.

In April 2002, the International Council for Science: Committee on Data for Science and Technology (CODATA) started the *Data Science Journal*, a publication focused on issues such as the description of data systems, their publication on the internet, applications and legal issues. Shortly thereafter, in January 2003, Columbia University began publishing *The Journal of Data Science*, which provided a platform for all data workers to present their views and exchange ideas. The journal was largely devoted to the application of statistical methods and quantitative research. In 2005, The National Science Board published "Long-lived Digital Data Collections: Enabling Research and Education in the 21st Century" defining data scientists as "the information and computer scientists, database and software and programmers, disciplinary experts, curators and expert annotators, librarians, archivists, and others, who are crucial to the successful management of a digital data collection" whose primary activity is to "conduct creative inquiry and analysis." In 2008, DJ Patil and Jeff Hammerbacher used the term "data scientist" to define their jobs at LinkedIn and Facebook, respectively.

In 2013, the IEEE Task Force on Data Science and Advanced Analytics was launched, and the first international conference: IEEE International Conference on Data Science and Advanced Analytics was launched in 2014. In 2015, the International Journal on Data Science and Analytics was launched by Springer to publish original work on data science and big data analytics (Brynjolfsson et al, 2011; Tambe, 2012; Fusfeld, 2010; Shah et al, 2012; Wirth et al, 2000; Hill et al, 2006; Martens 2011; "Wikipedia Data Science" n.d.).

3. HOW TO DO DATA SCIENCE

The three components involved in data science are organising, packaging and delivering data (the OPD of data). Organising is where the physical location and structure of the data is planned and executed. Packaging is where the prototypes are build, the statistics is performed and the visualisation is created. Delivering is where the story gets told and the value is obtained. However what separates data science from all other existing roles is that they also need to have a continual awareness of

What, How, Who and Why. A data scientist needs to know what will be the output of the data science process and have a clear vision of this output. A data scientist needs to have a clearly defined plan on how will this output be achieved within the restraints of available resources and time. A data scientist needs to deeply understand who the people are that will be involved in creating the output. And most of all the data scientist must know why there is a motivation behind attempting to manifest the creative visualization ("What is Data Science" n.d.)

The 3 Step OPD Data Science Process

Step 1: Organize Data. Organizing data involve the physical storage and format of data and incorporated best practices in data management.
Step 2: Package Data. Packaging data involve logically manipulating and joining the underlying raw data into a new representation and package.
Step 3: Deliver Data. Delivering data involve ensuring that the message data has is being accessed by those that need to hear it.

The OPD process answers to the questions like:

- What is being created?
- How will it be created?
- Who will be involved in creating it?
- Why is it to be created?

The Data Science Process is shown in Figure 1. The raw data is collected from the world wide web and used for the Data Science process. The collected Data is processed based on the requirements and applicability; then it is cleaned for missing values, inconsistencies and incompatibilites. Then the exploratory analysis is done if required; the data may be reprocessed based on the necessity of the analysis. The models and algorithms used in the data mining process are applied. The results are visualized as reports in the format required by the end user. These results are further used by the analyst and scientist in decision making ("What is Data Science" n..d).

4. DATA SCIENCE IN ACTION

Data science in action it is simply about moving people and/or systems between current and new technologies and between beginner and expert skills.

The matrix is shown in Figure 2. Technology is represented on the horizontal axis and the skills are represented on the vertical axis.

Figure 1. Data Science Process

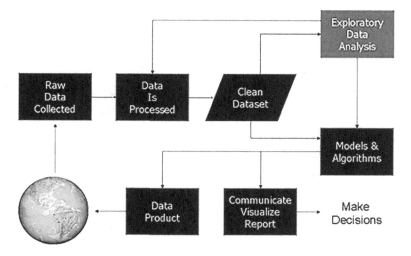

Figure 2.

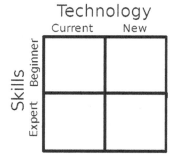

Step 1: Organizing Data. Organizing data involve moving people and systems from current to new (left to right) and from beginner to expert (top to bottom). Advancing technologies and skills is the essence of innovation. The movement is represented in Figure 3.

Step 2: Packaging Data. Packaging data is the reverse of organizing data and involves moving people and systems from new to current (right to left) and from expert to beginner (bottom to top). This is the art of making things simple but not simpler. The process is depicted in Figure 4.

Step 3: Delivering Data. Delivering data are enabling the movement from one view to another, enabling a beginner to become an expert, enabling current technology to seem new, enabling expert data to be understood by beginners

Figure 3. *Figure 4.*

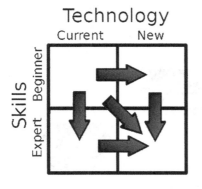 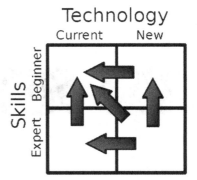

and enabling new technology to seem like it has been a part of your life since you were born. This transformational education is depicted in Figure 5.

5. DATA SCIENTISTS

Data Scientists perform data science. They use technology and skills to increase awareness, clarity and direction for those working with data. The data scientist role is here to accommodate the rapid changes that occur in our modern day environment and are bestowed the task of minimizing the disruption that technology and data is having on the way we work, play and learn. Data Scientists don't just present data, data scientists present data with an intelligent awareness of the consequences of presenting that data.

Figure 5.

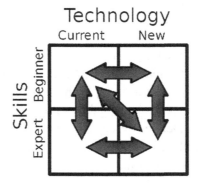

Data scientists should also have good computer science skills—including data structures, algorithms, systems and scripting languages—as well as a good understanding of correlation, causation and related concepts which are central to modeling exercises involving data.

The final skill set is the least standardized and somewhat elusive and to some extent a craft, but also a key differentiator to be an effective data scientist – the ability to formulate problems in a way that results in effective solutions. . . formulation expertise involves the ability to see commonalities across very different problems.

6. NEED FOR DATA SCIENCE

Data Science is emerging as one of the hottest new professions and academic disciplines in these early years of the 21st century. A number of articles have noted that the demand for data scientists is racing ahead of supply. People with the necessary skills are scarce, primarily because the discipline is so new. But, the situation is rapidly changing, as universities around the world have started to offer different kinds of graduate programs in data science.

It's very exciting to contemplate the emergence of a major new discipline. Like data science, computer science had its roots in a number of related areas, including math, engineering and management. In its early years, the field attracted people from a variety of other disciplines who started out using computers in their work or studies, and eventually switched to computer science from their original field.

Not unlike data science today, computing had to overcome the initial resistance of some prominent academics. Computer science has since become a well respected academic discipline. It has grown extensively since its early days and expanded in many new directions.

The raw materials of data science are not independent data sets, no matter how large they are, but heterogeneous, unstructured data set of all kinds – text, images, video. The data scientist will not simply analyze the data, but will look at it from many angles, with the hope of discovering new insights. One of the problems with conducting in-depth, exploratory analysis is that the multiple data sets that are typically required to do so are often found within organizational *silos;* be they different lines of business in a company, different companies in an industry or different institutions across society at large. Data science platforms and tools aim to address this problem by working with, linking together and analyzing data sets previously locked away in disparate *silos.*

Like computing, one of the most exciting part of data science is that it can be applied to many domains of knowledge. But doing so effectively requires domain expertise to identify the important problems to solve in a given area, the kinds of questions we should be asking and the kinds of answers we should be looking for, as well as how to best present whatever insights are discovered so they can be understood by domain practitioners in their own terms. *Garbage-in, garbage-out*, a phrase I often heard in the early days of computing, is just as applicable to data science today ("Wall Street Journal Blog: Why do we Need Data Science" n.d.)

7. IMPACT

A quick search for data jobs on LinkedIn yields over 61,000 results and Google Trends continues to show strong growth for Data Science and Big Data. The Insight Data Science Fellows Program continues to receive over 500 applicants for each class of 30 students, with a 100% placement rate in data careers afterwards. At the same time there are serious debates about the acceptable use of data.

Data is coming under a new level of scrutiny. Combining this approach with data science, the entire system is built. This includes everything from actionable dashboards to data products that help make counselors both more efficient and effective. For example, predicting when texting volume will be high, developing queues for which counsellors are most effective, and a unique interface for counsellors to work with multiple teenagers simultaneously. These approaches have enabled them to deliver more than a million text messages in the short time the service has been running ("Three Ways Data Science Changes the World" n.d.).

8. ETHICS

A Lapse in Ethics Can Be a Conscious Choice...

When we think of right and wrong, we often think of conscious choices. There are a ton of ways to purposefully commit fraud with data. Fabricating data, manipulating experiments, removing outliers are just a few. A 2005 study of questionable behavior in the scientific community shows that 15% of scientists report changing their experimental methodology in response to funding pressures.Another, more recent, survey of medical scientists reports that six of the twelve scientists surveyed had witnessed some sort of scientific fraud. The damage to the scientific community and society at large can be staggering.

A Lapse in Ethics Can Also Be Negligence

Of course not all ethics violations are malicious. Major retailers and lending institutions have a lot of our data. In aggregate, it helps them better understand our behavior and target products to us. In the best case, this data can be used to fight fraud and provide useful products. In the worst case, it can lead to serious privacy leaks.

Data leaks are not uncommon, even at high tech institutions that should know better. Google, leaked personal contact information when they launched their Buzz social networking system. This leak ultimately cost them 8.5 million dollars. Facebook has mistakenly leaked it's 'shadow profiles for 6.5 million users. These profiles contain information that Facebook inferred about it's users, information that the users themselves did not provide.

Creating Standards of Conduct

These lapses put the ethical considerations front and center, as data science rises in popularity. Some groups of data scientists have created codes of conduct. For example, the Data Science Association has a code of conduct. The code of conduct covers a number of things from defintions of common terms to ethical responsibilities of data scientists. "Things were really getting out of control in terms of the definition of 'data science, lot of people who really weren't data scientists started calling themselves data scientists and a lot of data science malpractice in the companies, or clients, that we work with."

Of course this isn't the only group that is trying to hammer out a code of conduct for data scientists. There are literally entire books on this topic and numerous articles discussing potential ethics concerns and values that data scientists should have. The codes of conduct directly address the frustrations felt by those in the community that have deep expertise. Pretty much everyone agrees that data scientists should not oversell their qualifications, and they should avoid letting external motivations influence their analyses.

Codes of conduct are important for maintaining quality and integrity. Of course they are evolving, and often lag behind the state of the art technology. And enforcement can often be difficult. However, it is important to think about the implications of the information you are gathering and the models of that you are creating. They have a real effect on the world ("Data Science Ethics" n.d.).

9. SUMMARY AND CONCLUSION

Data science is making us smarter and more innovative in so many ways. How does it all work? This article gives an insight into the data science model, need, ethics, model and its impact. The article addresses the key questions related to the explosion of interest in the emerging fields of big data, analytics, and data science. However, there is confusion about what exactly data science is, and this confusion could lead to cynicism as the concept diffuses into meaningless buzz. In this article, it is argued that there are good reasons why it has been hard to pin down exactly what is data science. The reason is that data science is intricately intertwined with other important concepts also of growing importance, such as big data and data-driven decision making. Another reason is the natural tendency to associate what a practitioner does with the definition of the practitioner's field; this can result in overlooking the fundamentals of the field. It is believed that trying to define the boundaries of data science precisely is not of the utmost importance. In this article, a perspective that addresses all the concepts of Data Science is presented. Finally the insights of the subsequent phases in research and development of Data Science is provided.

REFERENCES

Brynjolfsson, E., Hitt, L. M., & Kim, H. H. (2011). *Strength in numbers: How does data-driven decision making affect firm performance?* Working paper. Available at SSRN: http://ssrn.com/abstract=1819486

Davenport, T. H., & Patil, D. J. (2012, October). Data scientist: The sexiest job of the 21st century. *Harvard Business Review*. PMID:23074866

Forsythe, D. E. (1993). The construction of work in artificial intelligence. *Science, Technology & Human Values*, *18*(4), 460–479. doi:10.1177/016224399301800404

Fusfeld A. (2010, September 23). The digital 100: the world's most valuable startups. *Bus Insider*.

Hays, C. L. (2004, November 14). What they know about you. *NY Times*.

Hill, S., Provost, F., & Volinsky, C. (2006). Network-based marketing: Identifying likely adopters via consumer networks. *Statistical Science*, *21*(2), 256–276. doi:10.1214/088342306000000222

Martens, D., & Provost, F. (2011). *Pseudo-social network targeting from consumer transaction data*. Working paper, CEDER-11-05. Stern School of Business.

Shah, S., Horne, A., & Capella´, J. (2012, April). Good data won't guarantee good decisions. *Harvard Business Review*.

Tambe, P. (2012). *Big data know-how and business value*. Working paper. NYU Stern School of Business.

Wirth, R., & Hipp, J. (2000). CRISP-DM: Towards a standard process model for data mining. *Proceedings of the 4th International Conference on the Practical Applications of Knowledge Discovery and Data Mining*, 29–39.

Chapter 9
Data Science and Computational Biology

Singaraju Jyothi
Sri Padmavati Mahila University, India

Bhargavi P
Sri Padmavati Mahila University, India

ABSTRACT

Data Science and Computational biology is an interdisciplinary program that brings together the domain specific knowledge of science and engineering with relevant areas of computing and bioinformatics. Data science has the potential to revolutionise healthcare, and respond to the increasing volume and complexity in biomedical and bioinformatics data. From genomics to clinical records, from imaging to mobile health and personalised medicine, the data volume in biomedical research presents urgent challenges for computer science. This chapter elevates the researchers in what way data science play important role in Computational Biology such as Bio-molecular Computation, Computational Photonics, Medical Imaging, Scientific Computing, Structural Biology, Bioinformatics and Bio-Computing etc. Big data analytics of biological data bases, high performance computing in large sequence of genome database and Scientific Visualization are also discussed in this chapter.

INTRODUCTION

The term "Data Science" has emerged only recently to specifically designate a new profession that is expected to make sense of the vast stores of big data. Data Science draws scientific inquiry from a broad range of subject areas such as statistics, mathematics, computer science, machine learning and optimization, signal

DOI: 10.4018/978-1-5225-3015-2.ch009

processing, information retrieval, databases, cloud computing, computer vision, natural language processing and etc. Data Science is on the essence of deriving valuable insights from data. It is emerging to meet the challenges of processing very large datasets, i.e. Big Data, with the explosion of new data continuously generated from various channels such as smart devices, web, mobile and social media. At a high level, data science is a set of fundamental principles that support and guide the principled extraction of information and knowledge from data. Possibly the most closely related concept to data science is data mining-the actual extraction of knowledge from data via technologies.

A data science perspective provides practitioners with structure and principles, which give the data scientist a framework to systematically treat problems of extracting useful knowledge from data. The past of data science was all about descriptive analytics, or describing what has already taken place. But the future of data science will hinge on advanced analytics, specifically using predictive analytics and real time analytics. In the future, "the tools are going to de-emphasize the mechanics of doing machine learning.

Underlying the extensive collection of techniques for mining data is a much smaller set of fundamental concepts comprising data science. In order for data science to flourish as a field, rather than to drown in the flood of popular attention, data science is thought as beyond the algorithms, techniques, and tools in common use. The core principles and concepts that underlie the techniques and also the systematic thinking that foster success in data-driven decision making. These data science concepts are general and very broadly applicable. Data science supports data-driven decision making and sometimes allows making decisions automatically at massive scale and depends upon technologies for ''big data'' storage and engineering. However, the principles of data science are its own and should be considered and discussed explicitly in order for data science to realize its potential.

Computational Biology or Bioinformatics has been defined as the application of mathematical and Computer Science methods to solving problems in Molecular Biology that require large scale data, computation, and analysis. As expected, Molecular Biology databases play an essential role in Computational Biology research and development. Computational biology is part of a larger revolution that will affect how all of science is conducted. This larger revolution is being driven by the generation and use of information in all forms and in enormous quantities and requires the development of intelligent systems for gathering, storing and accessing information (Clutter, 1996).

Extracting knowledge from data is a defining challenge of science. Computational genomics has been an important area since the beginning of the Human Genome Project. Today, however, advances in tools and techniques for data generation are rapidly increasing the amount of data available to researchers, particularly in genomics.

This increase requires researchers to rely ever more heavily on computational and data science tools for the storage, management, analysis, and visualization of data. These efforts support research and development of transformative approaches and tools that maximize the integration of Big Data (like genomics data) and data science into biomedical research.

1. DATA SCIENCE

Day to day the amount of data produced across the world has been exponentially increasing and will continue to grow in the future. At companies across all industries, servers are overflowing with usage logs, message streams, transaction records, sensor data, business operations records and mobile device data. Effectively analyzing these huge collections of data, can create significant value for the world economy by enhancing productivity, increasing efficiency and delivering more value to consumers. Studies estimate that trillions of dollars of value in efficiency improvements and economic growth can be unlocked by extracting actionable knowledge from the deluge of data now being collected in almost every sector of the economy.

At a high level, data science is a set of fundamental principles that support and guide the principled extraction of information and knowledge from data. Possibly the most closely related concept to data science is data mining—the actual extraction of knowledge from data via technologies that incorporate these principles. There are hundreds of different data-mining algorithms, and a great deal of detail to the methods of the field. We argue that underlying all these many details is a much smaller and more concise set of fundamental principles. These principles and techniques are applied broadly across functional areas in business. Probably the broadest business applications are in marketing for tasks such as targeted marketing, online advertising, and recommendations for cross-selling. Also Data science is applied for general customer relationship management to analyze customer behavior in order to manage attrition and maximize expected customer value. The finance industry uses data science for credit scoring and trading and in operations via fraud detection and workforce management. Major retailers from Wal-Mart to Amazon apply data science throughout their businesses, from marketing to supply-chain management. Many firms have differentiated themselves strategically with data science, sometimes to the point of evolving into data-mining companies.

But data science involves much more than just data-mining algorithms. Successful data scientists must be able to view business problems from a data perspective. There is a fundamental structure to data-analytic thinking and basic principles that should be understood. Data science draws from many ''traditional'' fields of study. Fundamental principles of causal analysis must be understood. A large portion of what has traditionally been studied within the field of statistics is fundamental to data science. Methods and methology for visualizing data are vital. There are also particular areas where intuition, creativity, common sense, and knowledge of a particular application must be brought to bear. A data-science perspective provides practitioners with structure and principles, which give the data scientist a framework to systematically treat problems of extracting useful knowledge from data.

2. COMPUTATIONAL BIOLOGY

Computational biology involves the development and application of data-analytical and theoretical methods, mathematical modeling and computational simulation techniques to the study of biological, behavioral, and social systems. The field of computational biology is defined broadly and includes in computer science, applied mathematics, animation, statistics, biochemistry, chemistry, biophysics, molecular biology, genetics, genomics, ecology, evaluation, anatomy, neuroscience, and visualization.

Computational biology is different from biological computation which is a subfield of computer science and computer engineering using bioengineering and biology to build computers, but is similar to bioinformatics, which is an interdisciplinary science using computers to store and process biological data.

Sometimes Computational Biology also referred to as bioinformatics where it is the science of using biological data to develop algorithms and relations among various biological systems. Prior to the development of computational biology, biologists were unable to access the large amounts of data. Researchers were able to develop analytical methods for interpreting biological information, but were unable to share them quickly among colleagues.

Bioinformatics began to develop in the early 1970s. It was considered the science of analyzing informatics processes of various biological systems. At this time, research in artificial intelligence was using network models of the human brain in order to generate new algorithm. This use of biological data to develop other fields pushed biological researchers to revisit the idea of using computers to evaluate and compare large data sets. By 1982, information was being shared amongst researchers through the use of punch cards. The amount of data being shared began to grow exponentially by the end of the 1980s. This required the development of new computational methods in order to quickly analyze and interpret relevant information.

Since the late 1990s, computational biology has become an important part of developing emerging technologies for the field of biology. The terms computational biology and evolutionary computation have a similar name, but are not to be confused. Unlike computational biology, evolutionary computation is not concerned with modeling and analyzing biological data. It instead creates algorithms based on the ideas of evolution across species. Sometimes referred to as genetic algorithms, the research of this field can be applied to computational biology. While evolutionary computation is not inherently a part of computational biology, Computational evolutionary biology is a subfield of it.

Computational biology has been used to help sequence the human genome, create accurate models of the human brain, and assist in modeling biological systems. The subfields of Computational Biology are:

Computational Biomodeling

Computational biomodeling is a field concerned with building computer models of biological systems. Computational biomodeling aims to develop and use visual simulations in order to assess the complexity of biological systems. This is accomplished through the use of specialized algorithms, and visualization software. These models allow for prediction of how systems will react under different environments. This is useful for determining if a system is robust. A robust biological system is one that "maintain their state and functions against external and internal perturbations", which is essential for a biological system to survive. Computational biomodeling generates a large archive of such data, allowing for analysis from multiple users. While current techniques focus on small biological systems, researchers are working on approaches that will allow for larger networks to be analyzed and modeled. A majority of researchers believe that this will be essential in developing modern medical approaches to creating new drugs and gene therapy.

Computational Genomics (Computational Genetics)

Computational genomics is a field within genomics which studies the genomes of cells and organisms. It is often referred to as computational and Statistical Genetics is one example of computational genomics. This project looks to sequence the entire human genome into a set of data. Once fully implemented, this could allow for doctors to analyze the genome of an individual patient. This opens the possibility of personalized medicine, prescribing treatments based on an individual's pre-existing genetic patterns. This project has created many similar programs. Researchers are looking to sequence the genomes of animals, plants, bacteria, and all other types of life.

One of the main tools used in comparing the genomes is homology. Homology is observing the same organ across species and seeing what different functions they have. Research suggests that between 80 to 90% of sequences genes can be identified this way. In order to detect potential cures from genomes, comparisons between genome sequences of related species and mRNA sequences are drawn. This method is not completely accurate however. It may be necessary to include the genome of a primate in order to improve current methods of unique gene therapy. This field is still in development. An untouched project in the development in computational genomics is analyzing intergenic regions. Studies show that roughly 97% of the human genome consists of these regions. Researchers in computational genomics are working on understanding the functions of non-coding regions of the human genome through computational and statistical method development and large consortia projects such as ENCODE (The Encyclopedia of DNA Elements). and the Roadmap Epigenomics Project

Computational Neuroscience

Computational neuroscience is the study of brain function in terms of the information processing properties of the structures that make up the nervous system. It is a subset of the field of neuroscience, and looks to analyze brain data to create practical applications. It looks to model the brain in order to examine specific types aspects of the neurological system. Various types of models of the brain include:

- **Realistic Brain Models:** These models look to represent every aspect of the brain, including as much detail at the cellular level as possible. Realistic models provide the most information about the brain, but also have the largest margin for error. More variables in a brain model create the possibility for more error to occur. These models do not account for parts of the cellular structure that scientists do not know about. Realistic brain models are the most computationally heavy and the most expensive to implement.
- **Simplifying Brain Models:** These models look to limit the scope of a model in order to assess a specific physical property of the neurological system. This allows for the intensive computational problems to be solved, and reduces the amount of potential error from a realistic brain model.

It is the work of computational neuroscientists to improve the algorithms and data structures currently used to increase the speed of such calculations.

Computational Pharmacology

Computational pharmacology (from a computational biology perspective) is "the study of the effects of genomic data to find links between specific genotypes and diseases and then screening drug data". The pharmaceutical industry requires a shift in methods to analyze drug data. Pharmacists were able to use Microsoft Excel to compare chemical and genomic data related to the effectiveness of drugs. However, the industry has reached what is referred to as the Excel barricade. This arises from the limited number of cells accessible on a spreadsheet. This development led to the need for computational pharmacology. Scientists and researchers develop computational methods to analyze these massive data sets. This allows for an efficient comparison between the notable data points and allows for more accurate drugs to be developed.

Analysts project that if major medications fail due to patents, that computational biology will be necessary to replace current drugs on the market. Doctoral students in computational biology are being encouraged to pursue careers in industry rather than take Post-Doctoral positions. This is a direct result of major pharmaceutical companies needing more qualified analysts of the large data sets required for producing new drugs.

Computational Evolutionary Biology

Computational biology has assisted the field of evolutionary biology in many capacities. This includes:

- Using DNA data to evaluate the evolutionary change of a species over time.
- Taking the results of computational genomics in order to evaluate the evolution of genetic disorders within a species.
- Build models of evolutionary systems in order to predict what types of changes will occur in the future.

Cancer Computational Biology

Cancer computational biology is a field that aims to determine the future mutations in cancer through an algorithmic approach to analyzing data. Research in this field has led to the use of high-throughput measurement. High throughput measurement allows for the gathering of millions of data points using robotics and other sensing devices. This data is collected from DNA, RNA, and other biological structures. Areas of focus include determining the characteristics of tumors, analyzing molecules that are deterministic in causing cancer, and understanding how the human genome relates to the causation of tumors and cancer.

3. DATA SCIENCE IN COMPUTATIONAL BIOLOGY

A particular active area of research in computational biology is the application and development of big data techniques to solve biological problems. Analyzing large biological data sets requires making sense of the data by inferring structure or generalizations from the data. Examples of this type of analysis include protein structure prediction, gene classification, cancer classification based on microarray data, clustering of gene expression data, statistical modeling of protein-protein interaction, etc. Therefore, we see a great potential to increase the interaction between big data and computational biology. Over the past few decades rapid developments in genomic and other molecular research technologies and developments in information technologies have combined to produce a tremendous amount of information related to molecular biology.

Data Science is an emerging field that aims to extract actionable insights from vast arrays of information. Drawing on techniques and theories from statistics, computer science and mathematics, the program focuses on the effective analysis and use of large data in the natural and social sciences. The explosion of data in today's world is rapidly shaping the landscape of our life. This has led to an urgent need to process massive amounts of data and obtain meaningful information.

Computational biology is part of a larger revolution that will affect how all of science is conducted. This larger revolution is being driven by the generation and use of information in all forms and in enormous quantities and requires the development of intelligent systems for gathering, storing and accessing information (Clutter, 1996). Most Molecular Biology databases provide with (Molecular Biology) data analysis tools. Also some data analysis tools rely on one or several Molecular Biology databases, possibly constructed for a specific analysis method. Thus, it is sometimes difficult to clearly distinguish between a Molecular Biology data analysis tool and the Molecular Biology database specifically constructed for this tool.

Many data mining techniques have been proposed to deal with the identification of specific DNA sequences. The most common include neural networks, Bayesian classifiers, decision trees, and Support Vector Machines (SVMs) (Ma and Wang, 1999; Hirsh and Noordweier 1994; Zein et al, 2000). Sequence recognition algorithms exhibit performance tradeoffs between increasing sensitivity and decreasing selectivity (Houle et al, 2004). However, traditional data mining techniques cannot be directly applied to this type of recognition problems (Li et al, 2003). Thus, there is the need to adapt the existing techniques to this kind of problems and overcome this problem using feature generation and feature selection (Zein et al, 2000). Another data mining application in genomic level is the use of clustering algorithms to group structurally related DNA sequences.

Gene Expression Data Mining, the main types of microarray data analysis include gene selection, clustering, and classification (Piatetsky-Shapiro and Tamayo, 2003). An important issue in data analysis is feature selection. In gene expression analysis the features are the genes. Gene selection is a process of finding the genes most strongly related to a particular class. One benefit provided by this process is the reduction of the foresaid dimensionality of dataset. Moreover, a large number of genes are irrelevant when classification is applied. The danger of overshadowing the contribution of relevant genes is reduced when gene selection is applied. Clustering is the far most used method in gene expression analysis where a classification of clustering methods in two categories are provided one-way clustering and two-way clustering (Aas, 2001; Tibshirani et al, 1999). Methods of the first category are used to group either genes with similar behavior or samples with similar gene expressions. Two-way clustering methods are used to simultaneously cluster genes and samples. Hierarchical clustering is currently the most frequently applied method in gene expression analysis. An important issue concerning the application of clustering methods in microarray data is the assessment of cluster quality. Many techniques such as bootstrap, repeated measurements, mixture model-based approaches, sub-sampling and others have been proposed to deal with the cluster reliability assessment (Yeung et al, 2003; Kerr and Churchill, 2001). In microarray analysis classification is applied to discriminate diseases or to predict outcomes based on gene expression patterns and perhaps even identify the best treatment for given genetic signature (Piatetsky-Shapiro and Tamayo, 2003). Most of the methods used to deal with microarray data analysis can be used for Serial analysis of gene expression (SAGE) data analysis. Machine learning and data mining can be applied in order to design microarray experiments except to analyze them.

Many modification sites can be detected by simply scanning a database that contains known modification sites. However, in some cases, a simple database scan is not effective. The use of neural networks provides better results in these cases. Similar approaches are used for the prediction of active sites. Neural network approaches and nearest neighbor classifiers have been used to deal with protein localization prediction (Whishart, 2002). Neural networks have also been used to predict protein properties such as stability, globularity and shape. Data mining has been applied for the protein secondary structure prediction. This problem has been studied for over than 30 years and many techniques have been developed. Initially, statistical approaches were adopted to deal with this problem. Later, more accurate techniques based on information theory, Bayes theory, nearest neighbors, and neural networks were developed. Combined methods such as integrated multiple sequence alignments with neural network or nearest neighbor approaches improve prediction accuracy. A density based clustering algorithm (GDBSCAN) (Sander et al, 1998) that can be used to deal with protein interactions. This algorithm is able to cluster point and spatial objects according to both, their spatial and non-spatial attributes.

Big Data Analytics Tools in Computational Biology

Big data is one of the general attribute of biological studies, and today, researchers are capable of generating terabytes of data in hours. Over the last decade, biological datasets have been grown massively in size, mostly because of advances in technologies for collection and recording of data. Therefore, big data possess a great impact on the bioinformatics field and a researcher in this field faces many difficulties in using biological big data. Thus, it is essential that bioinformatics develop tools and techniques for big data analysis so as to keep pace with our ability to extract valuable information from the data easily thereby enhancing further advancement in the decision-making process related to diverse biological process, diseases and disorders (Kumari et al, 2004).

There are primarily five types of data that are massive in size and used heavily in bioinformatics research: i) gene expression data, ii) DNA, RNA, and protein sequence data, iii) protein-protein interaction (PPI) data, iv) pathway data, and v) gene ontology (GO). Although, other types of data such as human disease network and disease gene association network are also used, and highly important for many research directions including disease diagnosis.

Various tools have been developed over the years to handle the bioinformatics problems. The tools developed before the big data era are mostly standalone and not designed for very large scale data. In the last decade many large scale data analysis tools have been developed for several problems, such as microarray data analysis to idetify coexpressed patterns, gene-gene network analysis and salient module extraction, PPI complex finding, and RNA/DNA and sequence analysis. However, apart from certain sequence analysis tools, the other exsting tools are not adequate for handling big data or not suitable for cloud computing infrastructures. Along with specific tools, several cloud-based bioinformatics platforms have also been developed to integrate specific tools and to provide a fast comprehensive solution to multiple problems, such as Galaxy (Goecks et al, 2010) and CloudBLAST (Matsunga et al, 2008).

Tools for Microarray Data Analysis

Large numbers of software tools are available to perform various analyses on microarray data. However, not all the software are designed to handle large scale data. With the increase in the size of data sets, the time required to generate samples and sequences to identify complexes and to process heterogeneous disease query to find relevant complexes has become prohibitive. Beeline22 handles big data size by parallel computations and reduction in the data size with adaptive filtering. A quality assurance tool called caCORRECT (Stokes et al, 2007). removes artifactual noises from high throughput microarray data. caCORRECT may be used to improve integrity and quality of both public microarray archives as well as reproduced data and to provide a universal

quality score for validation. A web-based application called omniBiomarker (Phan et al, 2013) uses knowledge-driven algorithms to find differentially expressed genes for biomarker identification from high throughput gene expression data. The approach requires complex computation and validation, and omni Biomarker helps in identifying stable and reproducible biomarkers.

Tools for Gene-Gene Network Analysis

Gene expression datasets are already massive in size and getting bigger every day. FastGCN (Liang et al, 2014) tool exploits parallelism with GPU architectures to find the co-expression networks in an optimized way. Similar GPU accelerated co-expression networks analysis methods are proposed for gene expression datasets (Arefin et al, 2013; McArt, 2013). The UCLA Gene Expression Tool (UGET) (Day et al, 2009) performs large scale co-expression analysis to find disease gene associations. Disease networks have significantly higher gene correlations and UGET calculates the correlations among all possible pairs of genes. UGET has been found effective when tested on Celsius (Day et al, 2007), which is the largest co-normalized microarray dataset of Affymetrix-based gene expression data warehouse. WGCNA (Langfelder et al, 2008) is a popular R package for performing weighted gene co-expression network analysis and can be used in an R-Hadoop distributed computing system.

Tools for PPI Data Analysis

PPI complex finding problem is a highly time consuming process. From our research experience, standalone implementations for both supervised and unsupervised PPI complex finding, such as MATLAB programs, require days or even weeks of time to find complexes from a dataset of approximately 1 million interactions on standard workstations. Therefore, there is an urgent need to develop fast big data tools for PPI complex finding and ranking, w.r.t. any heterogeneous disease network query. Several relatively fast tools have been developed for PPI complex (isolated and overlapping) finding, such as NeMo (Rivera, 2010), MCODE (Bader and Hogue, 2003), and ClusterONE (Nepusz et al, 2012), either as a standalone tool or as a Cytoscape plugin. However, these tools cannot be used in distributed systems for better efficiency on large-scale PPI data. Finally, PathBLAST (Kelley et al, 2004) is an important web-based tool for fast alignment of protein interaction networks.

Tools for Sequence Analysis

For sequence analysis problems, several tools have been developed on top of the Hadoop MapReduce platform to perform analytics on large scale sequence data. BioPig (Nordberg et la, 2013) is a notable hadoop-based tool for sequence analysis that scales automatically with the data size and can be ported directly to many hadoop infrastructures. SeqPig (Schumacher et al, 2014) is another such tool. The Crossbow (Langmead et al, 2009) tool combines Bowtie (Langmead, Trapnell, Pop, Salzberg et al, 2009), an ultrafast and memory efficient short read aligner, and SoapSNP (Li, Li, Fang, Yang, Wang, Kristiansen, Wang, 2009), an accurate genotyper, to perform large scale whole genome sequence analytics on cloud platforms or on a local hadoop cluster. Other cloudbased tools that have been developed for large scale sequence analysis are Stormbow (Zhao, Prenger, Smith, 2013), CloVR (Angiuoli et al, 2011), and Rainbow (Zhao et al, 2013). There exist other programs for large scale sequence analysis that do not use big data technologies, such as Vmatch (Kurtz, 2003) and SeqMonk23.

Tools for Pathway Analysis

To support pathway analysis, a good number of tools have been developed for pathway analysis, such as GO-Elite (Zambon et al, 2012) to describe particular genes or metabolites, PathVisio (Iersel et al, 2008) for analysis and drawing, directPA (Yang et al, 2014) to perform analysis in a high-dimensional space for identifying pathways, Pathway Processor (GRosu et al, 2002) to analyze expression data regarding metabolic pathways, Pathway-PDT (Park, 2013) to perform analysis using raw genotypes in general nuclear families, and Pathview (Luo et al, 2013) for pathway based data integration. However, neither these tools use distributed computing platforms, nor they are developed as a cloud-based application, for high scalability.

Although evolutionary research may use tools developed for more specific problems, such as sequence analysis or gene-gene network analysis, a big data tool for comprehensive evolutionary research is still not known. The existing tools for evolution research, such as MEGA (Kumar et al, 2008) and EvoPipes.net (Barker et al, 2010) are not developed for big data in evolutionary research.

In the past five years, genetic association studies have evaluated the contribution of common SNP variation to complex traits at an unprecedented level of detail. These genome wide studies relied not only on advances in genotyping technologies but also on improved study designs and advances in statistical and computational methods - ranging from the development of cost-effective two stage designs, to new strategies to control for population structure, to methods and software for genotype imputation and for cross study meta-analyses. In the next five years, great advances are again expected in genotyping and sequencing technologies. Effectively using these technologies to further our understanding of complex traits will require continued advances in methods for the design and analysis of genetic studies. In this application, we build on our record of developing practical useful analytical methods, computational tools, and study designs for human genetic studies. Computational and statistical methods can be developed that will enable studies of complex traits in humans to effectively exploit the new technologies. Specifically, new methods and computational tools for genotype imputation and for the interpretation of short read sequence data, evaluate sequence and genotyping based design strategies for complex trait studies can be developed, and can also develop statistical methods that facilitate the prioritization of likely functional variants in genetic association studies (Kumari et al, 2014).

Computational and Statistical Models for Human Genetics

In the next few years, continued advances in laboratory methods will allow geneticists to examine sequence variation in great detail and in progressively larger numbers of individuals. Statistical tools, computational methods and study designs that will allow geneticists to more fully exploit these new laboratory methods to study complex traits in humans. The methods developed here will lead directly to improve understanding of the molecular basis of many human traits and diseases - an important step in the path towards new treatments and therapies. In recent years, Computational and Statistical Models for Human Genetics play important role. Figure 1 describes the Computational and Statistical Models for Human Genetics.

A Knowledge Base for Clinically Relevant Genes and Variants

Fundamental advances in genetic sequencing technologies were stimulated by the human genome project and are now in turn transforming genome science and medicine. Yet the promise of genomic medicine remains limited by the lack of definitive sources of information about the genetic contributions to disease. Although many groups are attempting to address this gap individually, such efforts will ultimately fall shor if they remain disconnected. The Clinically Relevant Variants Resource represents a collaborative effort of the genetics community to establish an evidence-based resource for the assessment of the clinical relevance of genes and variants. This knowledge base is critical for confident, efficient analysis and interpretation of genome-scale sequence data. The objective is to provide a publicly available consensus summary of the evidence from the medical literature, basic science researchers, and clinical laboratories regarding the genes and variants that are implicated in human health and disease. Dedicated portals will be provided for researchers, clinical laboratories,

Figure 1. Computational and statistical models for human genetics

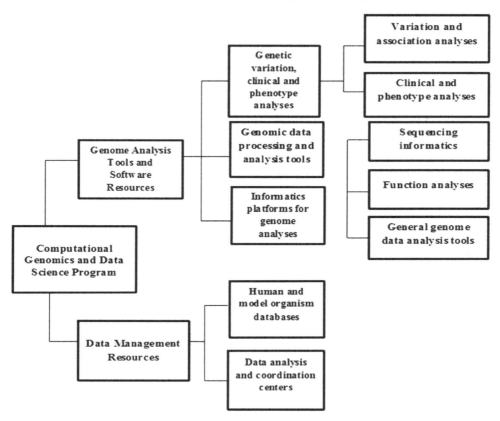

physicians, patients, and electronic health records to ensure that the resource is widely accessible. The consortium of investigators will accomplish this objective by pursuing five specific aims: 1) developing a semi-quantitative methodology for assessing the "clinical action ability" of gene- phenotype pairs, which will allow stakeholder groups to provide guidance on the reporting and use of such genetic results; 2) establishing a standardized process for evaluating whether variants are benign, related to disease, or of uncertain significance; 3) deploying an informatics infrastructure to support the activities of the consortiu by aggregating information from disparate sources and presenting it for human evaluation; 4) assembling clinical domain-specific working groups to systematically evaluate the genes that are clinically relevant; and 5) ensuring the interoperability of he resource with electronic medical record systems. The approach innovates by developing novel approaches for the assessment of genes and variants that are robust and reproducible, and by establishing a distributed informatics system for aggregating and displaying information, with mechanisms for updating and reanalysis. The proposal is forward-thinking in that attention will be paid to ensuring the interoperability of the resource with diverse end-users, including electronic health records. The proposed resource project is significant because it will provide freely available expert curation of the human genome across a substantial number of clinical domains, with a transparent and evidence-based approach (Kumari et al, 2014).

Statistical Methods for Population and Family-Based Whole-Genome Sequence Data

Emerging sequencing technologies have made whole-genome sequencing become available for researches to study various phenotypes/diseases of interest, particularly focusing on rare variants sites. Although the first batch of sequencing projects has mainly focused on the analysis of unrelated individuals, numerous sequencing studies including related individuals have been carried out or launched recently as the sequencing cost reduces rapidly. However, the methodologies for analyzing family-based sequence data are largely falling behind partially due to the complexity of family structures and computational barrier. In this study, our primary goals are to efficiently and accurately infer individual genotypes and haplotypes - the key component of any sequencing project - by combining information from both family and population levels, and to study how differential sequencing errors will affect downstream association analysis. To achieve these goals, we propose specific aims as follows: 1) Propose a novel statistical framework for genotyping calling and haplotype inference of sequence data including relative individuals. The new method takes advantages of both short stretches shared between unrelated individuals and long stretches shared between family members in a computationally feasible manner while retaining a high degree of accuracy via the synergy between two classic approaches: hidden Markov model (HMM) for linkage disequilibrium information and Lander-Green algorithm for inheritance vectors; 2) Develop an exact algorithm for HMM computation to speed up a class of widely use genetics programs, including the method developed in Aim 1, without any sacrifice of accuracy; 3) Assess the impact of sequencing errors on family-based association methods for rare variants and use the intrinsic stochastic nature of the proposed methods in Aim 1 to reduce the false positives under a framework of multiple imputation; 4) Test and recalibrate our developed methods in collaboration with ongoing sequencing projects and systematically investigate different study designs. Successful completion of these aims will yield state-of-the-art statistical methods and software, which will facilitate the fast growing sequencing projects including family members and guide the design and analysis of future studies (Kumari et al, 2014)

Enhanced Gene Identification in Complex Traits using Kernel Machines

Project Summary/Abstract Genome-wide association studies (GWAS) have mapped thousands of common trait-influencing variants yet the overwhelming majority of trait loci have yet to be discovered. The goal of this proposal is to develop and apply statistical approaches that move beyond the standard GWAS paradigm to map additional trait-influencing variation within the human genome (Kumari et al, 2014) Most of our proposed tools are based on a flexible high-dimensional framework called kernel machine regression, which we have had past success employing for powerful gene mapping of complex traits in GWAS and next-generation sequencing (NGS) studies. We believe the inherent flexibility of the kernel framework makes it ideal for exploring new paradigms in gene mapping of complex human traits. Aim 1 proposes novel kernel methods for integrated analysis of both single-nucleotide variation data (derived from GWAS and/or NGS) and genomic data (such as gene-expression and methylation patterns) that we believe will provide improved power for trait mapping. Aim 2 proposes novel kernel methods for large scale gene-gene interaction analysis across the genome, as well as a computational approach that enables efficient adjustment for multiple testing when applying such exhaustive testing procedures. Aim 3 establishes novel kernel methods for association mapping of SNVs on the X chromosome. The flexible nature of kernel machines makes it ideal for modeling potential sex-specific effects on this chromosome and the methods further can accommodate random X inactivation. Aim 4 proposes novel kernel approach for robust analysis of rare trait-influencing variation within families; such family-based designs are generally not considered in current rare-variant procedures. Aim 5 evaluates these methods on large-scale datasets that we are actively involved in and will implement the methods in user-friendly software for public distribution.

4. CONCLUSION

This chapter discusses the use of Data Science in Computational Biology. These areas have risen from the needs of biologists to utilize and help interpret the vast amounts of data that are constantly being gathered in computational biology research. Also this chapter elevates the researchers in what way data science play important role in Computational Biology such as Bio-molecular Computation, Computational Photonics, Medical Imaging, Scientific Computing, Structural Biology, Bioinformatics and Bio-Computing etc. Big data analytics of biological data bases, high performance computing in large sequence of genome database.

REFERENCES

Aas, K. (2001). *Microarray Data Mining: A Survey. NR Note, SAMBA*. Norwegian Computing Center.

Angiuoli, S. V., Matalka, M., Gussman, A., Galens, K., Vangala, M., Riley, D. R., & Fricke, W. F. et al. (2011). CloVR: A virtual machine for automated and portable sequence analysis from the desktop using cloud computing. *BMC Bioinformatics, 12*(1), 356. doi:10.1186/1471-2105-12-356 PMID:21878105

Arefin, A. S., Berretta, R., & Moscato, P. (2013). A GPU-based method for computing eigenvector centrality of gene-expression networks. In *Proceedings of the Eleventh Australasian Symposium on Parallel and Distributed Computing (vol. 140)*. Australian Computer Society, Inc.

Bader, G. D., & Hogue, C. W. (2003). An automated method for finding molecular complexes in large protein interaction networks. *BMC Bioinformatics, 4*(1), 2. doi:10.1186/1471-2105-4-2 PMID:12525261

Barker, M. S., Dlugosch, K. M., Dinh, L., Challa, R. S., Kane, N. C., King, M. G., & Rieseberg, L. H. (2010). EvoPipes. net: Bioinformatics tools for ecological and evolutionary genomics. *Evolutionary Bioinformatics Online, 6*, 143. doi:10.4137/EBO.S5861 PMID:21079755

Clutter, M. (1996). *Hearing on Computational Biology. Statement before the subcommittee on Science, Technology and Space Committee on Commerce, Science, and Transportation*. U.S. Senate.

Day, A., Carlson, M. R., Dong, J., OConnor, B. D., & Nelson, S. F. (2007). Celsius: A community resource for Affymetrix microarray data. *Genome Biology, 8*(6), R112. doi:10.1186/gb-2007-8-6-r112 PMID:17570842

Day, A., Dong, J., Funari, V. A., Harry, B., Strom, S. P., Cohn, D. H., & Nelson, S. F. (2009). Disease gene characterization through largescale co-expression analysis. *PLoS ONE, 4*(12), e8491. doi:10.1371/journal.pone.0008491 PMID:20046828

Goecks, J., Nekrutenko, A., Taylor, J., & Galaxy Team, T. (2010). Galaxy: A comprehensive approach for supporting accessible, reproducible, and transparent computational research in the life sciences. *Genome Biology, 11*(8), R86. doi:10.1186/gb-2010-11-8-r86 PMID:20738864

Grosu, P., Townsend, J. P., Hartl, D. L., & Cavalieri, D. (2002). Pathway Processor: A tool for integrating whole-genome expression results into metabolic networks. *Genome Research, 12*(7), 1121–1126. doi:10.1101/gr.226602 PMID:12097350

Hirsh, H., & Noordewier, M. (1994). Using Background Knowledge to Improve Inductive Learning of DNA Sequences. *Proceedings of the 10th IEEE Conference on Artificial Intelligence for Applications*, 351-357. doi:10.1109/CAIA.1994.323654

Houle, J. L., Cadigan, W., Henry, S., Pinnamaneni, A., & Lundahl, S. (2004, March 10). Database Mining in the Human Genome Initiative. Whitepaper. Amita Corporation.

Kashyap, Ahmed, Hoque, Roy, & Bhattacharyya. (2014). Big Data Analytics in Bioinformatics: A Machine Learning Perspective. *Journal of Latex Class Files, 13*(9).

Kelley, Yuan, Lewitter, Sharan, Stockwell, & Ideker. (2004). PathBLAST: A tool for alignment of protein interaction networks. *Nucleic Acids Research, 32*(S2), W83–W88.

Kerr, M. K., & Churchill, G. A. (2001). Bootstrapping Cluster Analysis: Assessing the Reliability of Conclusions from Microarray Experiments. *Proceedings of the National Academy of Sciences of the United States of America, 98*(16), 8961–8965. doi:10.1073/pnas.161273698 PMID:11470909

Kumar, S., Nei, M., Dudley, J., & Tamura, K. (2008). MEGA: A biologistcentric software for evolutionary analysis of DNA and protein sequences. *Briefings in Bioinformatics, 9*(4), 299–306. doi:10.1093/bib/bbn017 PMID:18417537

Kumari & Kumar. (2014). Impact of Biological Big Data in Bioinformatics. *International Journal of Computer Applications, 101*(11).

Kurtz, S. (2003). The vmatch large scale sequence analysis software. Academic Press.

Langfelder, P., & Horvath, S. (2008). WGCNA: An R package for weighted correlation network analysis. *BMC Bioinformatics, 9*(1), 559. doi:10.1186/1471-2105-9-559 PMID:19114008

Langmead, B., Schatz, M. C., Lin, J., Pop, M., & Salzberg, S. L. (2009). Searching for SNPs with cloud computing. *Genome Biology, 10*(11), R134. doi:10.1186/gb-2009-10-11-r134 PMID:19930550

Langmead, B., Trapnell, C., Pop, M., & Salzberg, S. L. (2009). Ultrafast and memory-efficient alignment of short DNA sequences to the human genome. *Genome Biology, 10*(3), R25. doi:10.1186/gb-2009-10-3-r25 PMID:19261174

Li, J., Ng, K.-S., & Wong, L. (2003). Bioinformatics Adventures in Database Research. *Proceedings of the 9th International Conference on Database Theory*, 31-46.

Li, R., Li, Y., Fang, X., Yang, H., Wang, J., Kristiansen, K., & Wang, J. (2009). SNP detection for massively parallel whole-genome resequencing. *Genome Research, 19*(6), 1124–1132. doi:10.1101/gr.088013.108 PMID:19420381

Liang, Zhang, Jin, & Zhu. (2014). FastGCN: A GPU Accelerated Tool for Fast Gene Co-Expression Networks. *PloS One, 10*(1).

Luo, W., & Brouwer, C. (2013). Pathview: An R/Bioconductor package for pathway-based data integration and visualization. *Bioinformatics (Oxford, England), 29*(14), 1830–1831. doi:10.1093/bioinformatics/btt285 PMID:23740750

Ma, Q., & Wang, J. T. L. (1999). Biological Data Mining Using Bayesian Neural Networks: A Case Study. *International Journal on Artificial Intelligence Tools, 8*(4), 433–451.

Matsunaga, A., Tsugawa, M., & Fortes, J. (2008). Cloudblast: Combining mapreduce and virtualization on distributed resources for bioinformatics applications. *eScience'08. IEEE Fourth International Conference on. IEEE*, 222–229. doi:10.1109/eScience.2008.62

McArt, D. G., Bankhead, P., Dunne, P. D., Salto-Tellez, M., Hamilton, P., & Zhang, S.-D. (2013). cudaMap: A GPU accelerated program for gene expression connectivity mapping. *BMC Bioinformatics, 14*(1), 305. doi:10.1186/1471-2105-14-305 PMID:24112435

Nepusz, T., Yu, H., & Paccanaro, A. (2012). Detecting overlapping protein complexes in protein-protein interaction networks. *Nature Methods, 9*(5), 471–472. doi:10.1038/nmeth.1938 PMID:22426491

Nordberg, H., Bhatia, K., Wang, K., & Wang, Z. (2013). BioPig: A Hadoop-based analytic toolkit for large-scale sequence data. *Bioinformatics (Oxford, England), 29*(23), 3014–3019. doi:10.1093/bioinformatics/btt528 PMID:24021384

Park, Y. S., Schmidt, M., Martin, E. R., Pericak-Vance, M. A., & Chung, R.-H. (2013). Pathway-PDT: A flexible pathway analysis tool for nuclear families. *BMC Bioinformatics, 14*(1), 267. doi:10.1186/1471-2105-14-267 PMID:24006871

Phan, J. H., Young, A. N., & Wang, M. D. (2013). omniBiomarker: A web-based application for knowledge-driven biomarker identification. *Biomedical Engineering, IEEE Transactions on, 60*(12), 3364–3367. doi:10.1109/TBME.2012.2212438 PMID:22893372

Piatetsky-Shapiro, G., & Tamayo, P. (2003). Microarray Data Mining: Facing the Challenges. *SIGKDD Explorations, 5*(2), 1–5. doi:10.1145/980972.980974

Rivera, Vakil, & Bader. (2010). NeMo: Network module identification in Cytoscape. *BMC Bioinformatics, 11*(S1), 61.

Sander, J., Ester, M., Kriegel, P.-H., & Xu, X. (1998). Density-Based Clustering in Spatial Databases: The Algorithm GDBSCAN and its Applications. *Data Mining and Knowledge Discovery, 2*(2), 169–194. doi:10.1023/A:1009745219419

Schumacher, A., Pireddu, L., Niemenmaa, M., Kallio, A., Korpelainen, E., Zanetti, G., & Heljanko, K. (2014). SeqPig: Simple and scalable scripting for large sequencing data sets in Hadoop. *Bioinformatics (Oxford, England), 30*(1), 119–120. doi:10.1093/bioinformatics/btt601 PMID:24149054

Stokes, T. H., Moffitt, R. A., Phan, J. H., & Wang, M. D. (2007). chip artifact CORRECTion (caCORRECT): A bioinformatics system for quality assurance of genomics and proteomics array data. *Annals of Biomedical Engineering, 35*(6), 1068–1080. doi:10.1007/s10439-007-9313-y PMID:17458699

Tibshirani, R., Hastie, T., Eisen, M., Ross, D., Botstein, D., & Brown, P. (1999). *Clustering methods for the analysis of DNA microarray data (Tech. Rep.).* Stanford, CA: Department of Statistics, Stanford University.

Tzanis, Berberidis, & Vlahavas. (n.d.). *Biological Data Mining.* Department of Informatics, Aristotle University of Thessaloniki.

van Iersel, M. P., Kelder, T., Pico, A. R., Hanspers, K., Coort, S., Conklin, B. R., & Evelo, C. (2008). Presenting and exploring biological pathways with PathVisio. *BMC Bioinformatics, 9*(1), 399. doi:10.1186/1471-2105-9-399 PMID:18817533

Whishart, D. S. (2002). Tools for Protein Technologies. In Biotechnology: Vol. 5b. Genomics and Bioinformatics (pp. 325-344). Wiley-VCH.

Yang, P., Patrick, E., Tan, S.-X., Fazakerley, D. J., Burchfield, J., Gribben, C., & Yang, Y. H. et al. (2014). Direction pathway analysis of large-scale proteomics data reveals novel features of the insulin action pathway. *Bioinformatics (Oxford, England), 30*(6), 808–814. doi:10.1093/bioinformatics/btt616 PMID:24167158

Yeung, Y. K., Medvedovic, M., & Bumgarner, R. E. (2003). Clustering GeneExpression Data with Repeated Measurements. *Genome Biology, 4*(5), R34. doi:10.1186/gb-2003-4-5-r34 PMID:12734014

Zambon, A. C., Gaj, S., Ho, I., Hanspers, K., Vranizan, K., Evelo, C. T., & Salomonis, N. et al. (2012). GO-Elite: A flexible solution for pathway and ontology over-representation. *Bioinformatics (Oxford, England), 28*(16), 2209–2210. doi:10.1093/bioinformatics/bts366 PMID:22743224

Zhao, S., Prenger, K., & Smith, L. (2013). *Stormbow: a cloud-based tool for reads mapping and expression quantification in largescale RNA-Seq studies* (Vol. 2013). International Scholarly Research Notices.

Zhao, S., Prenger, K., Smith, L., Messina, T., Fan, H., Jaeger, E., & Stephens, S. (2013). Rainbow: A tool for large-scale whole-genome sequencing data analysis using cloud computing. *BMC Genomics*, *14*(1), 425. doi:10.1186/1471-2164-14-425 PMID:23802613

Zien, A., Ratsch, G., Mika, S., Scholkopf, B., Lengauer, T., & Muller, R.-K. (2000). Engineering Support Vector Machine Kernels that Recognize Translation Initiation Sites. *Bioinformatics (Oxford, England)*, *16*(9), 799–807. doi:10.1093/bioinformatics/16.9.799 PMID:11108702

Zien, A., Ratsch, G., Mika, S., Scholkopf, B., Lengauer, T., & Muller, R.-K. (2000). Engineering Support Vector Machine Kernels that Recognize Translation Initiation Sites. *Bioinformatics (Oxford, England)*, *16*(9), 799–807. doi:10.1093/bioinformatics/16.9.799 PMID:11108702

Chapter 10
After Cloud:
In Hypothetical World

Shigeki Sugiyama
Independent Researcher, Japan

ABSTRACT

It is just now at the top of an aggregation point of globalization's era in terms of things and living creatures. And the communication methods including in many sorts of transfers like commodity, facility, information, system, thought, knowledge, human, etc. may cause many kinds of and many types of interactions among us. And those many kinds of and many types of interactions have been again causing many sorts of problems. Under these situations, Cloud has come out as a smart solution to these problems. However, "Cloud is the final ultimate solution to offer to these problems' solving?" On this chapter, this question is deeply concerned from various aspects. And it is studied on this regard for getting a new paradigm.

INTRODUCTION

It is just now at the top of an aggregation point of globalizations' era in terms of things and living creatures. And the communication methods including in many sorts of transfers like commodity, facility, information, system, thought, knowledge, people, culture, heritage, etc. may cause many kinds of and many types of interactions among us, which may have made the world closer but complex, smaller but intense, influential but solitude, networked but dividable, accumulated but distributed, direct but standstill, stable but chaotic, abstracted but differentiated loosely, many possibilities but almost none, free but controlled, unique but ubiquitous, solitude but mass, directed but diverge, and accumulated knowledge but ordinal. As the results

DOI: 10.4018/978-1-5225-3015-2.ch010

of these situations, they may cause even an individual world much wider or smaller, closer or divided, quicker or slower, dependent or independent, massive or nothing, unique or ubiquitous, far expanded or shrunk, any opportunity expected or nothing desired, viewable or invisible, manageable or uncontrollable, simple or chaotic, and limited or borderless. That is to say, it can be seen that these phenomenon in the world is being existed as an extreme opposite twin (dipole, pair) unit at the same moment. And so, this has been the causations of the Multi Dipoles. This phenomenon of the Multi Dipoles has caused the situations of many kinds of Mini Clouds by use of the Information Technology (IT) in order to offer necessary information to us individually. This phenomenon of the Multi Dipoles seems to be further deepened and extended under this phenomenon. But on the contrary, this phenomenon turns out to be the opposite direction, that is to say, this phenomenon will make the Multi Dipoles converge into Unique Dipole in the very near future as the public will go to the two kinds of categories (groups) of people; Simple Users and Controlled Venders.

Talking about the functions of Mini Clouds in the same flow, it will become possible to access seamlessly to any Mini Cloud whose phenomenon will make the Mini Clouds converge into the Unique Cloud. And so, under these situations, an individual is able to get a thing and information as many and as much as being wanted in order to accomplish one's desire, which is very easy to do. But on the other hand, it is very true to say that the thing and the information will be offered to anybody as "a unit (a black box)" that it is not possible to go into further details to change, moderate, and manage a concerned matter. This phenomenon will likely lose a thing and information of originated matters silently without being recognized by users as many and as much as users used to have.

And also it can be said that, under these situations, almost everything in the world may be interfered one another randomly, massively, closely, seamlessly, dividedly without being noticed to us. And what is more, this phenomenon will go on further beyond year by year aggressively.

So here studies on the problems caused by these situations, and will propose a method to resolve some of the problems caused by these situations by an idea of "After Cloud" in terms of Individual Cloud.

BACKGROUND

There are so many kinds of tool, system, software, hardware, knowledge, thought, idea, principle, theory, and various kinds of human behaviors linked with Internetworking by Information Technologies that have been facilitating human actions even in cases at Dense Interference Space (DIS). DIS is a place where so many people or information is gathered randomly unintentionally on a networking or at a physical place. In the

Interfering One Another (IOA) at DIS, it will be able to take any actions, for example, manufacturing fine goods, transporting goods, reducing a cost, solving a problem in managing a company, keeping an environment as they should be, making money, getting an information, making a new idea, learning, communicating, knowing, creating, diverging, etc. DIS could be appearing anywhere with any idea at any time purposely or coincidentally as long as a history tells us in the networked societies. And DIS may have an influential aspect in guiding a social and a technical direction without giving us any intention beforehand. And this tendency could not be stopped by anybody with any idea under the conventional ideas, thoughts, knowledge, and actions even though the tendency would be wanted to avoid.

In the present societies under these situations as mentioned above, there should be bearing various sorts of and many levels of DIS here and there. And some of them are brand new ones with a brand new knowledge, and others are mixed with new knowledge and conventional ones, and another are with stuck of "obsoledge" ("obsoledge" means "obsolete" + "knowledge" by Toffler, 2010.).

Under this circumstance, any output of a service processing at DIS, for example, will be easily affected goodly or badly by Handling Method Of Knowledge (HMOK), Handling Method Of Knowledge Value (HMOKV), and Intelligence Of Knowledge (IOK) itself, which are closely related with cores of Clouds.

Technically speaking, it is now under "Techno National", "Techno Hybrid", and "Techno Global". Under these situations, industries have been transferring their production spots to abroad from a developed country in order to reduce a production cost and a labor cost. And as a result of this, some of technologies of industries in those countries should be fading away and down to nothing (zero), and what is more, a deflation will be going on in those countries. Under these situations, ordinal machines equipped industries and traditional production methods used industries may have a hard time for surviving at the places where they used to have situated at. On the other hand, it is not so easy matter to create a new industry or a company in the replaces of the conventional companies. That is to say, there is not any stable space for any purpose to be achieved easily in reality.

However, at present, in terms of this matter, it could be and can be thought of some of the methods to overcome these problems and the situations for surviving. And they are shown in the followings.

1. **To Become "Far Advanced Company in Technology and Management":**
   This means that a company has the following functions.
   a. A company has a far advanced core technology.
   b. A company has the top share of distinguished goods in a limited field.
   c. A company has the best engineers and technicians in a field.
   d. A company has a unique management strategy and a good turnover.

e. A company has constantly a new development.

f. A company has collaboration with Universities.

g. A company has good concerns with an environment and a natural resource.

h. A company may give employees nice motivations for working.

2. **To Have "Alliance with Company in Developing Country":** This means that a company has a production spot in Asia or in South America in order to reduce a production cost and labor cost.

a. A company has a distinguished management.

b. A company has a strategy of "Goods from Asia or from South America to the world", for example.

c. A company has a unique planning section.

d. A company has a multiple management.

3. **To Become "Global Company":** A company will become a global company. That is to say, a company will stay at the best place (in any country) for production and management as multi-nationals.

4. **To Become "Environment Concern Type of Company":** This means that a company has the core direction in sustainability in all. A company has the best concerns with the nature, the natural resources, and responsibilities for the goods produced.

5. **To Become "Knowledge Accumulated Company":** Whatever we understand about the world, it is very hard to maintain an established position as a company for good. Generally speaking, it is understood that a company has to have an advanced thought comparing with others'. That is to say, it is very closely related with an idea how much knowledge, which is far advanced compared with others', a company has. In this case, Knowledge is in a technical field and in a management field, which are closely related with Cloud.

6. **To Become "Advanced Information Technology Equipped Company":** A company has the advanced Information Technologies that may replace a human job by using Cloud.

7. **To Become "Company with Niche Goods Production":** A company has goods that might not interest in the major companies.

8. **To Become "Company only in Net" Company in Digital:** A company does not have a physical office at all but it has all the necessary actions in Networking. This is a unique case of using Cloud as Knowledge.

9. **To Become "Non Profit Organization (NPO)":** An organization does not have a targeted making money motivation but has a loosely environment interfered action orientation with a nature, people, economy, culture, education, and the earth. This will be able to become a global but in the sense of economy mono pole.

Whichever the case to face to adopt, all these matters of 1 to 9 are closely related with "Cloud" for the necessary usages in planning, production, management, marketing, service, and sales.

PRESENT PHENOMENON IN SOCIETY AND PROBLEMS FACING

By taking an idea from 1 to 9 described in the previous chapter, a company may have any direction of the methods in order to keep its position in the world and in order to overcome the problems facing for being survived or for getting a higher position with shares and sales. However, it is very true to say that the economic situation in the world is not vivid like many decades ago, generally speaking. And what is worse, the consumers do not have much intention to buy goods and foods, etc. comparing with the decades ago. Because almost everything can be got in the world when it is desired through Networking, for example. They can be easily transported even if they are away from us in distance. And also they can be simply transferred through a computer networking if they are data, images, and information technology related matters. That is to say, they are able to come upon to us by the transfers without any information contained just as a matter of "THING", which means that Goods has been arrived upon us just as a final matter of "THING" without making us known its Contents, Relations, and Meanings.

If it is allowed to describe the above phenomenon with a bit of over expression, they may have lost these Contents, Relations, and Meanings of Goods and Foods before they have been delivered to us. So it is quite natural and easy to lose the values of them too at the time when they are used or are eaten. As the result of this, it is quite natural that the interests on Goods or Foods might be lost too although the producers and raisers have been doing much effort on adding the values onto them.

In another words, if it will be concluded to say, the world will be surrounded by full of simple matters of "THING", which might make us easily loose interests on Goods and Foods. And ultimately, the world will be surrounded by "simply a function" and "simply a matter" by "THING" that have been asked to possess. So a consumer will be fed up with them sooner or later by "a function" and "a simple matter". And a new Goods or Foods will be asked for soon after by a consumer. And in this vicious circle, it might be said that a deflation will be on, which will make an economic basic ground become smaller and smaller and will be likely shrunk to zero without any notice to us.

So, in short, what are the problems under this phenomenon in the case of production, market, and sales? They will be the followings.

1. A consumer will easily loose an interest in Goods, etc. sooner or later, and so the values that are existed on Goods, etc. will be fading away to nothing suddenly and instantly. As the result of this, a market size will have a tendency to diminish itself suddenly and instantly.

2. DIS will come up to the world suddenly and without any notice. So a new market will have a tendency to come up to the world suddenly without any notice to us.

3. Tendency is not a matter that is able to control easily.

4. A value is not a matter that is able to create easily.

5. Consumers are independent nowadays, and so they are independently taking any thought and action in all over the world. As the result of this, to grasp and to know a mass behavior is not an easy matter.

6. Data processing methods are in full for use today but it is hard to use them properly. So it is asked to have a method to use them simply, intentionally, knowledgably, and intelligently. This situation is really the matter of "Cloud" to come up and to use.

KEY FACTOR IN THE PROBLEMS SOLVING

In the previous chapter, the problems facing are extracted and are discussed. And here they will be studied further in order to find the core matter to cause the problems if there is any.

It will not take much time to find the core matter of the problems studied in the above chapter when it is thought out.

A new product has been asked almost every instance in commodities, in hobbies, and in lives. Or in another expression, a company has been offering a new product at every instance. This phenomenon shows that values, meanings, and relations of them have been lost sooner or later, which were existed on them. But what happens if those things likely loose values, meanings, and relations of them in much longer time. That is to say, if much important and vivid information are kept on a certain goods, they will be kept for them until the mechanical functions are damaged for use. In another words, "Contents (C)", "Relations (R)", and "Meanings (M)" of Goods, for example, are the core matters (the core factors) for us to keep our interests on Goods. And also it can be concluded by looking back of this phenomenon that those core matters (C, R, and M) should be strongly combined with "an intention to buy".

So it is quite obvious to say that the following two subjects of 1 and 2 are important actions and functions if there is a sale of Goods on a market;

1. Goods should have good reasons of "Contents", "Relations", and "Meanings" that belong to its own.
2. "Contents", "Relations", and "Meanings" should be within a quite understandable situation for anybody. And so, those things should be seen or taken or used quite easily by "anybody" at "any time" when those are wanted to.

Today, there are the following systems and functions in order to produce Goods in a costless and labor saving manner as a broad sense of a management field.

*   **SAP:** (Enterprise Resource Planning)
*   **SOA:** Service Oriented Architecture
*   **SaaS:** Software as a Service
*   **Mash Up:** Mashing Up software
*   **Meta Frame:** (peer to peer relation)
*   **PaaS:** Platform as a Service
*   **HaaS:** Hardware as a Service
*   **IaaS:** Infrastructure as a Service
*   **Cloud:** Cloud Computing within a particular area
*   **Mini Clouds:** Various Kinds of Small Cloud.

Those systems and functions mentioned above have been concluded as a part of "Cloud" computing in order to solve any kind of problem.

But nowadays there is the fact that it is not possible to invest so much money on a company system for solving the problems. Because skilled and educated engineers might be offered in the areas of developing countries, and those won't cost so much comparing to the systems mentioned above. And they may be creative which cannot be done by the computer systems mentioned above. So the companies try to use those engineers instead of using a high cost of the computer systems with SAP, SOA, SaaS, PaaS, HaaS, IaaS, Cloud, etc. And what is more, it is quite hard to create and add the two subjects mentioned above on Goods, for example, by using the above computer systems and the functions instantly.

CLOUD ORIENTED SERVICE IN SERVICE SCIENCE

Here introduces a new idea of "CLOUD ORIENTED SERVICE IN SERVICE SCIENCE" by using the method of "Accumulation and Integration in Seamless Knowledge", which will be able to solve those problems mentioned in a sense of "Service" with a low labor cost and a low production cost.

Definition of CLOUD ORIENTED SERVICE by Behavior

"By entering into the "CLOUD ORIENTED SERVICE" system, the desire (subject, problem) will be solved and offered by means of SERVICE; BPOSS, POSS, BFOSS, BSOSS, and IMOS. And this SERVICE consists of Field Analysis, Categorical Analysis, Functional Analysis, and Knowledge Enhancement in the mixed ways. And the services will be mainly offered by the computer systems, which may need some simple data-input."

In this manner, Service as Field Analysis will be firstly defined with five service systems as described below.

Service

Service Field

1. **Business Plan Oriented Service (BPOS):** Generally speaking, there are so many businesses in this world and also there will come up new businesses to the world day by day. It is true to say that each business itself is slightly different from one another in a sense of goods, a shape, a production method, a market, a customer, an environment, etc. But they may be divided as field (gathered as a bundle of groups) by a system structure, a kind of goods, a process kind, a market kind, etc., which should make the number of the businesses' fields small in quantity. That is to say, it will be possible to have a business plan for each field as "A Generalized System of Service" (Business Plan Oriented Service System: BPOS), which will be able to offer the following Service.
    a. BPOS can make use of database for a new generalized business plan (Contents).
    b. BPOS is able to offer one of the business plans for planning and controlling, or for getting assistance out of BPOS in managing.
    c. BPOS may make use of the database for using other purposes (Relations) by connecting to other systems with IT facilities like Printer, CAD/CAM, etc.
2. **Project Oriented Service (POS):** Now it is a common thing that we have some projects derived from a public sector (government, or NPO, etc.), a private sector, and an Academy Sector. These are Project Oriented Service (a theme of a project purpose is defined), which means that these are usually processed by collaboration among Private Sector, Academy Sector, and Public Sector. That is to say, each sector should be responsible for some parts in the project in order to get a purpose accomplished. In this case, the things that are needed

will be decided before starting a project. So the services offered for projects will be the followings.

a. POS can manage the whole project and can do "Check – Plan – Do – Evaluation - Action" circle. And this can offer and create Meanings.

b. POS has flexibility for adding and reducing a process of the system targeted.

c. POS may have a human interaction (of a coordinator) from time to time. In this case, a purpose of a project will be clearly decided before the start but not for methods to get the output.

3. **Business Fostering Oriented Service (BFOS):** When a business plan starts, it is a usual thing to say that there might be a problem for processing at some part during the operation. This kind of problem should be sort out by as soon as possible. For doing this kind of problem solving, it is very useful to have a similar kind of process example, which will give and offer a solution tips for the problem facing. So the services offered will be the followings. After having gone through this process, a new knowledge will be created, or value added knowledge will be made on.

a. BFOS can offer necessary information (Contents, Relations, and Meanings) including a method from the database accumulated from day by day processing when the business has a problem.

b. BFOS can offer a new-targeted mass (Relations) for sales, a new strategy for processing, and a new category for promotion, etc. by using an information retrieval system and GPS system.

c. BFOS can offer a market research activity (Relations) by using the several analysis methods offered by the BFOS.

4. **Business Skill Oriented Service (BSOS):** There are many skills and tactics in a field of business when a business is under operation. And these skills will be usually stored in a computer system as a knowledge base in order to use them for future. And an old knowledge will be transformed into a new knowledge through this process.

a. BSOS can offer business skills and tactics (Relations).

b. BSOS can store the skills and the tactics by the system in Database.

5. **Information Management Oriented Service (IMOS) (Suzuki 2013):** It always happens to get new information, and to process it, and to accumulate it by adding other related information. And those of many kinds of accumulated information need to be managed in the way to facilitate a problem solving and desired structure formation in processing.

a. IMOS can offer a problem solving technique by using various kinds of information on one computer screen. And those kinds of information can be searched, accumulated, processed, and added onto a system as a new knowledge by using Web., Google, and Data stored.

b. IMOS can offer the publication processes in any stage. And also this can offer an increment in knowledge enhancement.

Here explains about the system behavior of "CLOUD ORIENTED SERVICE" system.

The system consists of the four categories (BPOS, POS, BFOS, BSOS, IMOS) as mentioned above. The processes for Service Action as Categorical Analysis will be explained in the following subsection.

Service Action (Sugiyama, Suzuki (2012))

1. **Enter with "Subject":** Go to the system with "a subject". And go further into BPOS, which will offer a related category with the subject. And find the categories related with the subject.
2. **Get Subject Required:** Find the category related with the subject that will offer a desired output.
3. **Processing with Service:** After having found the related category, it will start processing for inputting the subject in order to get a desired output.
4. **Evaluate Output:** It is very important to know whether the output offered is valuable/acceptable or not. If the output is all right for use, this will be terminated.
5. **Goto First Stage:** If the output is not valuable for use, go to the "first stage of the system" to find more appropriate category.

The processes for Service Improvement as Functional Analysis will be explained in the following subsection.

Service Improvement

1. **Get Unsolved Subject:** Get an unsolved subject.
2. **Resolve It with Services:** Find the related functions for the subject by using the related categories. And then by using the categories, find out relatively influenced functions by the subject. If there are adding factors and functions, manipulate them by using this system. And then store it as a generalized system for service.
3. **Evaluate It with Output:** Find out the output whether it is good for use or not. It is good for use, and then stores it as one of the services onto Service Category with the functions used.

4. **Store It as Service:** If the output is not valuable for use, go to the "first stage of the system".

The General System Behavior

By using the method studied in the above sub chapters, we can create "CLOUD ORIENTED SERVICE" system of which the general system behavior is described below.

The system INPUT is for the desire at the place for "Service with Subject in a certain field", and then the desire will be categorized according to the content (elements) of the desire. And then the process center will be transferred to "Mini Cloud" of which is the most suitable for the desire. And then "Mini Cloud" will be getting an appropriate answer by interchanging the information with "CLOUD ORIENTED SERVICE". And then, the general behavior of this system will give us a notice what sort of service field and category that we are interested. By then, necessary functions will be ready for processing. By telling the category which we need to system, the system lures us one of Mini Cloud, which will give us an answer as OUTPUT.

However, there should be one more thing to think about regarding this matter. That is to say, "Whether or not that there is any limitation in Cloud?" Or "Mini Cloud is good enough for use ?".

In the next chapter, the limitation will be considered by using a mini Cloud.

Simple Example: Gshop and Information Management Oriented System
Gshop Structure in Field, Category, and Function

Here shows a simple example for making the Mini Cloud system by using Gshop in order to show a limitation if there is any.

The whole system consists of the major five subsystems.

1. "Process Template" is to show the present processing contents and the processing results.
2. "ScriptEngine" is for various kinds of Data processing, like "print, mail, SNS, etc.", "Search and Recommend by using GIS", "various analysis", etc.
3. "Database" is for Information, Object, and Person.
4. "Various Field Definitions"
5. "Project Plans and related"

The system behavior for the processing will be shown below.

1. **First Stage of the Processing:** From "Analysis Threshold", the system understands which field this subject is related with by using the "Evaluations". And the system will find that this subject is related with "Project B" mostly. And at the same time, the system knows that "Project B" consists of "Processes A to E". Each "Process" will get Data from "ScriptEngine" one by one. And the system will give necessary outputs.
2. **Second Stage of the Processing:** If the outputs are not as suitable as expected, then change the parameters on Process A and Process D. And get the outputs. If the results were good enough to proceed in the real world, then this system ceases to close.
3. **Third Stage of the Processing:** If the outputs are not as suitable as expected, then change the Processes Methods to Process E and etc. provided. And get the outputs. If the results were good enough to proceed in the real world, then this system ceases to close.
4. **Fourth Stage of the Processing:** If the outputs are not as suitable as expected, then try to search a new processing method by using a networking, from books, and with computer systems. And this processing will be able to add a new knowledge onto this system as shown in Figure (2) Seamless Knowledge in Gshop. The Knowledge in this processing is to add a new technical processing, a new data processing, a new manipulation, a new thought, a new behavior, a new transformation, and a new relation. That is to say, this is a processing route to find a new knowledge/rule by abstracting the methods used here repeatedly.
5. **Fifth Stage of the Processing:** The information and the knowledge that will be accumulated in the Fourth Stage will be able to be enhanced, comprehended, inferred, and enhanced in order to fulfill the information and the knowledge.

These processes from 1 to 5 will be repeated endlessly until one is able to get the output satisfied.

By this method in the seamless knowledge creation processes, one can create a new project which will give a new plan with a new knowledge.

However, it is easy to see that it is very hard to moderate the output after the processes have been completed.

Information Management Oriented System (IMOS) (Suzuki (2013))

Here shows a simple example for making Mini Cloud system by using Information Management Oriented System whether or not that there is any limitation for use.

This system consists of the following structures.

1.   **Subject (Category):** Each subject consists of project. And each project consists of Contents, Categories, and Objects. Each one of them (Contents, Categories, and Objects) has a seamless relation in the project. So a project is able to be directed onto a certain purpose in order to accomplish a desire by accumulating, enhancing, managing, restructuring, and concluding.
2.   **Process (Link and Database):** Each process consists of Link and Database. Link and Database have related data, searching data by related data, enhanced knowledge, related data (document, Web, geographical data, XML data, etc.) And each process has a seamless relation in the process.

Through these processes, it is possible to make and enhance "knowledge" in *Mini Cloud.*

However, Mini Cloud may behave only in a limited space which has been created by the above process. So this intelligence of Mini Cloud goes under "static behavior" and "closed space (not open for public)".

AFTER CLOUD

From the above chapters, it is quite natural to see the following things.

1.   Things and living creatures are transformed into "a digital world".
2.   The digital world consists of a world of "data".
3.   It might be said that the digital world is "a virtual world".
4.   The virtual world is "a simulation world", which is not real.
5.   "A hypothetical world" leads to the most of the simulation world.
6.   It might be said that Cloud goes under the hypothetical world.

So if Clouds are "static" and "closed" for users, the output given by Clouds will be the rigid ones. That is to say, they are all from the virtual world that Cloud has made them by itself. Under this circumstance, the space that the world is facing is really virtual world. The space must not be care about whether or not the world is real or not.

There are many kinds of and many types of Mini Clouds in the world. They are individually existed for a targeted customer. But Mini Cloud is a Mini Cloud that is able to foster in a very limited category or within a closed area. So it can be said that users have to use many kinds of and many types of Mini Clouds in order to accomplish ones desires. That is to say, it has come to the time which all of the Mini Cloud in the world may act as "knowledge of the world" uniquely. At this time, it will be necessary to access each related Mini Cloud in order to construct "each own knowledge for use". This is able to be done by the idea of Dynamic Knowledge Wisdom (Sugiyama 2013).

This behaves like "knowledge enhancement cloud" by Net Surfing with the data taken by the structure of groups of URL and groups of Mini Clouds with processing and restructuring.

Dynamic Knowledge Wisdom is a kind of "Smart Cloud (SC)", which will get and accumulate necessary information by Net Surfing on Webs (Mini Clouds) one after another. SC is formed as series of Mini Clouds (MC), those related data, and those related knowledge as described below.

$$
SC = \begin{bmatrix} MC, Data, Knowledge, Hypothetical\ World \mid MC1, MC2, \ldots, MCn, Data, Knowledge\ 1, \\ Knowledge\ 2, \ldots, Knowledge\ n, Simulation\ World\ 1, \ldots, Simulation\ World\ n \end{bmatrix}
$$

Inside of Cloud content is searched basically by Behavior of State Comprehension and State Inference, which might be an extension of Eigen Vector and Eigen Value behaviors.

CONCLUSION

Here argued about the following things.

The present real world is equal to the digital world offered by group of Mini Clouds. The digital world is equal to the virtual world offered by Clouds. The virtual world is equal to the hypothetical world that will be made by knowledge computer and the humans. And the hypothetical world is equal to a kind of Cloud.

So those can be expressed as follows.

"The Present Real World" = "The Digital World" = "The Virtual World"
= "The Hypothetical World by Simulation"
= "Clouds; Mini Cloud, Unique Cloud, Smart Cloud"

And the hypothetical world is able to be manipulated by a brand new method of "Accumulation and Integration in Seamless Knowledge" by using the knowledge processing mechanisms of "CLOUD ORIENTED SEVICE", so called Smart Cloud, within a principle of Service Science.

And the following results have been given.

1. It is shown that "SUBJECT in demand and need" will be resolved by means of the idea of "CLOUD ORIENTED SERVICE; BPOS, POS, BFOS, BSOS, and IMOS in a sense of "Service Science" with the knowledge processing mechanisms of "Accumulation and Integration in Seamless Knowledge".
2. By using this method, it will be quite possible to transform "Obsoledge" into "Brand New Knowledge".
3. HMOK, HMOKV, and IOK are able to be done by using this method.
4. It is obvious that this method can contribute to "Cost Reduction and Labor Savings".
5. This method can offer any type of fostering to an individual by accumulating and integrating knowledge seamlessly that is likely creating a brand new knowledge.
6. By using this method, an individual is able to do anything by oneself from the first stage to the final stage for a desire accomplishment assisted by Gshop.
7. As a next phenomenon in Clouds, an idea of Dynamic Knowledge Wisdom as Smart Cloud is introduced.
8. Smart Cloud will have an ability and knowledge to escape from the hypothetical world.

FUTURE WORK AND DIRECTION

It will be thought for sure that any kinds of knowledge will be accumulated and enhanced as Unique Cloud and Smart Cloud. And as a result of this phenomenon, the related space for the world will be able to be indulged in the world of getting processed information as a final use of data for a daily life. This is a very comfortable world to live, but, on the other hand, there might be a possibility which there will be many or some who live only under the offered information and knowledge from intelligent computer systems (Mini Cloud, Unique Cloud, Smart Cloud).

So, it is very important to have knowledge of us in investigating whether or not Unique Cloud and Smart Cloud are useful enough to use by inspecting from the outside world even though we are to live in the hypothetical world. Or, in another words, whether or not an individual wants to live in its own individual hypothetical world, or an individual wants to live in another's hypothetical world ?

REFERENCES

Sugiyama, S. (2008). Fundamental Behavior In Communication Method. IEEE/ SOLI, Beijing, China.

Sugiyama, S. (2013). Intangible Capital Management Method As Dynamic Knowledge Wisdom. In *Intellectual Capital Management For Knowledge-Based Organizations*. IGI Global.

Sugiyama, S., & Suzuki, J. (2012). Accumulation and Integration in Seamless Knowledge. *International Journal of Asian Business and Information Management*.

Suzuki, J. (2009). *Gshop*. PITS.

Suzuki, J. (2013). *Multi Publications*. PITS.

Toffler, A., & Toffler, H. (2010). *40 for the next 40*. Toffler Associates.

Chapter 11
Cloud–Based Big Data Analytics in Smart Educational System

Newlin Rajkumar Manokaran
Anna University – Coimbatore, India

Venkatesa Kumar Varathan
Anna University – Coimbatore, India

Shalinie Deepak
United Institute of Technology, India

ABSTRACT

In this modern Digital era, Technology is a key player in transforming the educational pedagogy for the benefit of students and society at large. Technology in the classroom allows the teacher to deliver more personalized learning to the student with better interaction through the internet. Humongous amount of digital data collected day by day increases has led to the use of big data. It helps to correlate the performance and learning pattern of individual students by analysing large amount of stored activity of the students, offering worthwhile feedback etc. The use of big data analytics in a cloud environment helps in providing an instant infrastructure with low cost, accessibility, usability etc. This paper presents an innovative means towards providing a smarter educational system in schools. It improves individual efficiency by providing a way to monitor the progress of individual student by maintaining a detailed profile. This framework has been established in a cloud environment which is an online learning system where the usage pattern of individual students are collected.

DOI: 10.4018/978-1-5225-3015-2.ch011

INTRODUCTION

Big Data

Analogously, the information and data have gone digital and is being hovering around. The amount of information that is rendezvous and stored seemed to be increasing triple folds every day. Although web makes the data apparent to interact, big data is more than just communicating. It has the capability to put forth many aspects of the world into the data that has never been calibrated before. This process is termed as "datafication". These volumes of data undergoes disparate transitions by collecting large amount of data rather than smaller samples, then setting predilection for a highly curated data, and lastly discovering various correlation among those data. This upsurge and explosion of data led to the rise of big data. Big data deals with a large and superfluous amount of data. The data is too big, too fast and does not fit the framework in the traditional data structure. Few applications of big data are stock market sentiment analysis, Picasa photo storing, recommendation systems, customer based analytics, machine generated data, booking systems, social networking for entertainment, medical diagnostics. Predominantly, big data is characterised by three 'V's that describe them. They are volume, velocity and variety.

The volume portrays the amount of data that are processed. It consumes colossal amount of data. These data are so mammoth that the conventional relational databases are hard to cope up with. There is growth in data deliberately that the database should be scaling to keep up with the growth. It is noted that big data handles more than 1 million transactions and can store a plethora of data to approximately 312 terabytes for a single unique transaction.

The velocity of the data explains the momentum in which they are processed. Various industries have to deal with the fast moving data flow into their system. Since the data are mostly processed in real time, the capability to process those data at high speed is required. It does not explain just the speed or the velocity of the incoming data, it embodies the surge of data into bulk storage for a later batch processing.

Variety depicts the disparate data that vary from structured data like numeric data in traditional databases to unstructured data that include text documents, email, video, audio, stack ticker data and financial transactions. Big data is the place where all types of data are being processed. It requires new technologies and techniques to capture, store, and analyze it. Figure 1 shows the amount of structured and unstructured data. Roughly, the unstructured data comprises of almost 80% of the databases while the structured data comprises of only 20%.

Figure 1. Structured and unstructured data

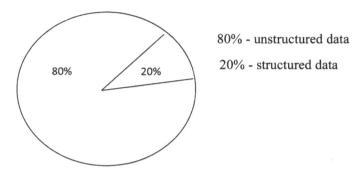

80% - unstructured data

20% - structured data

In conjunction with these 3 V's, big data includes veracity and value.

The big data analytics here is done providing a sophisticated way of accessing the students by predicting the behaviour of the student. With those predictions as a feedback, personalized and appropriate learning materials are issued as well as help the teachers to intervene if necessary. The database used here is HBase and the data analytics are performed in a hadoop environment. This educational system provides a holistic approach by gradually moving towards teacher centric to the student centric environment.

CLOUD COMPUTING

Cloud computing is the one that reckon on sharing computing resources rather than having local servers or personal devices to handle applications. There are few traits that makes the cloud computing desirable. First of all it can be easily managed; secondly it can be got on demand which may be public, private or hybrid. The services offered on a cloud are software as a service, infrastructure as a service and platform as a service.

These above discussed technologies are expeditiously emerging to deliver powerful results and benefits for most of the forward thinking companies. By converging the big data analytics operations into cloud environment, firms can increase the efficiency and productivity, while saving time and effort. This cloud-based approach to big data analytics serves to be more beneficial as it helps reduce cost, to take fast and better decision making and to create prominent new products and services.

UPHEAVAL OF TECHNOLOGY IN EDUCATION

Traditionally, educational system was based only on formal learning interventions which required the use of chalk pieces and blackboard. This teacher – driven style pedagogy required disquisition of any knowledgeable lecturers where multiple students gather to learn in a specific time and space. Not all the students have the same pace of learning and neither have they had the same learning styles. While some of the students could follow up with the teacher, the others should work on it. For the students with different learning styles will have the inability to grasp the key ideas and concepts at that particular time of lecture. These stumbling blocks led to the use of technology in the educational sector.

Recently, technology has been creeping with its usage is all the aspects including the educational system. The ability to transform the most exigent and the stodgy concepts into more interesting ones through the video and virtual lessons has led to this substantial transition. This e-learning system helps access the real time, humongous amount of educational resources that are available online. It establishes a dynamic learning environment with resilience, adaptability and differentiated learning. These colossal data tends to increase manifold everyday which led to the concept of big data in this field of education. Implementing these analytics in a cloud based big data environment benefits the education system by providing a service that is expeditious to start, easy to adopt, mobile and flexible. Perseverance of a larger infrastructure is not needed. Conglomerate data can be accessed with a good speed. Since they are executed in parallel, real time data access can be done efficiently. The Figure 2 describes the implementation of the educational data analytics in cloud based big data environment. It explains the working of online educational system using cloud based big data concepts. It starts with the online learning system implemented in the cloud. The end user is allowed to access any type of educational contents based on their category. The usage pattern of the database is then collected. These patterns are collected on real time. These patterns are used to predict the behaviour of the particular end user or student. These predictions are then given to the concerned staff as a feedback. According to the behaviour prediction of the student, personalized syllabus is allotted to him. These feedbacks also help the teacher to intervene and help the student in his personal development.

EXISTING SYSTEM

Recently, cities are getting smatter as IoT has been evolving. A smart city can be fabricated by the use of these IoT in our daily lives. Real life urban challenges are dealt with the use of these IoT tools. Some of the confrontations include environmental sustainability, socioeconomic innovation, participatory governance, better public services, planning and synergistic decision-making. Various indicators were used to represent a city's different application domain, which was used for the development of a city. The data can be congregated through various smart tools such as mobile, sensors, etc. These collected data are then fed into the system. The information collected from these tools are then scrutinized and correlated with the other functional indicators. This process helps in the development of the city through better planning and decision making. Using cloud computing resources for the large scale data analytics provides a very promising platform for a better execution and performance. A prototype has been constructed and the samples were taken from Bristol open dataset to identify the correlations between selected urban environment indicators such as Quality of Life. This Big Data analysis platform provides to be pragmatic for smart cities as it would allow decision-makers to collect and analyse data from many sources in a timely manner. The implementation was done by using hadoop and spark, which is a map reduce based prototype, in the cloud platform for analysing the sample data through a survey method.

In an educational background, a trial of an educational modelling is done based on big data techniques. With more and more online courses commencing at various websites and with the increasing population of learners, vast amounts of data are getting generated. Many educational institutions are now providing more and more learning material online, giving rise to Big Data storage requirements. These big data platforms primarily focuses on data storage schema-less and highly scalable, and data analytics that deals with management, processing and distribution of data. The existing system includes the use of data on a large scale. They used different methods to implement syllabuses and courses online. Different data analysis and tools were used here for the comparison of different learning methods. Using those details, these data analytics were done to introduce changes in course with a better scheme and syllabus.

The educational system so far implemented in cloud was used to set up the online classrooms. Here the teachers and students were allowed to interact. This was just like providing the interactive digital classrooms with the same syllabus for the appropriate cadre. The database was stored in MongoDB which is a NoSQL database. MongoDB, a NoSQL open source document-oriented database system, stores structured data as JSON-like heterogeneous documents with dynamic schemas. MongoDB scales horizontally through sharding. It provides the map Reduce database command for MapReduce operations. MongoDB queries can be much faster sometimes. It also does not require the unified data structure across all objects which make it much simpler to use than the RDBMS. The adaptive learning tool used in big data was wega. Wega is fully implemented in java programming language and it is platform independent and portable. It also contains graphical user interface, so the system is very easy to access.

DISADVANTAGES OF EXISTING SYSTEM

The various disadvantages in the existing system are as follows.

- The smart educational systems were not implemented in cloud architecture.
- The cloud implemented educational data analytics dealt only with the change in the course scheme and syllabus.
- The adaptive learning schemes were not implemented in cloud infrastructure.
- Only survey methods were used in a cloud based big data platform.

PROBLEM DESCRIPTION

Generally, an education system does not require the access to vast amount of data online. They are limited to a particular syllabus. They don't provide a platform where the students of different learning capabilities could grasp the concept. The pedagogy includes a one- way communication which is more teacher- centric which hinders the development of the student who is in a need. A digital smart educational system has not been implemented in cloud platform. This does not provide a better scalability. It is not the best fit for reporting style workloads. It is not a good choice for complex transactions. The adaptive learning schemes were not implemented in a cloud platform.

PROPOSED SYSTEM

The proposed system includes the student –centric pedagogy with a high knowledge retention rate. The system provides a smart education with an exposure to a vast amount of data and information online. Our approach here is to provide a better platform to implement the educational data analytics with greater scalability and flexibility. A prototype of the smart educational system implemented in cloud platform is put forth. It includes an online educational system. The contents contain large amount and variety of data. The students can access the contents belonging to the particular category. The student's usage pattern is tracked and the behaviour of the student is predicted. The progress of the student is maintained. The feedback about the behaviour is given to the teacher for the further assistance of the student.

ADVANTAGES

The advantages of the proposed system are as follows.

- It provides fast and a flexible platform to implement the educational data analytics.
- Proper authentication is given to the different cadre of end user accessing them.
- Proper security is given to the profile databases.
- The contents are categorised at the backend so that any student of the particular cadre can access the particular category allotted to them.
- It helps in improving individual improvement.
- They are scalable.

OVERALL ARCHITECTURE

The architecture of cloud based big data analytics of smart educational system can be described in Figure 2.

The user interaction is done through the web based application which uses the hadoop platform through the Java API. The contents are stored in the column –

Figure 2. Architecture

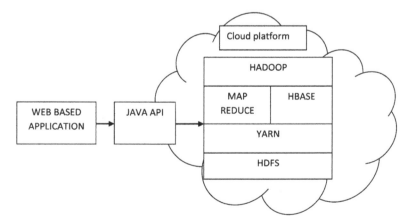

oriented Hbase which combines the scalability of the Hadoop Distributed file system with the real – time data access and a deep analytic capability of Map Reduce. The profile details and the content they are to access are stored in hbase. The working of the architecture is explained as follows.

- The student access the contents through the internet stored in hadoop environment.
- Usage patterns are collected and all the details are analytics are performed.
- The results are then generated.
- Usage behaviour is then predicted.
- This prediction and the analytics results are sent as feedback to the teachers.
- This helps the teachers to intervene if necessary.

This working can be put in a flowchart as shown Figure 3.

END USERS

The end users who use these databases include the students, teachers, school management of a particular school and the administrator. An authentication hierarchy is required for the users. Figure 4 explains the hierarchy here.

Here the administrator is in the highest level of the authentication hierarchy who has the access to all other end users and the content. He has the authority to add, delete or edit the contents. The other end users provide the details and register here if they are would prefer to. The next lower level of hierarchy is the school management who has the access to the staffs or the students of the particular school. They provide the details to the administrator and get themselves enrolled in the smart educational system. Then goes the staff that could access the contents and the students they are responsible for. The last one is the students who benefits from this online educational system.

CONTENT UPLOAD

Here the contents are vast and may be of any type like audio, video, pdf, podcast, gaming etc. A same concept is uploaded in different formats. The students have access to the variety of information provided in the web. The information and the content is categorised as per the grade of the appropriate student. The administrator has total access i.e. adds, deletes and edits the contents.

Figure 3. Flowchart

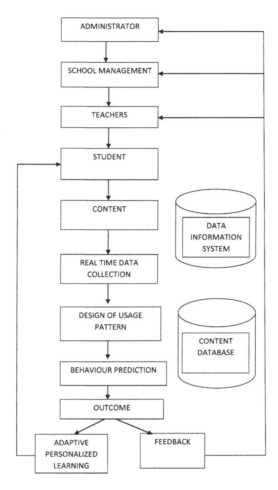

EXPERIMENTS AND RESULTS

Figure 5 describes the overall experiment of the smart educational system with the help of big data analytics in a cloud platform.

An experiment was conducted for a set of 50 students for 5 subjects. The subjects include maths, science, English, history and geography. Each subject included 10 units. Profile details were created for the students, the staffs and the school administration. A unique username and password was assigned to all the students, principal, teachers. As the student enters the website through the user name and the password, the profile details would be displayed. They are then open to all the information relating to the

Figure 4. Authentication hierarchy

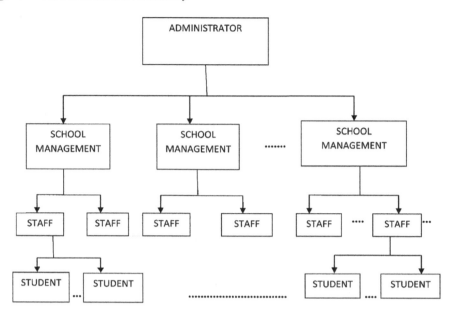

Figure 5. Smart educational system

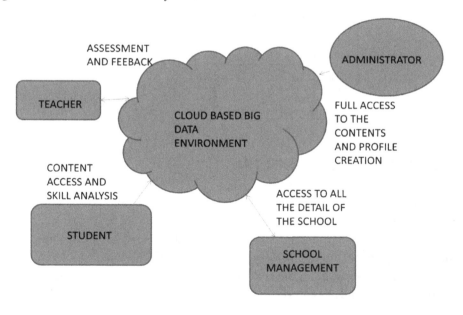

subject. The students can access the contents of their respective cadre. The contents are of various types like pdf, podcasts, video, gaming etc.

ANALYSIS AND FEEDBACK

The students were then subjected to tests. These tests were required to test their learning skills. Among various skill sets, only four set of skills namely knowledge based skills, comprehensive skills, analytical skills and synthetic skills were analysed here. The test pattern was split up such that the skills can be analysed separately. For each and every subjects and concepts that are included, these analyses were done. The results were obtained and statistical analyses were performed on them individually. The analysis reveals the behaviour of the student. The time of login and the logout are also noted. Finally, an overall predictive analysis was performed. These results are put in the feedback page of the student. This helps the teacher in assessing the students and intervenes and assists them if necessary.

CONCLUSION

Technology is one of the most valuable tools that are available every day. Providing education using this technology has transformed the traditional educational system from teacher centric to learner centric. This system of education using big data provides a platform where all kinds of data are available to the student. This exhibits as an information highway. The big data platform helps to analyze the performance and skill levels of individual students and create a personalized learning experience that meets the specific needs. Dropout rates in schools can be reduced by enhancing the learning experience and improving the performance of the students. Implementing this big data concept in cloud increases the flexibility and scalability.

Related References

To continue IGI Global's long-standing tradition of advancing innovation through emerging research, please find below a compiled list of recommended IGI Global book chapters and journal articles in the areas of risk assessment, project management, and portfolio management. These related readings will provide additional information and guidance to further enrich your knowledge and assist you with your own research.

Abdullah, M., Ahmad, R., Peck, L. S., Kasirun, Z. M., & Alshammari, F. (2014). Benefits of CMM and CMMI-based software process improvement. In *Software design and development: Concepts, methodologies, tools, and applications* (pp. 1385–1400). Hershey, PA: IGI Global. doi:10.4018/978-1-4666-4301-7.ch067

Abu-Shanab, E., & Ghaleb, O. (2012). Adoption of mobile commerce technology: An involvement of trust and risk concerns. *International Journal of Technology Diffusion*, 3(2), 36–49. doi:10.4018/jtd.2012040104

Adapa, S. (2013). Electronic retailing of prepared food in Australia. In K. Tarnay, S. Imre, & L. Xu (Eds.), *Research and development in e-business through service-oriented solutions* (pp. 280–292). Hershey, PA: IGI Global. doi:10.4018/978-1-4666-4181-5.ch014

Aklouf, Y., & Drias, H. (2011). An adaptive e-commerce architecture for enterprise information exchange. In *Enterprise information systems: Concepts, methodologies, tools and applications* (pp. 329–345). Hershey, PA: IGI Global. doi:10.4018/978-1-61692-852-0.ch202

Al-Nawayseh, M. K., Alnabhan, M. M., Al-Debei, M. M., & Balachandran, W. (2013). An adaptive decision support system for last mile logistics in e-commerce: A study on online grocery shopping. *International Journal of Decision Support System Technology*, 5(1), 40–65. doi:10.4018/jdsst.2013010103

Al-Somali, S. A., Clegg, B., & Gholami, R. (2013). An investigation into the adoption and implementation of electronic commerce in Saudi Arabian small and medium enterprises. In *Small and medium enterprises: Concepts, methodologies, tools, and applications* (pp. 816–839). Hershey, PA: IGI Global. doi:10.4018/978-1-4666-3886-0.ch040

Al-Somali, S. A., Gholami, R., & Clegg, B. (2013). An investigation into the adoption of electronic commerce among Saudi Arabian SMEs. In M. Khosrow-Pour (Ed.), *E-commerce for organizational development and competitive advantage* (pp. 126–150). Hershey, PA: IGI Global. doi:10.4018/978-1-4666-3622-4.ch007

Alavi, S. (2013). Collaborative customer relationship management-co-creation and collaboration through online communities. *International Journal of Virtual Communities and Social Networking*, *5*(1), 1–18. doi:10.4018/jvcsn.2013010101

Alavi, S., & Ahuja, V. (2013). E-commerce in a web 2.0 world: Using online business communities to impact consumer price sensitivity. *International Journal of Online Marketing*, *3*(2), 38–55. doi:10.4018/ijom.2013040103

Alawneh, A., Al-Refai, H., & Batiha, K. (2011). E-business adoption by Jordanian banks: An exploratory study of the key factors and performance indicators. In A. Tatnall (Ed.), *Actor-network theory and technology innovation: Advancements and new concepts* (pp. 113–128). Hershey, PA: IGI Global. doi:10.4018/978-1-60960-197-3.ch008

Albuquerque, S. L., & Gondim, P. R. (2012). Applying continuous authentication to protect electronic transactions. In T. Chou (Ed.), *Information assurance and security technologies for risk assessment and threat management: Advances* (pp. 134–161). Hershey, PA: IGI Global. doi:10.4018/978-1-61350-507-6.ch005

Alfahl, H., Sanzogni, L., & Houghton, L. (2012). Mobile commerce adoption in organizations: A literature review and future research directions. *Journal of Electronic Commerce in Organizations*, *10*(2), 61–78. doi:10.4018/jeco.2012040104

Aloini, D., Dulmin, R., & Mininno, V. (2013). E-procurement: What really matters in B2B e-reverse auctions. In P. Ordóñez de Pablos, J. Lovelle, J. Gayo, & R. Tennyson (Eds.), *E-procurement management for successful electronic government systems* (pp. 87–113). Hershey, PA: IGI Global. doi:10.4018/978-1-4666-2119-0.ch006

Amer, M., & Gómez, J. M. (2010). Measuring B2C quality of electronic service: Towards a common consensus. In I. Lee (Ed.), *Encyclopedia of e-business development and management in the global economy* (pp. 135–143). Hershey, PA: IGI Global. doi:10.4018/978-1-61520-611-7.ch014

Amer, M., & Gómez, J. M. (2012). Measuring quality of electronic services: Moving from business-to-consumer into business-to-business marketplace. In E. Kajan, F. Dorloff, & I. Bedini (Eds.), *Handbook of research on e-business standards and protocols: Documents, data and advanced web technologies* (pp. 637–654). Hershey, PA: IGI Global. doi:10.4018/978-1-4666-0146-8.ch029

Andriole, S. J. (2010). Business technology strategy for an energy information company. *Journal of Information Technology Research*, *3*(3), 19–42. doi:10.4018/jitr.2010070103

Andriole, S. J. (2010). Templates for the development of business technology strategies. *Journal of Information Technology Research*, *3*(3), 1–10. doi:10.4018/jitr.2010070101

Archer, N. (2010). Electronic marketplace support for B2B business transactions. In *Electronic services: Concepts, methodologies, tools and applications* (pp. 85–93). Hershey, PA: IGI Global. doi:10.4018/978-1-61520-967-5.ch007

Archer, N. (2010). Management considerations for B2B online exchanges. In *Business information systems: Concepts, methodologies, tools and applications* (pp. 1740–1747). Hershey, PA: IGI Global. doi:10.4018/978-1-61520-969-9.ch105

Arduini, D., Nascia, L., & Zanfei, A. (2012). Complementary approaches to the diffusion of innovation: Empirical evidence on e-services adoption in Italy. *International Journal of E-Services and Mobile Applications*, *4*(3), 42–64. doi:10.4018/jesma.2012070103

Arh, T., Dimovski, V., & Blažic, B. J. (2011). ICT and web 2.0 technologies as a determinant of business performance. In M. Al-Mutairi & L. Mohammed (Eds.), *Cases on ICT utilization, practice and solutions: Tools for managing day-to-day issues* (pp. 59–77). Hershey, PA: IGI Global. doi:10.4018/978-1-60960-015-0.ch005

Arikpo, I., Osofisan, A., & Eteng, I. E. (2012). Enhancing trust in e-commerce in developing IT environments: A feedback-based perspective. In A. Usoro, G. Majewski, P. Ifinedo, & I. Arikpo (Eds.), *Leveraging developing economies with the use of information technology: Trends and tools* (pp. 193–203). Hershey, PA: IGI Global. doi:10.4018/978-1-4666-1637-0.ch011

Aryanto, V. D., & Chrismastuti, A. A. (2013). Model for digital economy in Indonesia. In I. Oncioiu (Ed.), *Business innovation, development, and advancement in the digital economy* (pp. 60–77). Hershey, PA: IGI Global. doi:10.4018/978-1-4666-2934-9.ch005

Asim, M., & Petkovic, M. (2012). Fundamental building blocks for security interoperability in e-business. In E. Kajan, F. Dorloff, & I. Bedini (Eds.), *Handbook of research on e-business standards and protocols: documents, data and advanced web technologies* (pp. 269–292). Hershey, PA: IGI Global. doi:10.4018/978-1-4666-0146-8.ch013

Askool, S., Jacobs, A., & Nakata, K. (2013). A method of analysing the use of social networking sites in business. In *IT policy and ethics: Concepts, methodologies, tools, and applications* (pp. 794–813). Hershey, PA: IGI Global. doi:10.4018/978-1-4666-2919-6.ch036

Association, I. R. (2013). Enterprise resource planning: Concepts, methodologies, tools, and applications (Vols. 1–3). Hershey, PA: IGI Global. doi:10.4018/978-1-4666-4153-2

Azab, N., & Khalifa, N. (2013). Web 2.0 and opportunities for entrepreneurs: How Egyptian entrepreneurs perceive and exploit web 2.0 technologies. In N. Azab (Ed.), *Cases on web 2.0 in developing countries: Studies on implementation, application, and use* (pp. 1–32). Hershey, PA: IGI Global. doi:10.4018/978-1-4666-2515-0.ch001

Azevedo, S. G., & Carvalho, H. (2012). RFID technology in the fashion supply chain: An exploratory analysis. In T. Choi (Ed.), *Fashion supply chain management: Industry and business analysis* (pp. 303–326). Hershey, PA: IGI Global. doi:10.4018/978-1-60960-756-2.ch017

Baporikar, N. (2013). ICT challenge for ebusiness in SMEs. *International Journal of Strategic Information Technology and Applications*, 4(1), 15–26. doi:10.4018/jsita.2013010102

Barbin Laurindo, F. J., Monteiro de Carvalho, M., & Shimizu, T. (2010). Strategic alignment between business and information technology. In M. Hunter (Ed.), *Strategic information systems: Concepts, methodologies, tools, and applications* (pp. 20–28). Hershey, PA: IGI Global. doi:10.4018/978-1-60566-677-8.ch002

Barjis, J. (2012). Software engineering security based on business process modeling. In K. Khan (Ed.), *Security-aware systems applications and software development methods* (pp. 52–68). Hershey, PA: IGI Global. doi:10.4018/978-1-4666-1580-9.ch004

Barnes, D., & Hinton, M. (2011). The benefits of an e-business performance measurement system. In N. Shi & G. Silvius (Eds.), *Enterprise IT governance, business value and performance measurement* (pp. 158–169). Hershey, PA: IGI Global. doi:10.4018/978-1-60566-346-3.ch011

Bask, A., Lipponen, M., & Tinnilä, M. (2012). E-commerce logistics: A literature research review and topics for future research. *International Journal of E-Services and Mobile Applications*, 4(3), 1–22. doi:10.4018/jesma.2012070101

Bask, A., & Tinnilä, M. (2013). Impact of product characteristics on supply chains: An analytical literature review. *International Journal of Applied Logistics*, 4(1), 35–59. doi:10.4018/jal.2013010103

Basu, S. (2012). Direct taxation and e-commerce: Possibility and desirability. In E. Druică (Ed.), *Digital economy innovations and impacts on society* (pp. 26–48). Hershey, PA: IGI Global. doi:10.4018/978-1-4666-1556-4.ch003

Beckinsale, M. (2010). E-business among ethnic minority businesses: The case of ethnic entrepreneurs. In B. Thomas & G. Simmons (Eds.), *E-commerce adoption and small business in the global marketplace: Tools for optimization* (pp. 187–207). Hershey, PA: IGI Global. doi:10.4018/978-1-60566-998-4.ch010

Beckinsale, M. (2011). eBusiness among ethnic minority businesses: Ethnic entrepreneurs' ICT adoption and readiness. In S. Sharma (Ed.), E-adoption and socio-economic impacts: Emerging infrastructural effects (pp. 168-189). Hershey, PA: IGI Global. doi:10.4018/978-1-60960-597-1.ch009

Bedini, I., Gardarin, G., & Nguyen, B. (2011). Semantic technologies and e-business. In E. Kajan (Ed.), *Electronic business interoperability: Concepts, opportunities and challenges* (pp. 243–278). Hershey, PA: IGI Global. doi:10.4018/978-1-60960-485-1.ch011

Beedle, J., & Wang, S. (2013). Roles of a technology leader. In S. Wang & T. Hartsell (Eds.), *Technology integration and foundations for effective leadership* (pp. 228–241). Hershey, PA: IGI Global. doi:10.4018/978-1-4666-2656-0.ch013

Belhajjame, K., & Brambilla, M. (2013). Ontological description and similarity-based discovery of business process models. In J. Krogstie (Ed.), *Frameworks for developing efficient information systems: Models, theory, and practice* (pp. 30–50). Hershey, PA: IGI Global. doi:10.4018/978-1-4666-4161-7.ch002

Benou, P., & Bitos, V. (2010). Developing mobile commerce applications. In M. Khosrow-Pour (Ed.), *E-commerce trends for organizational advancement: New applications and methods* (pp. 1–15). Hershey, PA: IGI Global. doi:10.4018/978-1-60566-964-9.ch001

Berisha-Namani, M. (2013). Information systems usage in business and management. In I. Oncioiu (Ed.), *Business innovation, development, and advancement in the digital economy* (pp. 48–59). Hershey, PA: IGI Global. doi:10.4018/978-1-4666-2934-9.ch004

Bermúdez, G. M., & Rojas, L. A. (2013). Model-driven engineering for electronic commerce. In V. Díaz, J. Lovelle, B. García-Bustelo, & O. Martínez (Eds.), *Progressions and innovations in model-driven software engineering* (pp. 196–208). Hershey, PA: IGI Global. doi:10.4018/978-1-4666-4217-1.ch007

Bernardino, J. (2013). Open business intelligence for better decision-making. *International Journal of Information Communication Technologies and Human Development*, 5(2), 20–36. doi:10.4018/jicthd.2013040102

Berzins, M. (2012). Scams and the Australian e-business environment. In K. Mohammed Rezaul (Ed.), *Strategic and pragmatic e-business: Implications for future business practices* (pp. 156–175). Hershey, PA: IGI Global. doi:10.4018/978-1-4666-1619-6.ch007

Binsaleh, M., & Hassan, S. (2011). Systems development methodology for mobile commerce applications. *International Journal of Mobile Computing and Multimedia Communications*, 3(4), 36–52. doi:10.4018/jmcmc.2011100103

Binsaleh, M., & Hassan, S. (2013). Systems development methodology for mobile commerce applications. In I. Khalil & E. Weippl (Eds.), *Contemporary challenges and solutions for mobile and multimedia technologies* (pp. 146–162). Hershey, PA: IGI Global. doi:10.4018/978-1-4666-2163-3.ch009

Blake, R., Gordon, S., & Shankaranarayanan, G. (2013). The role of case-based research in information technology and systems. In P. Isaias & M. Baptista Nunes (Eds.), *Information systems research and exploring social artifacts: approaches and methodologies* (pp. 200–220). Hershey, PA: IGI Global. doi:10.4018/978-1-4666-2491-7.ch011

Boateng, R., Heeks, R., Molla, A., & Hinson, R. (2013). Advancing e-commerce beyond readiness in a developing country: Experiences of Ghanaian firms. In M. Khosrow-Pour (Ed.), *E-commerce for organizational development and competitive advantage* (pp. 1–17). Hershey, PA: IGI Global. doi:10.4018/978-1-4666-3622-4.ch001

Bonfatti, F., Monari, P. D., & Martinelli, L. (2011). Business document exchange between small companies. In E. Kajan (Ed.), *Electronic business interoperability: Concepts, opportunities and challenges* (pp. 482–510). Hershey, PA: IGI Global. doi:10.4018/978-1-60960-485-1.ch020

Boucadair, M., & Binet, D. (2014). Issues with current internet architecture. In M. Boucadair & D. Binet (Eds.), *Solutions for sustaining scalability in internet growth* (pp. 1–16). Hershey, PA: IGI Global. doi:10.4018/978-1-4666-4305-5.ch001

Bouras, A., Gouvas, P., & Mentzas, G. (2009). A semantic service-oriented architecture for business process fusion. In I. Lee (Ed.), *Electronic business: Concepts, methodologies, tools, and applications* (pp. 504–532). Hershey, PA: IGI Global. doi:10.4018/978-1-60566-056-1.ch032

Braun, P. (2011). Advancing women in the digital economy: eLearning opportunities for meta-competency skilling. In *Global business: Concepts, methodologies, tools and applications* (pp. 1978–1990). Hershey, PA: IGI Global. doi:10.4018/978-1-60960-587-2.ch708

Brown, M., & Garson, G. (2013). Organization behavior and organization theory. In *Public information management and e-government: Policy and issues* (pp. 160–195). Hershey, PA: IGI Global. doi:10.4018/978-1-4666-3003-1.ch007

Brown, M., & Garson, G. (2013). The information technology business model. In *Public information management and e-government: Policy and issues* (pp. 76–98). Hershey, PA: IGI Global. doi:10.4018/978-1-4666-3003-1.ch004

Burete, R., Badica, A., Badica, C., & Moraru, F. (2011). Enhanced reputation model with forgiveness for e-business agents. *International Journal of Agent Technologies and Systems*, 3(1), 11–26. doi:10.4018/jats.2011010102

Business Research and Case Center. (2011). *Cases on business and management in the MENA region: New trends and opportunities.* Hershey, PA: IGI Global. doi:10.4018/978-1-60960-583-4

Bwalya, K. J. (2011). E-commerce penetration in the SADC region: Consolidating and moving forward. In M. Cruz-Cunha & J. Varajão (Eds.), *E-business managerial aspects, solutions and case studies* (pp. 235–253). Hershey, PA: IGI Global. doi:10.4018/978-1-60960-463-9.ch014

Charbaji, R., Rebeiz, K., & Sidani, Y. (2010). Antecedents and consequences of the risk taking behavior of mobile commerce adoption in Lebanon. In H. Rahman (Ed.), *Handbook of research on e-government readiness for information and service exchange: Utilizing progressive information communication technologies* (pp. 354–380). Hershey, PA: IGI Global. doi:10.4018/978-1-60566-671-6.ch018

Chaturvedi, N. (2013). Collaborative web for natural resources industries. In *Supply chain management: Concepts, methodologies, tools, and applications* (pp. 601–614). Hershey, PA: IGI Global. doi:10.4018/978-1-4666-2625-6.ch035

Chen, C., & Yang, S. C. (2008). E-commerce and mobile commerce application adoptions. In A. Becker (Ed.), *Electronic commerce: Concepts, methodologies, tools, and applications* (pp. 826–836). Hershey, PA: IGI Global. doi:10.4018/978-1-59904-943-4.ch068

Chen, Q., & Zhang, N. (2013). IT-supported business performance and e-commerce application in SMEs. *Journal of Electronic Commerce in Organizations, 11*(2), 41–52. doi:10.4018/jeco.2013040104

Chen, T. F. (2011). Emerging business models: Value drivers in e-business 2.0 and towards enterprise 2.0. In T. Chen (Ed.), *Implementing new business models in for-profit and non-profit organizations: Technologies and applications* (pp. 1–28). Hershey, PA: IGI Global. doi:10.4018/978-1-60960-129-4.ch001

Chen, T. F. (2011). The critical success factors and integrated model for implementing e-business in Taiwan's SMEs. In *Global business: Concepts, methodologies, tools and applications* (pp. 1109–1133). Hershey, PA: IGI Global. doi:10.4018/978-1-60960-587-2.ch416

Chew, E., & Gottschalk, P. (2013). Critical success factors of IT strategy. In *Knowledge driven service innovation and management: IT strategies for business alignment and value creation* (pp. 185–220). Hershey, PA: IGI Global. doi:10.4018/978-1-4666-2512-9.ch006

Chew, E., & Gottschalk, P. (2013). Strategic alignment and IT-enabled value creation. In *Knowledge driven service innovation and management: IT strategies for business alignment and value creation* (pp. 141–184). Hershey, PA: IGI Global. doi:10.4018/978-1-4666-2512-9.ch005

Chew, E., & Gottschalk, P. (2013). Theories and models of service-oriented firms. In *Knowledge driven service innovation and management: IT strategies for business alignment and value creation* (pp. 1–34). Hershey, PA: IGI Global. doi:10.4018/978-1-4666-2512-9.ch001

Chiang, L. (2010). Digital confidence in business: A perspective of information ethics. In M. Pankowska (Ed.), *Infonomics for distributed business and decision-making environments: Creating information system ecology* (pp. 288–300). Hershey, PA: IGI Global. doi:10.4018/978-1-60566-890-1.ch017

Chugh, R., & Gupta, P. (2011). A unified view of enablers, barriers, and readiness of small to medium enterprises for e-business adoption. In M. Cruz-Cunha & J. Varajão (Eds.), *E-business issues, challenges and opportunities for SMEs: Driving competitiveness* (pp. 291–312). Hershey, PA: IGI Global. doi:10.4018/978-1-61692-880-3.ch017

Clear, F., Woods, A., & Dickson, K. (2013). SME adoption and use of ICT for networked trading purposes: The influence of sector, size and age of firm. In *Small and medium enterprises: Concepts, methodologies, tools, and applications* (pp. 774–791). Hershey, PA: IGI Global. doi:10.4018/978-1-4666-3886-0.ch038

Connolly, R. (2013). eCommerce trust beliefs: Examining the role of national culture. In P. Isaias & M. Baptista Nunes (Eds.), Information systems research and exploring social artifacts: Approaches and methodologies (pp. 20-42). Hershey, PA: IGI Global. doi:10.4018/978-1-4666-2491-7.ch002

Cormican, K. (2013). Collaborative networks: Challenges for SMEs. In *Small and medium enterprises: Concepts, methodologies, tools, and applications* (pp. 1638–1653). Hershey, PA: IGI Global. doi:10.4018/978-1-4666-3886-0.ch083

Costante, E., Petkovic, M., & den Hartog, J. (2013). Trust management and user's trust perception in e-business. In *IT policy and ethics: Concepts, methodologies, tools, and applications* (pp. 64–83). Hershey, PA: IGI Global. doi:10.4018/978-1-4666-2919-6.ch004

Costin, Y. (2012). Adopting ICT in the mompreneurs business: A strategy for growth? In C. Romm Livermore (Ed.), *Gender and social computing: Interactions, differences and relationships* (pp. 17–34). Hershey, PA: Information Science Publishing. doi:10.4018/978-1-60960-759-3.ch002

Cox, S. (2013). E-business planning in morphing organizations: Maturity models of business transformation. In E. Li, S. Loh, C. Evans, & F. Lorenzi (Eds.), *Organizations and social networking: Utilizing social media to engage consumers* (pp. 286–312). Hershey, PA: IGI Global. doi:10.4018/978-1-4666-4026-9.ch015

Cruz-Cunha, M. M., Moreira, F., & Varajão, J. (2014). *Handbook of research on enterprise 2.0: Technological, social, and organizational dimensions*. Hershey, PA: IGI Global. doi:10.4018/978-1-4666-4373-4

D'Aubeterre, F., Iyer, L. S., Ehrhardt, R., & Singh, R. (2011). Discovery process in a B2B emarketplace: A semantic matchmaking approach. In V. Sugumaran (Ed.), *Intelligent, adaptive and reasoning technologies: New developments and applications* (pp. 80–103). Hershey, PA: IGI Global. doi:10.4018/978-1-60960-595-7.ch005

Dabbagh, R. A. (2011). E-business: Concepts and context with illustrative examples of e-business and e-commerce in education. In A. Al Ajeeli & Y. Al-Bastaki (Eds.), *Handbook of research on e-services in the public sector: E-government strategies and advancements* (pp. 450–462). Hershey, PA: IGI Global. doi:10.4018/978-1-61520-789-3.ch033

Demirkan, H., & Spohrer, J. C. (2012). Servitized enterprises for distributed collaborative commerce. In S. Galup (Ed.), *Technological applications and advancements in service science, management, and engineering* (pp. 70–83). Hershey, PA: IGI Global. doi:10.4018/978-1-4666-1583-0.ch005

Denno, P. (2013). Trade collaboration systems. In *Supply chain management: Concepts, methodologies, tools, and applications* (pp. 615–633). Hershey, PA: IGI Global. doi:10.4018/978-1-4666-2625-6.ch036

Djoleto, W. (2011). E-business efficacious consequences the etiquettes and the business decision making. In O. Bak & N. Stair (Eds.), *Impact of e-business technologies on public and private organizations: Industry comparisons and perspectives* (pp. 278–295). Hershey, PA: IGI Global. doi:10.4018/978-1-60960-501-8.ch017

Djoleto, W. (2013). Information technology and organisational leadership. In *Electronic commerce and organizational leadership: Perspectives and methodologies*. Hershey, PA: IGI Global. doi:10.4018/978-1-4666-2982-0.ch003

Djoleto, W. (2013). Cloud computing and ecommerce or ebusiness: "The now it way" – An overview. In *Electronic commerce and organizational leadership: Perspectives and methodologies* (pp. 239–254). Hershey, PA: IGI Global. doi:10.4018/978-1-4666-2982-0.ch010

Djoleto, W. (2013). eCommerce and organisational leadership. In Electronic commerce and organizational leadership: Perspectives and methodologies (pp. 99-121). Hershey, PA: IGI Global. doi:10.4018/978-1-4666-2982-0.ch005

Djoleto, W. (2013). eCommerce: An overview. In Electronic commerce and organizational leadership: Perspectives and methodologies (pp. 74-98). Hershey, PA: IGI Global. doi:10.4018/978-1-4666-2982-0.ch004

Djoleto, W. (2013). Empirical analyses of ecommerce: The findings – A mixed methodology perspective. In *Electronic commerce and organizational leadership: Perspectives and methodologies* (pp. 150–189). Hershey, PA: IGI Global. doi:10.4018/978-1-4666-2982-0.ch007

Djoleto, W. (2013). Future endeavours. In *Electronic commerce and organizational leadership: Perspectives and methodologies* (pp. 269–280). Hershey, PA: IGI Global. doi:10.4018/978-1-4666-2982-0.ch012

Djoleto, W. (2013). Information technology: The journey. In *Electronic commerce and organizational leadership: Perspectives and methodologies* (pp. 32–54). Hershey, PA: IGI Global. doi:10.4018/978-1-4666-2982-0.ch002

Doolin, B., & Ali, E. I. (2012). Mobile technology adoption in the supply chain. In *Wireless technologies: Concepts, methodologies, tools and applications* (pp. 1553–1573). Hershey, PA: IGI Global. doi:10.4018/978-1-61350-101-6.ch603

Duin, H., & Thoben, K. (2011). Enhancing the preparedness of SMEs for e-business opportunities by collaborative networks. In M. Cruz-Cunha & J. Varajão (Eds.), *E-business issues, challenges and opportunities for SMEs: Driving competitiveness* (pp. 30–45). Hershey, PA: IGI Global. doi:10.4018/978-1-61692-880-3.ch003

Dulai, T., Jaskó, S., & Tarnay, K. (2013). IOTP and payments protocols. In K. Tarnay, S. Imre, & L. Xu (Eds.), *Research and development in e-business through service-oriented solutions* (pp. 20–56). Hershey, PA: IGI Global. doi:10.4018/978-1-4666-4181-5.ch002

Dza, M., Fisher, R., & Gapp, R. (2013). Service-dominant logic and supply network management: An efficient business mix? In N. Ndubisi & S. Nwankwo (Eds.), *Enterprise development in SMEs and entrepreneurial firms: Dynamic processes* (pp. 376–389). Hershey, PA: IGI Global. doi:10.4018/978-1-4666-2952-3.ch021

Ehsani, E. (2011). Defining e-novation in action. In H. Pattinson & D. Low (Eds.), *E-novation for competitive advantage in collaborative globalization: Technologies for emerging e-business strategies* (pp. 58–74). Hershey, PA: IGI Global. doi:10.4018/978-1-60566-394-4.ch005

Ekong, U. O., Ifinedo, P., Ayo, C. K., & Ifinedo, A. (2013). E-commerce adoption in Nigerian businesses: An analysis using the technology-organization-environmental framework. In *Small and medium enterprises: Concepts, methodologies, tools, and applications* (pp. 840–861). Hershey, PA: IGI Global. doi:10.4018/978-1-4666-3886-0.ch041

Emens, S. (2010). The new paradigm of business on the internet and its ethical implications. In D. Palmer (Ed.), *Ethical issues in e-business: Models and frameworks* (pp. 15–27). Hershey, PA: IGI Global. doi:10.4018/978-1-61520-615-5.ch002

Eriksson, P., Henttonen, E., & Meriläinen, S. (2011). Managing client contacts of small KIBS companies: Turning technology into business. *International Journal of Innovation in the Digital Economy*, 2(3), 1–10. doi:10.4018/jide.2011070101

Escofet, E., Rodríguez-Fórtiz, M. J., Garrido, J. L., & Chung, L. (2012). Strategic e-business/ IT alignment for SME competitiveness. In *Computer engineering: Concepts, methodologies, tools and applications* (pp. 1427–1445). Hershey, PA: IGI Global. doi:10.4018/978-1-61350-456-7.ch604

Eze, U. C., & Poong, Y. S. (2013). Consumers' intention to use mobile commerce and the moderating roles of gender and income. In I. Lee (Ed.), *Strategy, adoption, and competitive advantage of mobile services in the global economy* (pp. 127–148). Hershey, PA: IGI Global. doi:10.4018/978-1-4666-1939-5.ch007

Eze, U. C., & Poong, Y. S. (2013). The moderating roles of income and age in mobile commerce application. *Journal of Electronic Commerce in Organizations*, *11*(3), 46–67. doi:10.4018/jeco.2013070103

Fehér, P. (2012). Integrating and measuring business and technology services in the context of enterprise architecture. In V. Shankararaman, J. Zhao, & J. Lee (Eds.), *Business enterprise, process, and technology management: Models and applications* (pp. 148–163). Hershey, PA: IGI Global. doi:10.4018/978-1-4666-0249-6.ch008

Feja, S., Witt, S., & Speck, A. (2014). Tool based integration of requirements modeling and validation into business process modeling. In *Software design and development: Concepts, methodologies, tools, and applications* (pp. 285–309). Hershey, PA: IGI Global. doi:10.4018/978-1-4666-4301-7.ch016

Fengel, J. (2012). Semantic alignment of e-business standards and legacy models. In E. Kajan, F. Dorloff, & I. Bedini (Eds.), *Handbook of research on e-business standards and protocols: Documents, data and advanced web technologies* (pp. 676–704). Hershey, PA: IGI Global. doi:10.4018/978-1-4666-0146-8.ch031

Ferreira, M. P. (2013). SMEs and e-business: Implementation, strategies and policy. In *Small and medium enterprises: Concepts, methodologies, tools, and applications* (pp. 97–117). Hershey, PA: IGI Global. doi:10.4018/978-1-4666-3886-0.ch006

Fluvià, M., & Rigall-I-Torrent, R. (2013). Public sector transformation and the design of public policies for electronic commerce and the new economy: Tax and antitrust policies. In N. Pomazalová (Ed.), *Public sector transformation processes and internet public procurement: Decision support systems* (pp. 32–57). Hershey, PA: IGI Global. doi:10.4018/978-1-4666-2665-2.ch003

Franquesa, J., & Brandyberry, A. (2011). Organizational slack and information technology innovation adoption in SMEs. In I. Lee (Ed.), *E-business applications for product development and competitive growth: emerging technologies* (pp. 25–48). Hershey, PA: IGI Global. doi:10.4018/978-1-60960-132-4.ch002

Fries, T. P. (2014). Reengineering structured legacy system documentation to UML object-oriented artifacts. In *Software design and development: Concepts, methodologies, tools, and applications* (pp. 749–771). Hershey, PA: IGI Global. doi:10.4018/978-1-4666-4301-7.ch036

Galinski, C., & Beckmann, H. (2014). Concepts for enhancing content quality and eaccessibility: In general and in the field of eprocurement. In *Assistive technologies: Concepts, methodologies, tools, and applications* (pp. 180–197). Hershey, PA: IGI Global. doi:10.4018/978-1-4666-4422-9.ch010

Gan, J., & Gutiérrez, J. A. (2011). Viable business models for m-commerce: The key components. In M. Cruz-Cunha & F. Moreira (Eds.), *Handbook of research on mobility and computing: Evolving technologies and ubiquitous impacts* (pp. 837–852). Hershey, PA: IGI Global. doi:10.4018/978-1-60960-042-6.ch052

Garito, M. (2012). Mobile business and mobile TV: Available technologies, future opportunities and new marketing trends. In E-marketing: Concepts, methodologies, tools, and applications (pp. 1240-1251). Hershey, PA: IGI Global. doi:10.4018/978-1-4666-1598-4.ch072

Ghobakhloo, M., & Zulkifli, N. (2013). Adoption of mobile commerce: The impact of end user satisfaction on system acceptance. *International Journal of E-Services and Mobile Applications*, 5(1), 26–50. doi:10.4018/jesma.2013010102

Gill, A. Q., & Bunker, D. (2014). SaaS requirements engineering for agile development. In *Software design and development: Concepts, methodologies, tools, and applications* (pp. 351–380). Hershey, PA: IGI Global. doi:10.4018/978-1-4666-4301-7.ch019

Gimenez, J. (2014). Reflections of professional practice: Using electronic discourse analysis networks (EDANs) to examine embedded business emails. In H. Lim & F. Sudweeks (Eds.), *Innovative methods and technologies for electronic discourse analysis* (pp. 327–345). Hershey, PA: IGI Global. doi:10.4018/978-1-4666-4426-7.ch015

Gionis, G. A., Schroth, C., & Janner, T. (2011). Advancing interoperability for agile cross-organisational collaboration: A rule-based approach. In Y. Charalabidis (Ed.), *Interoperability in digital public services and administration: Bridging e-government and e-business* (pp. 238–253). Hershey, PA: IGI Global. doi:10.4018/978-1-61520-887-6.ch013

Gnoni, M. G., & Rollo, A. (2011). A content analysis for evaluating RFID applications in supply network management. In I. Mahdavi, S. Mohebbi, & N. Cho (Eds.), *Electronic supply network coordination in intelligent and dynamic environments: Modeling and implementation* (pp. 93–112). Hershey, PA: IGI Global. doi:10.4018/978-1-60566-808-6.ch004

Gonçalves, A., Serra, N., Serra, J., & Sousa, P. (2011). How to use information technology effectively to achieve business objectives. In M. Cruz-Cunha & J. Varajao (Eds.), *Enterprise information systems design, implementation and management: Organizational applications* (pp. 21–37). Hershey, PA: IGI Global. doi:10.4018/978-1-61692-020-3.ch002

Gordini, N., & Veglio, V. (2014). Customer relationship management and data mining: A classification decision tree to predict customer purchasing behavior in global market. In P. Vasant (Ed.), *Handbook of research on novel soft computing intelligent algorithms: Theory and practical applications* (pp. 1–40). Hershey, PA: IGI Global. doi:10.4018/978-1-4666-4450-2.ch001

Gottschalk, P. (2007). The CIO developing e-business. In P. Gottschalk (Ed.), *CIO and corporate strategic management: Changing role of CIO to CEO* (pp. 148–185). Hershey, PA: IGI Global. doi:10.4018/978-1-59904-423-1.ch007

Goutam, S. (2010). Analysis of speedy uptake of electronic and digital signatures in digital economy with special reference to India. In E. Adomi (Ed.), *Frameworks for ICT policy: Government, social and legal issues* (pp. 76–88). Hershey, PA: IGI Global. doi:10.4018/978-1-61692-012-8.ch005

Grieger, M., Hartmann, E., & Kotzab, H. (2011). E-markets as meta-enterprise information e systems. In *Enterprise information systems: Concepts, methodologies, tools and applications* (pp. 638–647). Hershey, PA: IGI Global. doi:10.4018/978-1-61692-852-0.ch306

Ha, H. (2012). Online security and consumer protection in ecommerce an Australian case. In K. Mohammed Rezaul (Ed.), *Strategic and pragmatic e-business: Implications for future business practices* (pp. 217–243). Hershey, PA: IGI Global. doi:10.4018/978-1-4666-1619-6.ch010

Ha, H., Coghill, K., & Maharaj, E. A. (2012). Current measures to protect e-consumers' privacy in Australia. In *Cyber crime: Concepts, methodologies, tools and applications* (pp. 1728–1755). Hershey, PA: IGI Global. doi:10.4018/978-1-61350-323-2.ch806

Halas, H., & Klobucar, T. (2011). Business models and organizational processes changes. In *Global business: Concepts, methodologies, tools and applications* (pp. 192–205). Hershey, PA: IGI Global. doi:10.4018/978-1-60960-587-2.ch113

Han, B. (2012). I play, I pay? An investigation of the users willingness to pay on hedonic social network sites. *International Journal of Virtual Communities and Social Networking*, 4(1), 19–31. doi:10.4018/jvcsn.2012010102

Harnesk, D. (2011). Convergence of information security in B2B networks. In E. Kajan (Ed.), *Electronic business interoperability: Concepts, opportunities and challenges* (pp. 571–595). Hershey, PA: IGI Global. doi:10.4018/978-1-60960-485-1.ch023

Harwood, T. (2012). Emergence of gamified commerce: Turning virtual to real. *Journal of Electronic Commerce in Organizations*, *10*(2), 16–39. doi:10.4018/jeco.2012040102

Heravi, B. R., & Lycett, M. (2012). Semantically enriched e-business standards development: The case of ebXML business process specification schema. In E. Kajan, F. Dorloff, & I. Bedini (Eds.), *Handbook of research on e-business standards and protocols: Documents, data and advanced web technologies* (pp. 655–675). Hershey, PA: IGI Global. doi:10.4018/978-1-4666-0146-8.ch030

Hill, D. S. (2012). An examination of standardized product identification and business benefit. In E. Kajan, F. Dorloff, & I. Bedini (Eds.), *Handbook of research on e-business standards and protocols: Documents, data and advanced web technologies* (pp. 387–411). Hershey, PA: IGI Global. doi:10.4018/978-1-4666-0146-8.ch018

Hoops, D. S. (2011). Legal issues in the virtual world and e-commerce. In B. Ciaramitaro (Ed.), *Virtual worlds and e-commerce: Technologies and applications for building customer relationships* (pp. 186–204). Hershey, PA: IGI Global. doi:10.4018/978-1-61692-808-7.ch010

Hu, W., Zuo, Y., Kaabouch, N., & Chen, L. (2010). A technological perspective of mobile and electronic commerce systems. In M. Khosrow-Pour (Ed.), *E-commerce trends for organizational advancement: New applications and methods* (pp. 16–35). Hershey, PA: IGI Global. doi:10.4018/978-1-60566-964-9.ch002

Hua, G. B. (2013). *Implementing IT business strategy in the construction industry*. Hershey, PA: IGI Global. doi:10.4018/978-1-4666-4185-3

Hua, S. C., Rajesh, M. J., & Theng, L. B. (2011). Determinants of e-commerce adoption among small and medium-sized enterprises in Malaysia. In S. Sharma (Ed.), *E-adoption and socio-economic impacts: Emerging infrastructural effects* (pp. 71–89). Hershey, PA: IGI Global. doi:10.4018/978-1-60960-597-1.ch005

Huang, J., & Dang, J. (2011). Context-sensitive ontology matching in electronic business. In E. Kajan (Ed.), *Electronic business interoperability: Concepts, opportunities and challenges* (pp. 279–301). Hershey, PA: IGI Global. doi:10.4018/978-1-60960-485-1.ch012

Hunaiti, Z., Tairo, D., Sedoyeka, E., & Elgazzar, S. (2010). Factors facing mobile commerce deployment in United Kingdom. In W. Hu & Y. Zuo (Eds.), *Handheld computing for mobile commerce: Applications, concepts and technologies* (pp. 109–123). Hershey, PA: IGI Global. doi:10.4018/978-1-61520-761-9.ch007

Hung, W. J., Tsai, C., Hung, S., McQueen, R., & Jou, J. (2011). Evaluating web site support capabilities in sell-side B2B transaction processes: A longitudinal study of two industries in New Zealand and Taiwan. *Journal of Global Information Management*, *19*(1), 51–79. doi:10.4018/jgim.2011010103

Hunter, M. G. (2013). The duality of information technology roles: A case study. In C. Howard (Ed.), *Strategic adoption of technological innovations* (pp. 38–49). Hershey, PA: IGI Global. doi:10.4018/978-1-4666-2782-6.ch003

Huq, N., Shah, S. M., & Mihailescu, D. (2012). Why select an open source ERP over proprietary ERP? A focus on SMEs and supplier's perspective. In R. Atem de Carvalho & B. Johansson (Eds.), *Free and open source enterprise resource planning: Systems and strategies* (pp. 33–55). Hershey, PA: IGI Global. doi:10.4018/978-1-61350-486-4.ch003

Ingvaldsen, J., & Gulla, J. (2010). Semantic business process mining of SAP transactions. In M. Wang & Z. Sun (Eds.), *Handbook of research on complex dynamic process management: Techniques for adaptability in turbulent environments* (pp. 416–429). Hershey, PA: IGI Global. doi:10.4018/978-1-60566-669-3.ch017

Ingvaldsen, J., & Gulla, J. (2011). Semantic business process mining of SAP transactions. In *Enterprise information systems: Concepts, methodologies, tools and applications* (pp. 866–878). Hershey, PA: IGI Global. doi:10.4018/978-1-61692-852-0.ch320

Ioannou, M. (2013). Customer relationship management (CRM): A one-size-fits-all philosophy? In H. Kaufmann & M. Panni (Eds.), *Customer-centric marketing strategies: Tools for building organizational performance* (pp. 150–170). Hershey, PA: IGI Global. doi:10.4018/978-1-4666-2524-2.ch008

Islam, M. S., & Scupola, A. (2013). E-service research trends in the domain of e-government: A contemporary study. In A. Scupola (Ed.), *Mobile opportunities and applications for e-service innovations* (pp. 152–169). Hershey, PA: IGI Global. doi:10.4018/978-1-4666-2654-6.ch009

Jailani, N., Patel, A., Mukhtar, M., Abdullah, S., & Yahya, Y. (2010). Concept of an agent-based electronic marketplace. In I. Lee (Ed.), *Encyclopedia of e-business development and management in the global economy* (pp. 239–251). Hershey, PA: IGI Global. doi:10.4018/978-1-61520-611-7.ch024

Johns, R. (2011). Technology, trust and B2B relationships: A banking perspective. In O. Bak & N. Stair (Eds.), *Impact of e-business technologies on public and private organizations: Industry comparisons and perspectives* (pp. 79–96). Hershey, PA: IGI Global. doi:10.4018/978-1-60960-501-8.ch005

Joshi, S. (2013). E-supply chain collaboration and integration: Implementation issues and challenges. In D. Graham, I. Manikas, & D. Folinas (Eds.), *E-logistics and e-supply chain management: Applications for evolving business* (pp. 9–26). Hershey, PA: IGI Global. doi:10.4018/978-1-4666-3914-0.ch002

Kamal, M., Qureshil, S., & Wolcott, P. (2013). Promoting competitive advantage in micro-enterprises through information technology interventions. In *Small and medium enterprises: Concepts, methodologies, tools, and applications* (pp. 581–606). Hershey, PA: IGI Global. doi:10.4018/978-1-4666-3886-0.ch030

Kamel, S. (2012). Electronic commerce prospects in emerging economies: Lessons from Egypt. In *Regional development: Concepts, methodologies, tools, and applications* (pp. 1104–1115). Hershey, PA: IGI Global. doi:10.4018/978-1-4666-0882-5.ch604

Kamoun, F., & Halaweh, M. (2012). User interface design and e-commerce security perception: An empirical study. *International Journal of E-Business Research*, 8(2), 15–32. doi:10.4018/jebr.2012040102

Karakaya, F. (2012). Business-to-consumers ecommerce: How companies use the internet in marketing products and services to consumers. In N. Delener (Ed.), *Service science research, strategy and innovation: Dynamic knowledge management methods* (pp. 227–244). Hershey, PA: IGI Global. doi:10.4018/978-1-4666-0077-5.ch014

Karakaya, F. (2013). B2B ecommerce: Current practices. In *Supply chain management: Concepts, methodologies, tools, and applications* (pp. 497–510). Hershey, PA: IGI Global. doi:10.4018/978-1-4666-2625-6.ch029

Karimov, F. P. (2013). Factors influencing e-commerce growth: A comparative study of central Asian transition economies. In S. Sharma (Ed.), *Adoption of virtual technologies for business, educational, and governmental advancements* (pp. 1–17). Hershey, PA: IGI Global. doi:10.4018/978-1-4666-2053-7.ch001

Kart, F., Moser, L. E., & Melliar-Smith, P. M. (2010). An automated supply chain management system and its performance evaluation. *International Journal of Information Systems and Supply Chain Management*, 3(2), 84–107. doi:10.4018/jisscm.2010040105

Kelarev, A. V., Brown, S., Watters, P., Wu, X., & Dazeley, R. (2011). Establishing reasoning communities of security experts for internet commerce security. In J. Yearwood & A. Stranieri (Eds.), *Technologies for supporting reasoning communities and collaborative decision making: Cooperative approaches* (pp. 380–396). Hershey, PA: IGI Global. doi:10.4018/978-1-60960-091-4.ch020

Kerr, D., Gammack, J. G., & Boddington, R. (2011). Overview of digital business security issues. In D. Kerr, J. Gammack, & K. Bryant (Eds.), *Digital business security development: Management technologies* (pp. 1–36). Hershey, PA: IGI Global. doi:10.4018/978-1-60566-806-2.ch001

Kerr, D., Gammack, J. G., & Bryant, K. (2011). *Digital business security development: Management technologies.* Hershey, PA: IGI Global. doi:10.4018/978-1-60566-806-2

Kett, H. (2013). A business model approach for service engineering in the internet of services. In P. Ordóñez de Pablos & R. Tennyson (Eds.), *Best practices and new perspectives in service science and management* (pp. 228–236). Hershey, PA: IGI Global. doi:10.4018/978-1-4666-3894-5.ch013

Khurana, R., & Aggarwal, R. (2013). *Interdisciplinary perspectives on business convergence, computing, and legality.* Hershey, PA: IGI Global. doi:10.4018/978-1-4666-4209-6

Kim, G., & Suh, Y. (2012). Building semantic business process space for agile and efficient business processes management: Ontology-based approach. In V. Shankararaman, J. Zhao, & J. Lee (Eds.), *Business enterprise, process, and technology management: Models and applications* (pp. 51–73). Hershey, PA: IGI Global. doi:10.4018/978-1-4666-0249-6.ch004

King, K. P., & Foley, J. J. (2012). 21st century learning opportunities for SME success: Maximizing technology tools and lifelong learning for innovation and impact. In *Human resources management: Concepts, methodologies, tools, and applications* (pp. 731–752). Hershey, PA: IGI Global. doi:10.4018/978-1-4666-1601-1.ch045

Kipp, A., & Schubert, L. (2011). E-business interoperability and collaboration. In E. Kajan (Ed.), *Electronic business interoperability: Concepts, opportunities and challenges* (pp. 153–184). Hershey, PA: IGI Global. doi:10.4018/978-1-60960-485-1.ch008

Klink, S., & Weiß, P. (2011). Social impact of collaborative services to maintain electronic business relationships. In *Virtual communities: Concepts, methodologies, tools and applications* (pp. 2011–2040). Hershey, PA: IGI Global. doi:10.4018/978-1-60960-100-3.ch609

Koumpis, A., & Protogeros, N. (2010). Doing business on the globalised networked economy: Technology and business challenges for accounting information systems. In M. Cruz-Cunha (Ed.), *Social, managerial, and organizational dimensions of enterprise information systems* (pp. 81–92). Hershey, PA: IGI Global. doi:10.4018/978-1-60566-856-7.ch004

Kritchanchai, D., Tan, A. W., & Hosie, P. (2010). An empirical investigation of third party logistics providers in Thailand: Barriers, motivation and usage of information technologies. *International Journal of Information Systems and Supply Chain Management, 3*(2), 68–83. doi:10.4018/jisscm.2010040104

Kritchanchai, D., Tan, A. W., & Hosie, P. (2012). An empirical investigation of third party logistics providers in Thailand: Barriers, motivation and usage of information technologies. In J. Wang (Ed.), *Information technologies, methods, and techniques of supply chain management* (pp. 272–288). Hershey, PA: IGI Global. doi:10.4018/978-1-4666-0918-1.ch016

Kumar, M. (2011). Role of web interface in building trust in B2B e-exchanges. In S. Chhabra & H. Rahman (Eds.), *Human development and global advancements through information communication technologies: New initiatives* (pp. 63–74). Hershey, PA: IGI Global. doi:10.4018/978-1-60960-497-4.ch005

Kumar, M., & Sareen, M. (2012). Trust theories and models of e-commerce. In *Trust and technology in B2B e-commerce: Practices and strategies for assurance* (pp. 58–77). Hershey, PA: IGI Global. doi:10.4018/978-1-61350-353-9.ch003

Kumar, M., Sareen, M., & Chhabra, S. (2013). Technology related trust issues in SME B2B e-commerce. In S. Chhabra (Ed.), *ICT influences on human development, interaction, and collaboration* (pp. 243–259). Hershey, PA: IGI Global. doi:10.4018/978-1-4666-1957-9.ch015

Kung, M. T., & Zhang, Y. (2011). Creating competitive markets for small businesses with new media and e-business strategy. *International Journal of E-Business Research, 7*(4), 31–49. doi:10.4018/jebr.2011100103

Kuo, D., Wong, D., Gao, J., & Chang, L. (2013). A 2D barcode validation system for mobile commerce. In W. Hu & S. Mousavinezhad (Eds.), *Mobile and handheld computing solutions for organizations and end-users* (pp. 1–19). Hershey, PA: IGI Global. doi:10.4018/978-1-4666-2785-7.ch001

Kyobe, M. (2010). E-crime and non-compliance with government regulations on e-commerce: Barriers to e-commerce optimization in South African SMEs. In B. Thomas & G. Simmons (Eds.), *E-commerce adoption and small business in the global marketplace: Tools for optimization* (pp. 47–66). Hershey, PA: IGI Global. doi:10.4018/978-1-60566-998-4.ch003

Lawrence, J. E. (2011). The growth of e-commerce in developing countries: An exploratory study of opportunities and challenges for SMEs. *International Journal of ICT Research and Development in Africa, 2*(1), 15–28. doi:10.4018/jictrda.2011010102

Lawrence, J. E. (2013). Barriers hindering ecommerce adoption: A case study of Kurdistan region of Iraq. In A. Zolait (Ed.), *Technology diffusion and adoption: Global complexity, global innovation* (pp. 152–165). Hershey, PA: IGI Global. doi:10.4018/978-1-4666-2791-8.ch010

Lee, I. (2012). B2B e-commerce, online auction, supply chain management, and e-collaboration. In *Electronic commerce management for business activities and global enterprises: Competitive advantages* (pp. 249–299). Hershey, PA: IGI Global. doi:10.4018/978-1-4666-1800-8.ch007

Lee, I. (2012). B2C online consumer behavior. In *Electronic commerce management for business activities and global enterprises: competitive advantages* (pp. 166–201). Hershey, PA: IGI Global. doi:10.4018/978-1-4666-1800-8.ch005

Lee, I. (2012). Introduction to e-commerce in the global economy. In *Electronic commerce management for business activities and global enterprises: Competitive advantages* (pp. 1–46). Hershey, PA: IGI Global. doi:10.4018/978-1-4666-1800-8.ch001

Lee, I. (2012). Mobile commerce. In *Electronic commerce management for business activities and global enterprises: Competitive advantages* (pp. 300–338). Hershey, PA: IGI Global. doi:10.4018/978-1-4666-1800-8.ch008

Lee, I. (2012). Online payment systems. In *Electronic commerce management for business activities and global enterprises: Competitive advantages* (pp. 340–365). Hershey, PA: IGI Global. doi:10.4018/978-1-4666-1800-8.ch009

Leonard, L. N. (2010). C2C mobile commerce: Acceptance factors. In I. Lee (Ed.), *Encyclopedia of e-business development and management in the global economy* (pp. 759–767). Hershey, PA: IGI Global. doi:10.4018/978-1-61520-611-7.ch076

Lertpittayapoom, N., & Paul, S. (2010). The roles of online intermediaries in collective memory-supported electronic negotiation. In *Electronic services: Concepts, methodologies, tools and applications* (pp. 1831–1847). Hershey, PA: IGI Global. doi:10.4018/978-1-61520-967-5.ch112

Li, L., Liu, C., Zhao, X., & Wang, J. (2011). Transactional properties of complex web services. In H. Leung, D. Chiu, & P. Hung (Eds.), *Service intelligence and service science: Evolutionary technologies and challenges* (pp. 21–34). Hershey, PA: IGI Global. doi:10.4018/978-1-61520-819-7.ch002

Li, X., & Lin, J. (2011). Call u back: An agent-based infrastructure for mobile commerce. *International Journal of E-Entrepreneurship and Innovation, 2*(2), 1–13. doi:10.4018/jeei.2011040101

Liao, Q., Luo, X., & Gurung, A. (2011). Trust restoration in electronic commerce. In S. Clarke & A. Dwivedi (Eds.), *Organizational and end-user interactions: New explorations* (pp. 72–88). Hershey, PA: IGI Global. doi:10.4018/978-1-60960-577-3.ch003

Liberato, N. A., Varajão, J. E., Correia, E. S., & Bessa, M. E. (2011). Location based e-commerce system: An architecture. In M. Cruz-Cunha & F. Moreira (Eds.), *Handbook of research on mobility and computing: Evolving technologies and ubiquitous impacts* (pp. 881–892). Hershey, PA: IGI Global. doi:10.4018/978-1-60960-042-6.ch055

Lim, S. Y., & Wong, S. F. (2012). Impact of applying aggregate query processing in mobile commerce. *International Journal of Business Data Communications and Networking, 8*(2), 1–17. doi:10.4018/jbdcn.2012040101

Lin, C., & Jalleh, G. (2013). Key issues and challenges for managing and evaluating B2B e-commerce projects within the Australian pharmaceutical supply chain. In *Supply chain management: Concepts, methodologies, tools, and applications* (pp. 1083–1100). Hershey, PA: IGI Global. doi:10.4018/978-1-4666-2625-6.ch064

Lin, C., Jalleh, G., & Huang, Y. (2013). E-business investment evaluation and outsourcing practices in Australian and Taiwanese hospitals: A comparative study. In K. Tarnay, S. Imre, & L. Xu (Eds.), *Research and development in e-business through service-oriented solutions* (pp. 244–266). Hershey, PA: IGI Global. doi:10.4018/978-1-4666-4181-5.ch012

Lin, C., Lin, H. K., Jalleh, G., & Huang, Y. (2011). Key adoption challenges and issues of B2B e-commerce in the healthcare sector. In M. Cruz-Cunha & F. Moreira (Eds.), *Handbook of research on mobility and computing: Evolving technologies and ubiquitous impacts* (pp. 175–187). Hershey, PA: IGI Global. doi:10.4018/978-1-60960-042-6.ch011

Liyanage, J. P. (2011). Copying with dynamic change: Collaborative business interfacing for SMEs under intergated eoperations. In M. Cruz-Cunha & J. Varajão (Eds.), *E-business managerial aspects, solutions and case studies* (pp. 136–147). Hershey, PA: IGI Global. doi:10.4018/978-1-60960-463-9.ch008

Liyanage, J. P. (2012). Hybrid intelligence through business socialization and networking: Managing complexities in the digital era. In M. Cruz-Cunha, P. Gonçalves, N. Lopes, E. Miranda, & G. Putnik (Eds.), *Handbook of research on business social networking: organizational, managerial, and technological dimensions* (pp. 567–582). Hershey, PA: IGI Global. doi:10.4018/978-1-61350-168-9.ch030

Loeser, F., Erek, K., & Zarnekow, R. (2013). Green IT strategies: A conceptual framework for the alignment of information technology and corporate sustainability strategy. In P. Ordóñez de Pablos (Ed.), *Green technologies and business practices: An IT approach* (pp. 58–95). Hershey, PA: IGI Global. doi:10.4018/978-1-4666-1972-2.ch004

Maamar, Z., Faci, N., Mostéfaoui, S. K., & Akhter, F. (2011). Towards a framework for weaving social networks into mobile commerce. *International Journal of Systems and Service-Oriented Engineering*, 2(3), 32–46. doi:10.4018/jssoe.2011070103

Mahmood, M. A., Gemoets, L., Hall, L. L., & López, F. J. (2011). Building business value in e-commerce enabled organizations: An empirical study. In *Global business: Concepts, methodologies, tools and applications* (pp. 229–253). Hershey, PA: IGI Global. doi:10.4018/978-1-60960-587-2.ch201

Mahran, A. F., & Enaba, H. M. (2013). Exploring determinants influencing the intention to use mobile payment service. In R. Eid (Ed.), *Managing customer trust, satisfaction, and loyalty through information communication technologies* (pp. 288–309). Hershey, PA: IGI Global. doi:10.4018/978-1-4666-3631-6.ch017

Marimuthu, M., Omar, A., Ramayah, T., & Mohamad, O. (2013). Readiness to adopt e-business among SMEs in Malaysia: Antecedents and consequence. In S. Sharma (Ed.), *Adoption of virtual technologies for business, educational, and governmental advancements* (pp. 18–36). Hershey, PA: IGI Global. doi:10.4018/978-1-4666-2053-7.ch002

Mayes, P. (2014). Interactive advertising: Displays of identity and stance on YouTube. In H. Lim & F. Sudweeks (Eds.), *Innovative methods and technologies for electronic discourse analysis* (pp. 260–284). Hershey, PA: IGI Global. doi:10.4018/978-1-4666-4426-7.ch012

McGrath, T. (2012). The reality of using standards for electronic business document formats. In E. Kajan, F. Dorloff, & I. Bedini (Eds.), *Handbook of research on e-business standards and protocols: Documents, data and advanced web technologies* (pp. 21–32). Hershey, PA: IGI Global. doi:10.4018/978-1-4666-0146-8.ch002

Meredith, J., & Potter, J. (2014). Conversation analysis and electronic interactions: Methodological, analytic and technical considerations. In H. Lim & F. Sudweeks (Eds.), *Innovative methods and technologies for electronic discourse analysis* (pp. 370–393). Hershey, PA: IGI Global. doi:10.4018/978-1-4666-4426-7.ch017

Millman, C., & El-Gohary, H. (2011). New digital media marketing and micro business: A UK perspective. *International Journal of Online Marketing*, *1*(1), 41–62. doi:10.4018/ijom.2011010104

Mishra, B., & Shukla, K. K. (2014). Data mining techniques for software quality prediction. In *Software design and development: Concepts, methodologies, tools, and applications* (pp. 401–428). Hershey, PA: IGI Global. doi:10.4018/978-1-4666-4301-7.ch021

Misra, H., & Rahman, H. (2013). *Managing enterprise information technology acquisitions: Assessing organizational preparedness*. Hershey, PA: IGI Global. doi:10.4018/978-1-4666-4201-0

Mohammadi, S., Golara, S., & Mousavi, N. (2012). Selecting adequate security mechanisms in e-business processes using fuzzy TOPSIS. *International Journal of Fuzzy System Applications*, *2*(1), 35–53. doi:10.4018/ijfsa.2012010103

Möhlenbruch, D., Dölling, S., & Ritschel, F. (2010). Interactive customer retention management for mobile commerce. In K. Pousttchi & D. Wiedemann (Eds.), *Handbook of research on mobile marketing management* (pp. 437–456). Hershey, PA: IGI Global. doi:10.4018/978-1-60566-074-5.ch023

Molla, A., & Peszynski, K. (2013). E-business in agribusiness: Investigating the e-readiness of Australian horticulture firms. In S. Chhabra (Ed.), *ICT influences on human development, interaction, and collaboration* (pp. 78–96). Hershey, PA: IGI Global. doi:10.4018/978-1-4666-1957-9.ch004

Monsanto, C., & Andriole, S. J. (2010). Business technology strategy for a major real estate and mortgage brokerage company. *Journal of Information Technology Research*, *3*(3), 43–53. doi:10.4018/jitr.2010070104

Montes, J. A., Gutiérrez, A. C., Fernández, E. M., & Romeo, A. (2013). Reality mining, location based services, and e-business opportunities: The case of city analytics. In S. Nasir (Ed.), *Modern entrepreneurship and e-business innovations* (pp. 87–99). Hershey, PA: IGI Global. doi:10.4018/978-1-4666-2946-2.ch007

Moqbel, A., Yani-De-Soriano, M., & Yousafzai, S. (2012). Mobile commerce use among UK mobile users: An experimental approach based on a proposed mobile network utilization framework. In A. Zolait (Ed.), *Knowledge and technology adoption, diffusion, and transfer: International perspectives* (pp. 78–111). Hershey, PA: IGI Global. doi:10.4018/978-1-4666-1752-0.ch007

Movahedi, B. M., Lavassani, K. M., & Kumar, V. (2012). E-marketplace emergence: Evolution, developments and classification. *Journal of Electronic Commerce in Organizations*, *10*(1), 14–32. doi:10.4018/jeco.2012010102

Mugge, R., & Schoormans, J. P. (2010). Optimizing consumer responses to mass customization. In C. Mourlas & P. Germanakos (Eds.), *Mass customization for personalized communication environments: Integrating human factors* (pp. 10–22). Hershey, PA: IGI Global. doi:10.4018/978-1-60566-260-2.ch002

Musso, F. (2012). Technology in marketing channels: Present and future drivers of innovation. *International Journal of Applied Behavioral Economics*, *1*(2), 41–51. doi:10.4018/ijabe.2012040104

Mutula, S. M. (2010). Digital economy components. In S. Mutula (Ed.), *Digital economies: SMEs and e-readiness* (pp. 29–38). Hershey, PA: IGI Global. doi:10.4018/978-1-60566-420-0.ch003

Mutula, S. M. (2010). Trends and best practices in the digital economy. In S. Mutula (Ed.), *Digital economies: SMEs and e-readiness* (pp. 283–301). Hershey, PA: IGI Global. doi:10.4018/978-1-60566-420-0.ch017

Nachtigal, S. (2011). E-business: Definition and characteristics. In O. Bak & N. Stair (Eds.), *Impact of e-business technologies on public and private organizations: Industry comparisons and perspectives* (pp. 233–248). Hershey, PA: IGI Global. doi:10.4018/978-1-60960-501-8.ch014

Nah, F. F., Hong, W., Chen, L., & Lee, H. (2012). Information search patterns in e-commerce product comparison services. In K. Siau (Ed.), *Cross-disciplinary models and applications of database management: Advancing approaches* (pp. 131–145). Hershey, PA: IGI Global. doi:10.4018/978-1-61350-471-0.ch006

Nair, P. R. (2010). Benefits of information technology implementations for supply chain management: An explorative study of progressive Indian companies. In S. Parthasarathy (Ed.), *Enterprise information systems and implementing IT infrastructures: Challenges and issues* (pp. 323–343). Hershey, PA: IGI Global. doi:10.4018/978-1-61520-625-4.ch021

Ndou, V., Del Vecchio, P., Passiante, G., & Schina, L. (2013). Web-based services and future business models. In P. Papajorgji, A. Guimarães, & M. Guarracino (Eds.), *Enterprise business modeling, optimization techniques, and flexible information systems* (pp. 1–13). Hershey, PA: IGI Global. doi:10.4018/978-1-4666-3946-1.ch001

Ndou, V., & Sadguy, N. (2013). Digital marketplaces as a viable model for SME networking. In *Supply chain management: Concepts, methodologies, tools, and applications* (pp. 275–288). Hershey, PA: IGI Global. doi:10.4018/978-1-4666-2625-6.ch016

Ochara, N. M., & Krauss, K. (2012). Towards a collaborative e-business vision for Africa. In K. Mohammed Rezaul (Ed.), *Strategic and pragmatic e-business: Implications for future business practices* (pp. 396–414). Hershey, PA: IGI Global. doi:10.4018/978-1-4666-1619-6.ch018

Oncioiu, I. (2013). *Business innovation, development, and advancement in the digital economy.* Hershey, PA: IGI Global. doi:10.4018/978-1-4666-2934-9

Ondimu, K. O., Muketha, G. M., & Ondago, C. O. (2013). E-business adoption framework in the hospitality industry: The case of Kenyan coast. In K. Tarnay, S. Imre, & L. Xu (Eds.), *Research and development in e-business through service-oriented solutions* (pp. 225–243). Hershey, PA: IGI Global. doi:10.4018/978-1-4666-4181-5.ch011

Ovaskainen, M., & Tinnilä, M. (2013). Megatrends in electronic business: An analysis of the impacts on SMEs. In S. Nasir (Ed.), *Modern entrepreneurship and e-business innovations* (pp. 12–27). Hershey, PA: IGI Global. doi:10.4018/978-1-4666-2946-2.ch002

Özcan, O., & Reeves, K. A. (2011). The firm boundary decision for sustainability-focused companies. *International Journal of Applied Logistics*, 2(2), 49–68. doi:10.4018/jal.2011040104

Öztayşi, B., & Kahraman, C. (2014). Quantification of corporate performance using fuzzy analytic network process: The case of e-commerce. In P. Vasant (Ed.), *Handbook of research on novel soft computing intelligent algorithms: Theory and practical applications* (pp. 385–413). Hershey, PA: IGI Global. doi:10.4018/978-1-4666-4450-2.ch013

Palmer, D. E. (2010). The transformative nature of e-business: Business ethics and stakeholder relations on the internet. In D. Palmer (Ed.), *Ethical issues in e-business: Models and frameworks* (pp. 1–14). Hershey, PA: IGI Global. doi:10.4018/978-1-61520-615-5.ch001

Pelet, J. É., & Papadopoulou, P. (2013). The effect of e-commerce websites' colors on customer trust. In I. Lee (Ed.), *Mobile applications and knowledge advancements in e-business* (pp. 167–185). Hershey, PA: IGI Global. doi:10.4018/978-1-4666-1960-9.ch011

Pennington, R. (2012). Enhanced social presence through ebranding the consumer in virtual communities. In A. Kapoor & C. Kulshrestha (Eds.), *Branding and sustainable competitive advantage: Building virtual presence* (pp. 189–206). Hershey, PA: IGI Global. doi:10.4018/978-1-61350-171-9.ch012

Peslak, A. R. (2012). Industry variables affecting ERP success and status. *International Journal of Enterprise Information Systems*, 8(3), 15–33. doi:10.4018/jeis.2012070102

Peterson, D., & Howard, C. (2012). Electronic payment systems evaluation: A case study to examine system selection criteria and impacts. *International Journal of Strategic Information Technology and Applications*, 3(1), 66–80. doi:10.4018/jsita.2012010105

Pflügler, C. (2012). Fostering networked business operations: A framework for B2B electronic intermediary development. *International Journal of Intelligent Information Technologies*, 8(2), 31–58. doi:10.4018/jiit.2012040103

Pillai, K., & Ozansoy, C. (2013). Web-based digital habitat ecosystems for sustainable built environments. In P. Ordóñez de Pablos (Ed.), *Green technologies and business practices: An IT approach* (pp. 185–199). Hershey, PA: IGI Global. doi:10.4018/978-1-4666-1972-2.ch011

Pinto, M., Rodrigues, A., Varajão, J., & Gonçalves, R. (2011). Model of funcionalities for the development of B2B e-commerce solutions. In M. Cruz-Cunha & J. Varajão (Eds.), *Innovations in SMEs and conducting e-business: Technologies, trends and solutions* (pp. 35–60). Hershey, PA: IGI Global. doi:10.4018/978-1-60960-765-4.ch003

Pires, J. A., & Gonçalves, R. (2011). Constrains associated to e-business evolution. In M. Cruz-Cunha & J. Varajão (Eds.), *E-business issues, challenges and opportunities for SMEs: Driving competitiveness* (pp. 335–349). Hershey, PA: IGI Global. doi:10.4018/978-1-61692-880-3.ch019

Polovina, S., & Andrews, S. (2011). A transaction-oriented architecture for structuring unstructured information in enterprise applications. In V. Sugumaran (Ed.), *Intelligent, adaptive and reasoning technologies: New developments and applications* (pp. 285–299). Hershey, PA: IGI Global. doi:10.4018/978-1-60960-595-7.ch016

Potocan, V., Nedelko, Z., & Mulej, M. (2011). What is new with organization of e-business: Organizational viewpoint of the relationships in e-business. In M. Cruz-Cunha & J. Varajão (Eds.), *E-business issues, challenges and opportunities for SMEs: Driving competitiveness* (pp. 131–148). Hershey, PA: IGI Global. doi:10.4018/978-1-61692-880-3.ch009

Potocan, V., Nedelko, Z., & Mulej, M. (2011). What is new with organization of e-business: Organizational viewpoint of the relationships in e-business. In M. Cruz-Cunha & J. Varajão (Eds.), *E-business issues, challenges and opportunities for SMEs: Driving competitiveness* (pp. 131–148). Hershey, PA: IGI Global. doi:10.4018/978-1-61692-880-3.ch009

Pucihar, A., & Lenart, G. (2011). eSME Slovenia: Initiative and action plan for the accelerated introduction of e-business in SMEs. In Global business: Concepts, methodologies, tools and applications (pp. 995-1022). Hershey, PA: IGI Global. doi:10.4018/978-1-60960-587-2.ch409

Quan, J. (2011). E-business strategy and firm performance. In *Global business: Concepts, methodologies, tools and applications* (pp. 56–66). Hershey, PA: IGI Global. doi:10.4018/978-1-60960-587-2.ch105

Quente, C. (2010). Brand driven mobile marketing: 5 theses for today and tomorrow. In K. Pousttchi & D. Wiedemann (Eds.), *Handbook of research on mobile marketing management* (pp. 468–483). Hershey, PA: IGI Global. doi:10.4018/978-1-60566-074-5.ch025

Qureshil, S., Kamal, M., & Wolcott, P. (2011). Information technology interventions for growth and competitiveness in micro-enterprises. In M. Tavana (Ed.), *Managing adaptability, intervention, and people in enterprise information systems* (pp. 106–137). Hershey, PA: IGI Global. doi:10.4018/978-1-60960-529-2.ch006

Rabaey, M. (2014). Complex adaptive systems thinking approach to enterprise architecture. In P. Saha (Ed.), *A systemic perspective to managing complexity with enterprise architecture* (pp. 99–149). Hershey, PA: IGI Global. doi:10.4018/978-1-4666-4518-9.ch003

Rahman, H., & Ramos, I. (2012). Trends of open innovation in developing nations: Contexts of SMEs. In H. Rahman & I. Ramos (Eds.), *Cases on SMEs and open innovation: Applications and investigations* (pp. 65–80). Hershey, PA: IGI Global. doi:10.4018/978-1-61350-314-0.ch004

Rahman, H., & Ramos, I. (2013). Implementation of e-commerce at the grass roots: Issues of challenges in terms of human-computer interactions. *International Journal of Information Communication Technologies and Human Development*, 5(2), 1–19. doi:10.4018/jicthd.2013040101

Rajagopal, D. (2010). Customer value and new product retailing dynamics: An analytical construct for gaining competetive advantage. In *Business information systems: Concepts, methodologies, tools and applications* (pp. 1998–2014). Hershey, PA: IGI Global. doi:10.4018/978-1-61520-969-9.ch121

Rajagopal, D. (2010). Internet, reengineering and technology applications in retailing. In *Business information systems: Concepts, methodologies, tools and applications* (pp. 1324–1342). Hershey, PA: IGI Global. doi:10.4018/978-1-61520-969-9.ch082

Rajagopal, D. (2011). Marketing strategy, technology and modes of entry in global retailing. In *Global business: Concepts, methodologies, tools and applications* (pp. 1–27). Hershey, PA: IGI Global. doi:10.4018/978-1-60960-587-2.ch101

Rajagopal, D. (2012). Convergence marketing. In *Systems thinking and process dynamics for marketing systems: Technologies and applications for decision management* (pp. 274–290). Hershey, PA: IGI Global. doi:10.4018/978-1-4666-0969-3.ch011

Rajagopal, D. (2012). Product development and market governance. In *Systems thinking and process dynamics for marketing systems: Technologies and applications for decision management* (pp. 88–117). Hershey, PA: IGI Global. doi:10.4018/978-1-4666-0969-3.ch004

Rajagopal, D. (2012). Systems thinking and cognitive process in marketing. In *Systems thinking and process dynamics for marketing systems: technologies and applications for decision management* (pp. 170–197). Hershey, PA: IGI Global. doi:10.4018/978-1-4666-0969-3.ch007

Rajagopal, D. (2013). Pricing for new products. In *Marketing decision making and the management of pricing: Successful business tools* (pp. 56–74). Hershey, PA: IGI Global. doi:10.4018/978-1-4666-4094-8.ch003

Ramayah, T., Popa, S., & Suki, N. M. (2013). Key dimensions on B2C e-business: An empirical study in Malaysia. *International Journal of Human Capital and Information Technology Professionals*, *4*(2), 43–55. doi:10.4018/jhcitp.2013040104

Rambo, K., & Liu, K. (2011). Culture-sensitive virtual e-commerce design with reference to female consumers in Saudi Arabia. In B. Ciaramitaro (Ed.), *Virtual worlds and e-commerce: Technologies and applications for building customer relationships* (pp. 267–289). Hershey, PA: IGI Global. doi:10.4018/978-1-61692-808-7.ch016

Ratnasingam, P. (2010). The evolution of online relationships in business to consumer e-commerce. In M. Khosrow-Pour (Ed.), *E-commerce trends for organizational advancement: New applications and methods* (pp. 167–176). Hershey, PA: IGI Global. doi:10.4018/978-1-60566-964-9.ch010

Ratnasingam, P. (2010). The impact of e-commerce customer relationship management in business-to-consumer e-commerce. In M. Hunter (Ed.), *Strategic information systems: Concepts, methodologies, tools, and applications* (pp. 2099–2111). Hershey, PA: IGI Global. doi:10.4018/978-1-60566-677-8.ch132

Razavi, A. R., Krause, P., & Moschoyiannis, S. (2010). Digital ecosystems: Challenges and proposed solutions. In N. Antonopoulos, G. Exarchakos, M. Li, & A. Liotta (Eds.), Handbook of research on P2P and grid systems for service-oriented computing: Models, methodologies and applications (pp. 1003-1031). Hershey, PA: IGI Global. doi:10.4018/978-1-61520-686-5.ch043

Regazzi, J. J. (2014). *Infonomics and the business of free: Modern value creation for information services*. Hershey, PA: IGI Global. doi:10.4018/978-1-4666-4454-0

Riaz, N., & Rehman, M. (2013). Negotiation by software agents in electronic business: An example of hybrid negotiation. In E. Li, S. Loh, C. Evans, & F. Lorenzi (Eds.), *Organizations and social networking: Utilizing social media to engage consumers* (pp. 327–349). Hershey, PA: IGI Global. doi:10.4018/978-1-4666-4026-9.ch017

Roberti, G., & Marinelli, A. (2012). Branding identity: Facebook, brands and self construction. In F. Comunello (Ed.), *Networked sociability and individualism: Technology for personal and professional relationships* (pp. 147–168). Hershey, PA: IGI Global. doi:10.4018/978-1-61350-338-6.ch008

Rodrigues, D. E. (2012). Cyberethics of business social networking. In M. Cruz-Cunha, P. Gonçalves, N. Lopes, E. Miranda, & G. Putnik (Eds.), *Handbook of research on business social networking: Organizational, managerial, and technological dimensions* (pp. 314–338). Hershey, PA: IGI Global. doi:10.4018/978-1-61350-168-9.ch016

Roos, G. (2013). The role of intellectual capital in business model innovation: An empirical study. In P. Ordóñez de Pablos, R. Tennyson, & J. Zhao (Eds.), *Intellectual capital strategy management for knowledge-based organizations* (pp. 76–121). Hershey, PA: IGI Global. doi:10.4018/978-1-4666-3655-2.ch006

Rowley, J., & Edmundson-Bird, D. (2013). Brand presence in digital space. *Journal of Electronic Commerce in Organizations, 11*(1), 63–78. doi:10.4018/jeco.2013010104

Rusko, R. (2013). The redefined role of consumer as a prosumer: Value co-creation, coopetition, and crowdsourcing of information goods. In P. Renna (Ed.), *Production and manufacturing system management: Coordination approaches and multi-site planning* (pp. 162–174). Hershey, PA: IGI Global. doi:10.4018/978-1-4666-2098-8.ch009

Sahi, G., & Madan, S. (2013). Developing a website usability framework for B2C e-commerce success. *International Journal of Information Communication Technologies and Human Development, 5*(1), 1–19. doi:10.4018/jicthd.2013010101

Sainz de Abajo, B., de la Torre Díez, I., & López-Coronado, M. (2010). Analysis of benefits and risks of e-commerce: Practical study of Spanish SME. In I. Portela & M. Cruz-Cunha (Eds.), *Information communication technology law, protection and access rights: Global approaches and issues* (pp. 214–239). Hershey, PA: IGI Global. doi:10.4018/978-1-61520-975-0.ch014

Samanta, I., & Kyriazopoulos, P. (2011). Can global environment influence B2B relationships? In P. Ordóñez de Pablos, M. Lytras, W. Karwowski, & R. Lee (Eds.), *Electronic globalized business and sustainable development through IT management: Strategies and perspectives* (pp. 54–69). Hershey, PA: IGI Global. doi:10.4018/978-1-61520-623-0.ch004

Sambhanthan, A., & Good, A. (2012). Implications for improving accessibility to e-commerce websites in developing countries: A study of hotel websites. *International Journal of Knowledge-Based Organizations, 2*(2), 1–20. doi:10.4018/ijkbo.2012040101

Sampaio, L., & Figueiredo, J. (2011). E-sourcing electronic platforms in real business. In M. Cruz-Cunha & J. Varajão (Eds.), *E-business managerial aspects, solutions and case studies* (pp. 185–205). Hershey, PA: IGI Global. doi:10.4018/978-1-60960-463-9.ch011

Seetharaman, A., & Raj, J. R. (2011). Evolution, development and growth of electronic money. In S. Sharma (Ed.), *E-adoption and socio-economic impacts: Emerging infrastructural effects* (pp. 249–268). Hershey, PA: IGI Global. doi:10.4018/978-1-60960-597-1.ch013

Sengupta, A., & Glavin, S. E. (2013). Predicting volatile consumer markets using multi-agent methods: Theory and validation. In B. Alexandrova-Kabadjova, S. Martinez-Jaramillo, A. Garcia-Almanza, & E. Tsang (Eds.), *Simulation in computational finance and economics: Tools and emerging applications* (pp. 339–358). Hershey, PA: IGI Global. doi:10.4018/978-1-4666-2011-7.ch016

Serpico, E., Aquilani, B., Ruggieri, A., & Silvestri, C. (2013). Customer centric marketing strategies: The importance and measurement of customer satisfaction – Offline vs. online. In H. Kaufmann & M. Panni (Eds.), *Customer-centric marketing strategies: Tools for building organizational performance* (pp. 315–357). Hershey, PA: IGI Global. doi:10.4018/978-1-4666-2524-2.ch016

Shareef, M. A., & Kumar, V. (2012). Prevent/control identity theft: Impact on trust and consumers purchase intention in B2C EC. *Information Resources Management Journal*, 25(3), 30–60. doi:10.4018/irmj.2012070102

Sherringham, K., & Unhelkar, B. (2011). Business driven enterprise architecture and applications to support mobile business. In *Enterprise information systems: Concepts, methodologies, tools and applications* (pp. 805–816). Hershey, PA: IGI Global. doi:10.4018/978-1-61692-852-0.ch316

Shin, N. (2011). Information technology and diversification: How their relationship affects firm performance. In N. Kock (Ed.), *E-collaboration technologies and organizational performance: Current and future trends* (pp. 65–79). Hershey, PA: IGI Global. doi:10.4018/978-1-60960-466-0.ch005

Sidnal, N., & Manvi, S. S. (2010). Service discovery techniques in mobile e-commerce. In I. Lee (Ed.), *Encyclopedia of e-business development and management in the global economy* (pp. 812–823). Hershey, PA: IGI Global. doi:10.4018/978-1-61520-611-7.ch081

Sidnal, N., & Manvi, S. S. (2013). English auction issues in mobile e-commerce. In K. Tarnay, S. Imre, & L. Xu (Eds.), *Research and development in e-business through service-oriented solutions* (pp. 208–223). Hershey, PA: IGI Global. doi:10.4018/978-1-4666-4181-5.ch010

Singh, S. (2010). Usability techniques for interactive software and their application in e-commerce. In T. Spiliotopoulos, P. Papadopoulou, D. Martakos, & G. Kouroupetroglou (Eds.), *Integrating usability engineering for designing the web experience: Methodologies and principles* (pp. 81–102). Hershey, PA: IGI Global. doi:10.4018/978-1-60566-896-3.ch005

Söderström, E. (2010). Guidelines for managing B2B standards implementation. In E. Alkhalifa (Ed.), *E-strategies for resource management systems: Planning and implementation* (pp. 86–105). Hershey, PA: IGI Global. doi:10.4018/978-1-61692-016-6.ch005

Sood, S. (2012). The death of social media in start-up companies and the rise of s-commerce: Convergence of e-commerce, complexity and social media. *Journal of Electronic Commerce in Organizations, 10*(2), 1–15. doi:10.4018/jeco.2012040101

Soto-Acosta, P. (2010). E-business and the resource-based view: Towards a research agenda. In I. Lee (Ed.), *Encyclopedia of e-business development and management in the global economy* (pp. 336–346). Hershey, PA: IGI Global. doi:10.4018/978-1-61520-611-7.ch033

Sourouni, A. M., Mouzakitis, S., Kourlimpini, G., Askounis, D., & Psarras, J. (2010). Ontology-based registries: An e-business transactions' registry. In E. Alkhalifa (Ed.), *E-strategies for resource management systems: Planning and implementation* (pp. 106–117). Hershey, PA: IGI Global. doi:10.4018/978-1-61692-016-6.ch006

Srinivasan, S., & Barker, R. (2012). Global analysis of security and trust perceptions in web design for e-commerce. *International Journal of Information Security and Privacy, 6*(1), 1–13. doi:10.4018/jisp.2012010101

Su, Q., & Adams, C. (2012). Consumers' attitudes toward mobile commerce: A model to capture the cultural and environment influences. In A. Scupola (Ed.), *Innovative mobile platform developments for electronic services design and delivery* (pp. 1–20). Hershey, PA: IGI Global. doi:10.4018/978-1-4666-1568-7.ch001

Swilley, E., Hofacker, C. F., & Lamont, B. T. (2012). The evolution from e-commerce to m-commerce: Pressures, firm capabilities and competitive advantage in strategic decision making. *International Journal of E-Business Research, 8*(1), 1–16. doi:10.4018/jebr.2012010101

Swimm, N., & Andriole, S. J. (2010). Business technology strategy for an energy management company. *Journal of Information Technology Research,* *3*(3), 54–65. doi:10.4018/jitr.2010070105

Tadjouddine, E. M. (2011). E-commerce systems for software agents: Challenges and opportunities. In M. Cruz-Cunha & J. Varajão (Eds.), *E-business issues, challenges and opportunities for SMEs: Driving competitiveness* (pp. 20–29). Hershey, PA: IGI Global. doi:10.4018/978-1-61692-880-3.ch002

Taylor, P. R. (2014). Enterprise architecture's identity crisis: New approaches to complexity for a maturing discipline. In P. Saha (Ed.), *A systemic perspective to managing complexity with enterprise architecture* (pp. 433–453). Hershey, PA: IGI Global. doi:10.4018/978-1-4666-4518-9.ch013

Tella, A. (2012). Determinants of e-payment systems success: A users satisfaction perspective. *International Journal of E-Adoption,* *4*(3), 15–38. doi:10.4018/jea.2012070102

Terjesen, A. (2010). Anonymity and trust: The ethical challenges of e-business transactions. In D. Palmer (Ed.), *Ethical issues in e-business: Models and frameworks* (pp. 40–57). Hershey, PA: IGI Global. doi:10.4018/978-1-61520-615-5.ch004

Tijsen, R., Spruit, M., van de Ridder, M., & van Raaij, B. (2011). BI-FIT: Aligning business intelligence end-users, tasks and technologies. In M. Cruz-Cunha & J. Varajao (Eds.), *Enterprise information systems design, implementation and management: Organizational applications* (pp. 162–177). Hershey, PA: IGI Global. doi:10.4018/978-1-61692-020-3.ch011

Toka, A., Aivazidou, E., Antoniou, A., & Arvanitopoulos-Darginis, K. (2013). Cloud computing in supply chain management: An overview. In D. Graham, I. Manikas, & D. Folinas (Eds.), *E-logistics and e-supply chain management: Applications for evolving business* (pp. 218–231). Hershey, PA: IGI Global. doi:10.4018/978-1-4666-3914-0.ch012

Tran, Q., Huang, D., & Zhang, C. (2013). An assessment method of the integrated e-commerce readiness for construction organizations in developing countries. *International Journal of E-Adoption,* *5*(1), 37–51. doi:10.4018/jea.2013010103

Tung, H., Kung, H., Lawless, D. S., Sofge, D. A., & Lawless, W. F. (2011). Conservation of information and e-business success and challenges: A case study. In M. Cruz-Cunha & J. Varajão (Eds.), *E-business managerial aspects, solutions and case studies* (pp. 254–269). Hershey, PA: IGI Global. doi:10.4018/978-1-60960-463-9.ch015

Unhelkar, B. (2011). *Handbook of research on green ICT: Technology, business and social perspectives*. Hershey, PA: IGI Global. doi:10.4018/978-1-61692-834-6

Unhelkar, B., Ghanbary, A., & Younessi, H. (2010). Collaborative business process engineering (CBPE) model. In B. Unhelkar, A. Ghanbary, & H. Younessi (Eds.), *Collaborative business process engineering and global organizations: Frameworks for service integration* (pp. 98–120). Hershey, PA: IGI Global. doi:10.4018/978-1-60566-689-1.ch004

Unhelkar, B., Ghanbary, A., & Younessi, H. (2010). Emerging technologies for business collaboration. In B. Unhelkar, A. Ghanbary, & H. Younessi (Eds.), *Collaborative business process engineering and global organizations: Frameworks for service integration* (pp. 37–64). Hershey, PA: IGI Global. doi:10.4018/978-1-60566-689-1.ch002

Unhelkar, B., Ghanbary, A., & Younessi, H. (2010). Fundamentals of collaborative business. In B. Unhelkar, A. Ghanbary, & H. Younessi (Eds.), *Collaborative business process engineering and global organizations: Frameworks for service integration* (pp. 1–36). Hershey, PA: IGI Global. doi:10.4018/978-1-60566-689-1.ch001

Van Huy, L., Rowe, F., Truex, D., & Huynh, M. Q. (2012). An empirical study of determinants of e-commerce adoption in SMEs in Vietnam: An economy in transition. *Journal of Global Information Management*, *20*(3), 23–54. doi:10.4018/jgim.2012070102

Vannoy, S. A. (2011). A structured content analytic assessment of business services advertisements in the cloud-based web services marketplace. *International Journal of Dependable and Trustworthy Information Systems*, *2*(1), 18–49. doi:10.4018/jdtis.2011010102

Vasconcelos, V., & Campos, P. (2012). The role of social networks in distributed informal information systems for innovation. In J. Varajão, M. Cruz-Cunha, & A. Trigo (Eds.), *Organizational integration of enterprise systems and resources: Advancements and applications* (pp. 60–75). Hershey, PA: IGI Global. doi:10.4018/978-1-4666-1764-3.ch004

Venkatraman, R., Venkatraman, S., & Asaithambi, S. P. (2013). A practical cloud services implementation framework for e-businesses. In K. Tarnay, S. Imre, & L. Xu (Eds.), *Research and development in e-business through service-oriented solutions* (pp. 167–198). Hershey, PA: IGI Global. doi:10.4018/978-1-4666-4181-5.ch008

Verkasalo, H. (2011). Analysis of the forces reshaping the mobile internet business. In M. Bartolacci & S. Powell (Eds.), *Interdisciplinary and multidimensional perspectives in telecommunications and networking: Emerging findings* (pp. 19–45). Hershey, PA: IGI Global. doi:10.4018/978-1-60960-505-6.ch003

Verma, A. (2013). Effects of phishing on e-commerce with special reference to India. In R. Khurana & R. Aggarwal (Eds.), *Interdisciplinary perspectives on business convergence, computing, and legality* (pp. 186–197). Hershey, PA: IGI Global. doi:10.4018/978-1-4666-4209-6.ch017

Walker, B., & Posey, E. (2013). Digital El Paso: A public-private business model for community wireless networks. In A. Abdelaal (Ed.), *Social and economic effects of community wireless networks and infrastructures* (pp. 94–111). Hershey, PA: IGI Global. doi:10.4018/978-1-4666-2997-4.ch006

Wan, Y., Clegg, B., & Dey, P. K. (2013). A framework for enabling dynamic e-business strategies via new enterprise paradigms and ERP solutions. In *Enterprise resource planning: Concepts, methodologies, tools, and applications* (pp. 1561–1595). Hershey, PA: IGI Global. doi:10.4018/978-1-4666-4153-2.ch083

Wang, F., Lupton, N., Rawlinson, D., & Zhang, X. (2012). EBDMSS: A web-based decision making support system for strategic e-business management. In P. Zaraté (Ed.), *Integrated and strategic advancements in decision making support systems* (pp. 265–284). Hershey, PA: IGI Global. doi:10.4018/978-1-4666-1746-9.ch019

Wenyin, L., Liu, A., Li, Q., & Huang, L. (2011). Business models for insurance of business web services. In H. Leung, D. Chiu, & P. Hung (Eds.), *Service intelligence and service science: Evolutionary technologies and challenges* (pp. 261–272). Hershey, PA: IGI Global. doi:10.4018/978-1-61520-819-7.ch014

Wiedmann, K., Reeh, M., & Schumacher, H. (2010). Employment and acceptance of near field communication in mobile marketing. In K. Pousttchi & D. Wiedemann (Eds.), *Handbook of research on mobile marketing management* (pp. 190–212). Hershey, PA: IGI Global. doi:10.4018/978-1-60566-074-5.ch011

Williams, J. G., & Premchaiswadi, W. (2011). On-line credit card payment processing and fraud prevention for e-business. In *Global business: Concepts, methodologies, tools and applications* (pp. 699–717). Hershey, PA: IGI Global. doi:10.4018/978-1-60960-587-2.ch312

Wilms, A., & Andriole, S. J. (2010). Business technology strategy for a specialty chemicals company. *Journal of Information Technology Research*, *3*(3), 11–18. doi:10.4018/jitr.2010070102

Winkler, U., & Gilani, W. (2012). Business continuity management of business driven IT landscapes. In S. Reiff-Marganiec & M. Tilly (Eds.), *Handbook of research on service-oriented systems and non-functional properties: Future directions* (pp. 381–399). Hershey, PA: IGI Global. doi:10.4018/978-1-61350-432-1.ch017

Wollenberg, A. (2013). Optimizing international joint venture (IJV) ownership structures: A technology and knowledge transfer-linked productivity growth perspective. In B. Christiansen, E. Turkina, & N. Williams (Eds.), *Cultural and technological influences on global business* (pp. 142–164). Hershey, PA: IGI Global. doi:10.4018/978-1-4666-3966-9.ch009

Wood, A. M., Moultrie, J., & Eckert, C. (2010). Product form evolution. In A. Silva & R. Simoes (Eds.), *Handbook of research on trends in product design and development: Technological and organizational perspectives* (pp. 499–512). Hershey, PA: IGI Global. doi:10.4018/978-1-61520-617-9.ch027

Wresch, W., & Fraser, S. (2011). Persistent barriers to e-commerce in developing countries: A longitudinal study of efforts by Caribbean companies. *Journal of Global Information Management, 19*(3), 30–44. doi:10.4018/jgim.2011070102

Wresch, W., & Fraser, S. (2013). Persistent barriers to e-commerce in developing countries: A longitudinal study of efforts by Caribbean companies. In F. Tan (Ed.), *Global diffusion and adoption of technologies for knowledge and information sharing* (pp. 205–220). Hershey, PA: IGI Global. doi:10.4018/978-1-4666-2142-8.ch009

Xiao, X., Liu, Y., & Zhang, Z. (2012). The analysis of the logistics mode decision to e-commerce. *Journal of Electronic Commerce in Organizations, 10*(4), 57–70. doi:10.4018/jeco.2012100105

Xu, L. (2010). Outsourcing and multi-party business collaborations modeling. In K. St.Amant (Ed.), *IT outsourcing: Concepts, methodologies, tools, and applications* (pp. 558–577). Hershey, PA: IGI Global. doi:10.4018/978-1-60566-770-6.ch033

Xu, M., Rohatgi, R., & Duan, Y. (2010). Engaging SMEs in e-business: Insights from an empirical study. In *Business information systems: Concepts, methodologies, tools and applications* (pp. 115–134). Hershey, PA: IGI Global. doi:10.4018/978-1-61520-969-9.ch009

Yermish, I., Miori, V., Yi, J., Malhotra, R., & Klimberg, R. (2010). Business plus intelligence plus technology equals business intelligence. *International Journal of Business Intelligence Research, 1*(1), 48–63. doi:10.4018/jbir.2010071704

Yeung, W. L. (2013). Specifying business-level protocols for web services based collaborative processes. In A. Loo (Ed.), *Distributed computing innovations for business, engineering, and science* (pp. 137–154). Hershey, PA: IGI Global. doi:10.4018/978-1-4666-2533-4.ch007

Z arour, M., Abran, A., & Desharnais, J. (2014). Software process improvement for small and very small enterprises. In *Software design and development: Concepts, methodologies, tools, and applications* (pp. 1363-1384). Hershey, PA: IGI Global. doi:10.4018/978-1-4666-4301-7.ch066

Zerenler, M., & Gözlü, S. (2012). Issues influencing electronic commerce activities of SMEs: A study of the Turkish automotive supplier industry. In *Human resources management: Concepts, methodologies, tools, and applications* (pp. 1035–1055). Hershey, PA: IGI Global. doi:10.4018/978-1-4666-1601-1.ch064

Compilation of References

140kit. (n.d.). Retrieved from https://github.com/WebEcologyProject/140kit

Aas, K. (2001). *Microarray Data Mining: A Survey. NR Note, SAMBA.* Norwegian Computing Center.

Agarwalla, S., & Sarma, K. K. (2016). Machine learning based sample extraction for automatic speech recognition using dialectal Assamese speech. *Neural Networks, 78,* 97–111. doi:10.1016/j.neunet.2015.12.010 PMID:26783204

Ahmad, A., Rathore, M. M., Paul, A., & Rho, S. (2016). Defining Human Behaviors Using Big Data Analytics in Social Internet of Things. *2016 IEEE 30th International Conference on Advanced Information Networking and Applications (AINA),* 1101-1107.

Ahmad, Paul, Rathore, & Chang. (2016). An Efficient Multidimensional Big Data Fusion Approach in Machine-to-Machine Communication. *ACM Trans. Embed. Comput. Syst., 15*(2).

Akyildiz, I. F., Lee, W., Vuran, M. C., & Mohanty, S. (2006). NeXt generation/dynamic spectrum access/cognitive radio wireless networks: A survey. *Elsevier Journal on Computer Networks, 50*(13), 2127–2159. doi:10.1016/j.comnet.2006.05.001

Akyildiz, I. F., Lee, W., Vuran, M. C., & Mohanty, S. (2008). A Survey on Spectrum Management in Cognitive Radio Networks. *IEEE Communications Magazine, 46*(4), 40–48. doi:10.1109/MCOM.2008.4481339

Akyildiz, I. F., Lo, B. F., & Balakrishnan, R. (2011). Cooperative spectrum sensing in cognitive radio networks: A survey. *Physical Communication, 4*(1), 40–62. doi:10.1016/j.phycom.2010.12.003

Ambati, S. (2016). Deep learning: A brief guide for practical problem solvers. *InfoWorld.* Retrieved 26 June 2016, from http://www.infoworld.com/article/3003315/big-data/deep-learning-a-brief-guide-for-practical-problem-solvers.html.html

Aminian, M., & Naji, H. R. (2013). *A Hospital Healthcare Monitoring System Using Wireless Sensor Networks,* Health &. *Medical Informatics, 4*(2).

Amit, Y., & Geman, D. (1997). Shape quantization and recognition with randomized trees. *Neural Computation, 9*(7), 1545–1588. doi:10.1162/neco.1997.9.7.1545

Anagnostou, E. N. (2004). A convective/stratiform precipitation classification algorithm for volume scanning weather radar observations. *Meteorological Applications, 11*(4), 291–300. doi:10.1017/S1350482704001409

Angiuoli, S. V., Matalka, M., Gussman, A., Galens, K., Vangala, M., Riley, D. R., & Fricke, W. F. et al. (2011). CloVR: A virtual machine for automated and portable sequence analysis from the desktop using cloud computing. *BMC Bioinformatics, 12*(1), 356. doi:10.1186/1471-2105-12-356 PMID:21878105

Archive Team. (n.d.). *The Twitter Stream Grab.* Retrieved from https://archive.org/details/twitterstream

Arefin, A. S., Berretta, R., & Moscato, P. (2013). A GPU-based method for computing eigenvector centrality of gene-expression networks. In *Proceedings of the Eleventh Australasian Symposium on Parallel and Distributed Computing (vol. 140).* Australian Computer Society, Inc.

Arel, I., Rose, D. C., & Karnowski, T. P. (2010). Deep machine learning-a new frontier in artificial intelligence research [research frontier]. *IEEE Comput Intell, 5*(4), 13–18. doi:10.1109/MCI.2010.938364

Ariananda, D. D., Lakshmanan, M. K., & Nikookar, H. (2009). A Survey on Spectrum Sensing Techniques for Cognitive Radio. *Proceedings of second International Workshop on Cognitive Radio and Advanced Spectrum Management (CogART),* 74-79. doi:10.1109/COGART.2009.5167237

Assunção, M. D., Calheiros, R. N., Bianchi, S., Netto, M. A. S., & Buyya, R. (2015). Big Data computing and clouds: Trends and future directions. *Journal of Parallel and Distributed Computing, 79,* 3–15. doi:10.1016/j.jpdc.2014.08.003

Bader, G. D., & Hogue, C. W. (2003). An automated method for finding molecular complexes in large protein interaction networks. *BMC Bioinformatics, 4*(1), 2. doi:10.1186/1471-2105-4-2 PMID:12525261

Baheti, R., & Gill, H. (2011). Cyber-physical systems. The Impact of Control Technology, IEEE, 161-166.

Barker, M. S., Dlugosch, K. M., Dinh, L., Challa, R. S., Kane, N. C., King, M. G., & Rieseberg, L. H. (2010). EvoPipes. net: Bioinformatics tools for ecological and evolutionary genomics. *Evolutionary Bioinformatics Online, 6,* 143. doi:10.4137/EBO.S5861 PMID:21079755

Becker, Caceres, Hanson, Loh, Urbanek, Varshavsky, & Volinsky. (2011). A tale of one city: Using cellular network data for urban planning. *IEEE Pervasive Computing, 10*(4), 18-26.

Beebe, N., & Clark, J. (2005). *Dealing with terabyte data sets in digital investigations.* Springer.

Bengio, Y. (2009). Learning deep architectures for AI. *Foundations and Trends® in Machine Learning, 2*(1), 1-127.

Bengio, Y., & LeCun, Y. (2007). Scaling learning algorithms towards, AI. In L. Bottou, O. Chapelle, D. DeCoste, & J. Weston (Eds.), Large Scale Kernel Machines (Vol. 34, pp. 321–360). Cambridge, MA: MIT Press. Retrieved from http://www.iro.umontreal.ca/~lisa/pointeurs/bengio+lecun_chapter2007.pdf

Bengio, Y. (2007). Greedy layer-wise training of deep networks. *Advances in Neural Information Processing Systems*, *19*, 153.

Bengio, Y. (2012). Deep Learning of Representations for Unsupervised and Transfer Learning. *Journal of Machine Learning Research*, *27*, 17–37.

Bengio, Y., & Bengio, S. (2000). *Modeling High-Dimensional Discrete Data*. Adv. Neural Inf. Process. Syst.

Ben-Zvi, G. (2016). Big data to the Rescue? Cyber Attacks Rank as Major Global Threat in 2016 - SQream. *SQream*. Retrieved 26 June 2016, from http://sqream.com/big-data-to-the-rescue-cyber-attacks-rank-as-major-global-threat-in-2016/

Bharill, N., & Tiwari, A. (2016). *Handling Big Data with Fuzzy Based Classification Approach*. Academic Press.

Big Data Working Group. (2013). *Big data analytics for security intelligence*. Cloud Security Alliance.

Bi, S., Zhang, R., Ding, Z., & Cui, S. (2015). Wireless communications in the era of big data. *IEEE Communications Magazine*, *53*(10), 190–199. doi:10.1109/MCOM.2015.7295483

Bobadilla, Ortega, Hernando, & Gutierrez. (2013). Recommender systems survey. *Knowledge-Based Systems*, *46*, 109-132.

Boken, V. K., Cracknell, A. P., & Heathcote, R. L. (2005). *Monitoring and predicting agricultural drought: a global study*. Oxford University Press.

Brahic, C. (2007). Sunshade "for global warming could cause drought". *New Scientist*.

Breiman, L. (2001). Random forests. *Machine Learning*, *45*(1), 5–32. doi:10.1023/A:1010933404324

Brynjolfsson, E., Hitt, L. M., & Kim, H. H. (2011). *Strength in numbers: How does data-driven decision making affect firm performance?* Working paper. Available at SSRN: http://ssrn.com/abstract=1819486

Casado, R., & Younas, M. (2015). Emerging trends and technologies in big data processing. *Concurrency and Computation*, *27*(8), 2078–2091. doi:10.1002/cpe.3398

Chen, C. L. (2014). Data-intensive applications, challenges, techniques and technologies: A survey on Big Data. *Information Sciences*, *275*, 314–347. doi:10.1016/j.ins.2014.01.015

Cheng, Z., Caverlee, J., Lee, K., & Sui, D. Z. (2011). Exploring millions of footprints in location sharing services. *ICWSM*, *2011*, 81–88.

Chen, M., Mao, S., & Liu, Y. (2014). Big data: A survey. *Mobile Networks and Applications, 19*(2), 171–209. doi:10.1007/s11036-013-0489-0

Chen, X. W., & Lin, X. (2014). Big data deep learning: Challenges and perspectives. *IEEE Access, 2*, 514–525. doi:10.1109/ACCESS.2014.2325029

Chien, J.-T., & Hsieh, H.-L. (2013). Nonstationary Source Separation Using Sequential and Variational Bayesian Learning. *IEEE Transactions on Neural Networks and Learning Systems, 24*(5), 681–694. doi:10.1109/TNNLS.2013.2242090 PMID:24808420

Chow, J. (2010). Towards location-based social networking services. *Proceedings of the 2nd ACM SIGSPATIAL International Workshop on Location Based Social Networks*, 31-38. doi:10.1145/1867699.1867706

Ciresan, D. C., Meier, U., Masci, J., Gambardella, L. M., & Schmidhuber, J. (2011). Flexible, high performance convolutional neural networks for image classification. *Proc. 22nd Int. Conf. Artif. Intell.*

Clutter, M. (1996). *Hearing on Computational Biology. Statement before the subcommittee on Science, Technology and Space Committee on Commerce, Science, and Transportation.* U.S. Senate.

Coates, A., Huval, B., Wang, T., Wu, D., Catanzaro, B., & Andrew, N. (2013). Deep learning with COTS HPC systems. *Journal of Machine Learning Research, 28*(3), 1337–1345.

Collaborative Defense Enriched by Dynamic Analysis. (2015). Business white paper I Collaborative Defense Enriched by Dynamic Analysis, Threat Central, developed with HP Labs.

Collaborative Information Exchange Models to Fight Cyber Threats. (2016). Retrieved 26 June 2016, from https://www.blueliv.com/corporate/the-use-of-social-media-models-in-the-fight-against-cyber-threats/

Coomans, D., & Massart, D. L. (1982). Alternative k-nearest neighbour rules in supervised pattern recognition: Part 1. k-Nearest neighbour classification by using alternative voting rules. *Analytica Chimica Acta, 136*, 15–27. doi:10.1016/S0003-2670(01)95359-0

Crooks, A. (2012). #Earthquake: Twitter as a distributed sensor system. *Transactions in GIS.*

Cui, L., Yu, F. R., & Yan, Q. (2016). When big data meets software-defined networking: SDN for big data and big data for SDN. *IEEE Network, 30*(1), 58–65. doi:10.1109/MNET.2016.7389832

Davenport, T. H., & Patil, D. J. (2012, October). Data scientist: The sexiest job of the 21st century. *Harvard Business Review.* PMID:23074866

Day, A., Carlson, M. R., Dong, J., OConnor, B. D., & Nelson, S. F. (2007). Celsius: A community resource for Affymetrix microarray data. *Genome Biology, 8*(6), R112. doi:10.1186/gb-2007-8-6-r112 PMID:17570842

Day, A., Dong, J., Funari, V. A., Harry, B., Strom, S. P., Cohn, D. H., & Nelson, S. F. (2009). Disease gene characterization through largescale co-expression analysis. *PLoS ONE*, *4*(12), e8491. doi:10.1371/journal.pone.0008491 PMID:20046828

Dean, J., & Ghemawat, S. (2008). MapReduce: Simplified data processing on large clusters. *Communications of the ACM*, *51*(1), 107–113. doi:10.1145/1327452.1327492

Dehuri, S., & Sanyal, S. (2015). Computational Intelligence for Big Data Analysis. Springer International Publishing.

Demchenko, Y., De Laat, C., & Membrey, P. (2014). Defining architecture components of the Big Data Ecosystem. *IEEE International Conference on Collaboration Technologies and Systems*. doi:10.1109/CTS.2014.6867550

DeWitt, D., & Gray, J. (1992). Parallel database systems: The future of high performance database systems. *Communications of the ACM*, *35*(6), 85–98. doi:10.1145/129888.129894

Dietterich, T. G. (2000). An experimental comparison of three methods for constructing ensembles of decision trees: Bagging, boosting, and randomization. *Machine Learning*, *40*(2), 139–157. doi:10.1023/A:1007607513941

Domingos, P. (2012). A few useful things to know about machine learning. *Communications of the ACM*, 55.

Dore, A. J., Mousavi-Baygi, M., Smith, R. I., Hall, J., Fowler, D., & Choularton, T. W. (2006). A model of annual orographic precipitation and acid deposition and its application to Snowdonia. *Atmospheric Environment*, *40*(18), 3316–3326. doi:10.1016/j.atmosenv.2006.01.043

Duffy, A. (2014). *CarveML: Application of machine learning to file fragment classification.*

Effective fraud protection relies on deep analytics. (2016). *IBM Big data & Analytics Hub*. Retrieved 26 June 2016, from http://www.ibmbigdatahub.com/blog/effective-fraud-protection-relies-deep-analytics

Eibagi, A. (2014). *Big Data Analysis Using Neuro-Fuzzy System* (Thesis). San Jose State University.

Eldar, Y. C., & Kutyniok, G. (2012). *Compressed Sensing: Theory and Applications*. Cambridge, UK: Cambridge University Press. doi:10.1017/CBO9780511794308

ElHihi, S., & Bengio, Y. (1995). Hierarchical recurrent neural networks for long-term dependencies. *Proc. Advances in Neural Information Processing Systems*, 8. Retrieved from http://papers.nips.cc/paper/1102-hierarchical-recurrent-neural-networks-for-long-term-dependencies

Eriksson, B., Barford, P., Sommers, J., & Nowak, R. A learning-based approach for IP geolocation. In A. Krishnamurthy & B. Plattner (Eds.), *Passive and Active Measurement* (Vol. 6032, pp. 171–180). Berlin: Springer Lecture Notes in Computer Science. doi:10.1007/978-3-642-12334-4_18

Falkenmark, M., Lundqvist, J., & Widstrand, C. (1989). Macro-scale water scarcity requires micro-scale approaches. Natural Resources Forum, 13(4).

Fanan, A. M., Riley, N. G., Mehdawi, M., Ammar, M., & Zolfaghari, M. (2014). Survey: A Comparison of Spectrum Sensing Techniques in Cognitive Radio. *Proceedings of International Conference on Image Processsing, Computers and Industrial Engineering (ICICIE)*, 65-69.

Ferrari, L., Rosi, A., Mamei, M., & Zambonelli, F. (2011). Extracting urban patterns from location-based social networks. *Proc. of the 3rd ACM LBSN*. doi:10.1145/2063212.2063226

Fielding, R. T. (n.d.). *Architectural styles and the design of network-based software architectures.* (PhD Thesis). University of California, Irvine, CA.

Forsythe, D. E. (1993). The construction of work in artificial intelligence. *Science, Technology & Human Values, 18*(4), 460–479. doi:10.1177/016224399301800404

Fossi, Egan, Haley, Johnson, Mack, Adams, … McKinney. (2011). *Symantec internet security threat report trends for 2010*. Symantec.

Fossi, M., Johnson, E., Turner, D., Mack, T., Blackbird, J., McKinney, D., & Gough, J. et al. (2008). *Symantec report on the underground economy: July 2007 to June 2008. Technical Report.* Symantec Corporation.

Friedman, J., Hastie, T., & Tibshirani, R. (2001). The elements of statistical learning (Vol. 1). Springer.

Fung, C. J., & Boutaba, R. (2013, May). Design and management of collaborative intrusion detection networks. In *2013 IFIP/IEEE International Symposium on Integrated Network Management (IM 2013)* (pp. 955-961). IEEE.

Fusfeld A. (2010, September 23). The digital 100: the world's most valuable startups. *Bus Insider*.

Gantz & Reinsel. (2010). *The Digital Universe Decade: Are You Ready*. Hopkinton, MA: EMC.

Gantz & Reinsel. (2011). *Extracting Value from Chaos*. Hopkinton, MA: EMC.

Gantz, J., & Reinsel, D. (2011). *Extracting Value from Chaos*. Available: https://www.emc.com/collateral/analyst-reports/idc-extracting-value-from-chaos-ar.pdf

Gantz, J., & Reinsel, D. (2011). Extracting value from chaos. *IDC Review, 1142*, 1-12.

Garrett, M. A. (2014). Big Data analytics and Cognitive Computing: future opportunities for Astronomical research. *IOP Conference Series Materials Science and Engineering, 67*(1). doi:10.1088/1757-899X/67/1/012017

Glantz, M. H. (1988). *Drought and hunger in Africa*. CUP Archive.

Glorot, X., Bordes, A., & Bengio, Y. (2011). Domain adaptation for large-scale sentiment classification: A deep learning approach. *28th International Conference on Machine Learning*.

Goecks, J., Nekrutenko, A., Taylor, J., & Galaxy Team, T. (2010). Galaxy: A comprehensive approach for supporting accessible, reproducible, and transparent computational research in the life sciences. *Genome Biology, 11*(8), R86. doi:10.1186/gb-2010-11-8-r86 PMID:20738864

Grosu, P., Townsend, J. P., Hartl, D. L., & Cavalieri, D. (2002). Pathway Processor: A tool for integrating whole-genome expression results into metabolic networks. *Genome Research, 12*(7), 1121–1126. doi:10.1101/gr.226602 PMID:12097350

Gunes, V., Peter, S., Givargis, T., & Vahid, F. (2014). A Survey on Concepts, Applications, and Challenges in Cyber-Physical Systems. *Transactions on Internet and Information Systems (Seoul), 8*(12), 4242–4268.

Gungor, V. C., Lu, B., & Hancke, G. P. (2010). Opportunities and Challenges of Wireless Sensor Networks in Smart Grid. *IEEE Transactions on Industrial Electronics, 57*(10), 10. doi:10.1109/TIE.2009.2039455

Guturu, P., & Bhargava, B. (2011). Cyber-Physical Systems: A Confluence of Cutting Edge Technological Streams. *Proceedings of International Conference on Advances in Computing and Communication ICACC-11.*

Haklay, M. (2010). How good is volunteered geographical information? A comparative study of OpenStreetMap and Ordnance Survey datasets. *Environment and Planning. B, Planning & Design, 37*(4), 682–703. doi:10.1068/b35097

Hasan, M. (2014). Genetic Algorithm and its application to Big Data Analysis. *International Journal of Scientific & Engineering Research, 5*(1).

Hays, C. L. (2004, November 14). What they know about you. *NY Times.*

Health Industry Cyber Threat Information Sharing and Analysis, Annual Review of HITRUST Cyber Threat XChange (CTX) -Summary of Findings and Recommendations, Public Discussion Document. (n.d.). Retrieved from www.HITRUSTalliance.net

Hefez, Kanza, & Levin. (2011). Tarsius: A system for traffic-aware route search under conditions of uncertainty. SIGSPATIAL'11, 517-520.

Henseler, H., Hofste, J., & van Keulen, M. (2013). Digital-forensics based pattern recognition for discovering identities in electronic evidence. European. *IEEE Intelligence and Security Informatics Conference (EISIC).* doi:10.1109/EISIC.2013.24

Hern. (2013). Online volunteers map Philippines after typhoon Haiyan. *The Guardian.* Retrieved from http://www.theguardian.com/technology/ 2013/nov/15/online-volunteers-mapphilippines-after-typhoon-haiyan

Hey, T., Tansley, S., & Tolle, K. M. (2009). The fourth paradigm: Data-intensive scientific discovery (Vol. 1). Redmond, WA: Microsoft Research.

Hill, S., Provost, F., & Volinsky, C. (2006). Network-based marketing: Identifying likely adopters via consumer networks. *Statistical Science, 21*(2), 256–276. doi:10.1214/088342306000000222

Hinton, G. (2002). Training products of experts by minimizing contrastive divergence. *Neural Computation, 14*(8), 1771–1800. doi:10.1162/089976602760128018 PMID:12180402

Hinton, G. (2010). *A practical guide to training restricted Boltzmann machines*. Toronto, Canada: Dept. Comput. Sci., Univ.

Hinton, G. E., Osindero, S., & Teh, Y.-W. (2006). A fast learning algorithm for deep belief nets. *Neural Computation*, *18*(7), 1527–1554. doi:10.1162/neco.2006.18.7.1527 PMID:16764513

Hinton, G., Deng, L., Yu, D., Mohamed, A.-R., Jaitly, N., Senior, A., & Kingsbury, B. et al. (2012). Deep neural networks for acoustic modeling in speech recognition: The shared views of four research groups. *Signal Process Mag IEEE*, *29*(6), 82–97. doi:10.1109/MSP.2012.2205597

Hirsh, H., & Noordewier, M. (1994). Using Background Knowledge to Improve Inductive Learning of DNA Sequences. *Proceedings of the 10th IEEE Conference on Artificial Intelligence for Applications*, 351-357. doi:10.1109/CAIA.1994.323654

Ho, T. K. (1995). Random decision forests. *Document Analysis and Recognition, 1995, Proceedings of the Third International Conference on*, 1.

Hochreiter, S., & Schmidhuber, J. (1997). Long short-term memory. *Neural Computation*, *9*(8), 1735–1780. doi:10.1162/neco.1997.9.8.1735 PMID:9377276

Hofman, V., & Franzen, D. (1997). Emergency tillage to control wind erosion. North Dakota State University.

Hootsuite. (n.d.). Retrieved from hootsuite.com

Ho, T. K. (1998). The random subspace method for constructing decision forests. *Pattern Analysis and Machine Intelligence, IEEE Transactions on*, *20*(8), 832–844. doi:10.1109/34.709601

Houle, J. L., Cadigan, W., Henry, S., Pinnamaneni, A., & Lundahl, S. (2004, March 10). Database Mining in the Human Genome Initiative. Whitepaper. Amita Corporation.

Hubel, D. H., & Wiesel, T. N. (1962). Receptive fields, binocular interaction, and functional architecture in the cats visual cortex. *The Journal of Physiology*, *160*(1), 106–154. doi:10.1113/jphysiol.1962.sp006837 PMID:14449617

Hu, H., Wen, Y., Chua, T. S., & Li, X. (2014). Toward scalable systems for big data analytics: A technology tutorial. *IEEE Access*, *2*, 652–687. doi:10.1109/ACCESS.2014.2332453

IBM X-Force Exchange. (2016). Retrieved 26 June 2016, from http://www-03.ibm.com/software/products/en/xforce-exchange

IDC. (2014). *The digital universe of opportunities: Rich data and the increasing value of the internet of things*. Retrieved from https://www.emc.com/leadership/digital-universe/2014iview/executive-summary.htm

Information Sharing Specifications for Cybersecurity | US-CERT. (2016). Retrieved 26 June 2016, from https://www.us-cert.gov/Information-Sharing-Specifications-Cybersecurity

Jaiswal, M., & Sharma, A. K. (2013). A Survey on Spectrum Sensing Techniques for Cognitive Radio. In *Proceedings of Conference on Advances in Communication and Control Systems (CAC2S)*. Atlantis Press.

Jardak, C., Mähönen, P., & Riihijärvi, J. (2014). Spatial big data and wireless networks: Experiences, applications, and research challenges. *IEEE Network, 28*(4), 26–31. doi:10.1109/MNET.2014.6863128

Jaskowiak, P. A., & Campello, R. J. G. B. (2011). Comparing correlation coefficients as dissimilarity measures for cancer classification in gene expression data. *Proceedings of the Brazilian Symposium on Bioinformatics.*

Johnson, C., Badger, L., & Waltermire, D. (2014). *Guide to cyber threat information sharing* (draft). NIST Special Publication 800-150 (Draft).

Kala, R., Shulkla, A., & Tiwari, R. (2009, March). *Fuzzy Neuro systems for machine learning for large data sets. Advance Computing Conference, 2009. IACC 2009. IEEE International,* 541-545. doi:10.1109/IADCC.2009.4809069

Kamal, M. (2012). Digital investigation concepts. *Security Kaizen Magazine, 2*(6), 6–10.

Kanza, Y., Kravi, E., & Motchan, U. (2014). City nexus: Discovering pairs of jointly-visited locations based on geo-tagged posts in social networks. SIGSPATIAL'14, 597-600.

Kashyap, Ahmed, Hoque, Roy, & Bhattacharyya. (2014). Big Data Analytics in Bioinformatics: A Machine Learning Perspective. *Journal of Latex Class Files, 13*(9).

Kaur, N., & Aulakh, I. K. (2015). A Survey of Cooperative Spectrum Sensing in Cognitive Radio Networks. *International Journal on Recent and Innovation Trends in Computing and Communication, 3*(11), 6313–6316.

Keddy, P. (2007). *Plants and vegetation: origins, processes, consequences.* Cambridge University Press. doi:10.1017/CBO9780511812989

Kelley, Yuan, Lewitter, Sharan, Stockwell, & Ideker. (2004). PathBLAST: A tool for alignment of protein interaction networks. *Nucleic Acids Research, 32*(S2), W83–W88.

Kerr, M. K., & Churchill, G. A. (2001). Bootstrapping Cluster Analysis: Assessing the Reliability of Conclusions from Microarray Experiments. *Proceedings of the National Academy of Sciences of the United States of America, 98*(16), 8961–8965. doi:10.1073/pnas.161273698 PMID:11470909

Kriegeskorte, N. (2015). Deep neural networks: *A new framework for modeling biological vision and brain information processing. Annual Review of Vision Science, 1*(1), 417–446. doi:10.1146/annurev-vision-082114-035447

Krizhevsky, I. S. G. H. A. (2012). *ImageNet classification with deep convolutional neural networks.* Proc. Adv. NIPS.

Kumari & Kumar. (2014). Impact of Biological Big Data in Bioinformatics. *International Journal of Computer Applications, 101*(11).

Kumar, S., Nei, M., Dudley, J., & Tamura, K. (2008). MEGA: A biologistcentric software for evolutionary analysis of DNA and protein sequences. *Briefings in Bioinformatics, 9*(4), 299–306. doi:10.1093/bib/bbn017 PMID:18417537

Kune, R., Konugurthi, P. K., Agarwal, A., Rao Chillarige, R., & Buyya, R. (2014). Genetic Algorithm based Data-aware Group Scheduling for Big Data Clouds. *International Symposium on Big Data Computing*, 96-104. doi:10.1109/BDC.2014.15

Kurtz, S. (2003). The vmatch large scale sequence analysis software. Academic Press.

Lan, R. (2014). Spatio-temporal disease tracking using news articles. HealthGIS'14, 31-38.

Lan, R., Lieberman, M. D., & Samet, H. (2012). The picture of health: map-based, collaborative spatio-temporal disease tracking. HealthGIS'12, 27-35.

Laney. (2001). *3D Data Management: Controlling Data Volume, Velocity and Variety*. Application Delivery Strategies, Meta Group, 1-4.

Langfelder, P., & Horvath, S. (2008). WGCNA: An R package for weighted correlation network analysis. *BMC Bioinformatics, 9*(1), 559. doi:10.1186/1471-2105-9-559 PMID:19114008

Langmead, B., Schatz, M. C., Lin, J., Pop, M., & Salzberg, S. L. (2009). Searching for SNPs with cloud computing. *Genome Biology, 10*(11), R134. doi:10.1186/gb-2009-10-11-r134 PMID:19930550

Langmead, B., Trapnell, C., Pop, M., & Salzberg, S. L. (2009). Ultrafast and memory-efficient alignment of short DNA sequences to the human genome. *Genome Biology, 10*(3), R25. doi:10.1186/gb-2009-10-3-r25 PMID:19261174

Larochelle, Y. B. J. L. P. L. H. (2009). Exploring strategies for training deep neural networks. *Journal of Machine Learning Research, 10*, 1–40.

Lawrence, S., Giles, C. L., Tsoi, A. C., & Back, A. D. (1997). Face recognition: A convolutional neural-network approach. *IEEE Transactions on Neural Networks, 8*(1), 98–113. doi:10.1109/72.554195 PMID:18255614

LeCun, Y., Bottou, L., Bengio, Y., & Haffner, P. (1998). Gradient-based learning applied to document recognition. *Proceedings of the IEEE, 86*(11), 2278–2324. doi:10.1109/5.726791

Lee, H., Battle, A., Raina, R., & Ng, A. (n.d.). Efficient sparse coding algorithms. Proc. Neural Inf. Procees. Syst.

Le, N. T., Martin, L., Mumme, C., & Pinkwart, N. (2012) Communication-free detection of resource conflicts in multi-agent-based cyber-physical systems. *Proceedings of the 6th IEEE International Conference on Digital Ecosystems Technologies (DEST)*, 1-6. doi:10.1109/DEST.2012.6227952

Leung, S. T., & Gobioff, H. (2003). The Google file system. *SOSP'03 Proceeding of Nineteenth ACM Symposium on Operating Systems Principles*, 29-43.

Levin, R., & Kanza, Y. (2014). Tars: Traffic-aware route search. *GeoInformatica*, *18*(3), 461–500. doi:10.1007/s10707-013-0185-z

Li & Yu. (2014). *Deep Learning: Methods and Applications*. Now Publishers.

Li, W. (2015). *Artificial intelligence laboratory*. Retrieved from https://ai.arizona.edu/sites/ai/files/resources/chen_deep_learningapril2015.pptx

Li. (2012). Three classes of deep learning architectures and their applications: a tutorial survey. *APSIPA Transactions on Signal and Information Processing*.

Liang, Zhang, Jin, & Zhu. (2014). FastGCN: A GPU Accelerated Tool for Fast Gene Co-Expression Networks. *PloS One, 10*(1).

Liang, Y., Zeng, Y., Peh, E. C. Y., & Hoang, A. T. H. (2008). Sensing-Throughput Tradeoff for Cognitive Radio Networks. *IEEE Transactions on Wireless Communications*, *7*(4), 1326–1337. doi:10.1109/TWC.2008.060869

Li, J., Ng, K.-S., & Wong, L. (2003). Bioinformatics Adventures in Database Research. *Proceedings of the 9th International Conference on Database Theory*, 31-46.

Li, R., Li, Y., Fang, X., Yang, H., Wang, J., Kristiansen, K., & Wang, J. (2009). SNP detection for massively parallel whole-genome resequencing. *Genome Research*, *19*(6), 1124–1132. doi:10.1101/gr.088013.108 PMID:19420381

Locasto, M. E., Parekh, J. J., Keromytis, A. D., & Stolfo, S. J. (2005, June). Towards collaborative security and p2p intrusion detection. In *Proceedings from the Sixth Annual IEEE SMC Information Assurance Workshop* (pp. 333-339). IEEE.

Luo, W., & Brouwer, C. (2013). Pathview: An R/Bioconductor package for pathway-based data integration and visualization. *Bioinformatics (Oxford, England)*, *29*(14), 1830–1831. doi:10.1093/bioinformatics/btt285 PMID:23740750

Lynggaard, P., & Skouby, K. E. (2015). Deploying 5G-technologies in smart city and smart home wireless sensor networks with interferences. *Wireless Personal Communications*, *81*(4), 1399–1413. doi:10.1007/s11277-015-2480-5

Ma, D., & Wang, Y. (2013). Network Threat Behavior Detection and Trend Analysis Based on the TDLC Model. *SmartCR*, *3*(4), 285–297. doi:10.6029/smartcr.2013.04.007

Mane, D., & Salian, S. (2015). Utilizing Big Data, Cognitive Computing and Big Data Testing to deduce optimized result based decisions. *International Journal of Engineering Research and General Science*, *3*(3), 351–356.

Manyika, J., Chui, M., Brown, B., Bughin, J., Dobbs, R., Roxburgh, C., & Byers, A. H. (2011). *Big data: The next frontier for innovation, competition, and productivity.* San Francisco, CA: McKinsey Global Institute.

Ma, Q., & Wang, J. T. L. (1999). Biological Data Mining Using Bayesian Neural Networks: A Case Study. *International Journal on Artificial Intelligence Tools, 8*(4), 433–451.

Martens, D., & Provost, F. (2011). *Pseudo-social network targeting from consumer transaction data.* Working paper, CEDER-11-05. Stern School of Business.

Matsunaga, A., Tsugawa, M., & Fortes, J. (2008). Cloudblast: Combining mapreduce and virtualization on distributed resources for bioinformatics applications. *eScience'08. IEEE Fourth International Conference on. IEEE,* 222–229. doi:10.1109/eScience.2008.62

Mazhar, Rathore, Ahmad, Paul, & Wu. (2016). Real-time continuous feature extraction in large size satellite images. *Journal of Systems Architecture, 64*(March), 122–132.

McAfee Threat Intelligence Exchange I Intel Security Products. (2016). Retrieved 26 June 2016, from http://www.mcafee.com/in/products/threat-intelligence-exchange.aspx

McArt, D. G., Bankhead, P., Dunne, P. D., Salto-Tellez, M., Hamilton, P., & Zhang, S.-D. (2013). cudaMap: A GPU accelerated program for gene expression connectivity mapping. *BMC Bioinformatics, 14*(1), 305. doi:10.1186/1471-2105-14-305 PMID:24112435

Mikolov, T., Sutskever, I., Chen, K., Corrado, G., & Dean, J. (2013). Distributed representations of words and phrases and their compositionality. Proc. Advances in Neural Information Processing Systems, 26, 3111–3119.

Mohan, U., & Salisu, S. (2015). The use of big data in the field of digital forensics investigations (comparative study between digital forensics in UK and Nigeria). *International Journal of New Technologies in Science and Engineering, 2*(4).

Najafabadi, M. M., Villanustre, F., Khoshgoftaar, T. M., Seliya, N., Wald, R., & Muharemagic, E. (2015). Deep learning applications and challenges in big data analytics. *Journal of Big Data, 2*(1), 1–21. doi:10.1186/s40537-014-0007-7

National Security Agency. (2013). *The National Security Agency: Missions, Authorities, Oversight and Partnerships.* Available: http://www.nsa.gov/public_info/__les/speeches_testimonies/2013_08_09_the_nsa_story.pdf

National Security Agency. (2013). *The National Security Agency: Missions, Authorities, Oversight and Partnerships.* Available: https://www.nsa.gov/public_info/_files/speeches_testimonies/2013_08_09_the_nsa_story.pdf

Nepusz, T., Yu, H., & Paccanaro, A. (2012). Detecting overlapping protein complexes in protein-protein interaction networks. *Nature Methods, 9*(5), 471–472. doi:10.1038/nmeth.1938 PMID:22426491

Ngiam, J., Khosla, A., Kim, M., Nam, J., Lee, H., & Ng, A. Y. (2011). Multimodal Deep Learning. *28th International Conference on Machine Learning.*

Nirkhi, S., & Dharaskar, R. V. (2015). Authorship Identification in Digital Forensics using Machine Learning Approach. *International Journal of Latest Trends in Engineering and Technology, 5*(1).

Nordberg, H., Bhatia, K., Wang, K., & Wang, Z. (2013). BioPig: A Hadoop-based analytic toolkit for large-scale sequence data. *Bioinformatics (Oxford, England), 29*(23), 3014–3019. doi:10.1093/bioinformatics/btt528 PMID:24021384

Nower, N., Tan, Y. S., & Lim, A. O. (2014). Efficient temporal and spatial data recovery scheme for stochastic and incomplete feedback data of cyber-physical systems. In *Proceedings of the 8th IEEE International Symposium on Service Oriented System Engineering (SOSE).* Oxford, UK: IEEE. doi:10.1109/SOSE.2014.29

O'Connor, Krieger, & Ahn. (2010). Tweetmotif: Exploratory search and topic summarization for twitter. ICWSM.

Paepe, R., Fairbridge, R. W., & Jelgersma, S. (Eds.). (2012). *Greenhouse effect, sea level and drought* (Vol. 325). Springer Science & Business Media.

Palmer, G. (2001). A road map for digital forensic research. *First Digital Forensic Research Workshop*, Utica, NY.

Palmer, W. C. (1965). *Meteorological drought* (Vol. 30). Washington, DC: US Department of Commerce, Weather Bureau.

Panchal, Ganatra, Kosta, & Panchal. (2011). Behavioral Analysis of Multilayer Perceptrons with Multiple hidden neurons and hidden layers. *IJCTE, 3*(2).

Papadimitriou, P. (2011). Geo-social recommendations. *ACM Recommender Systems 2011 (RecSys) Workshop on Personalization in Mobile Applications.*

Park, Y. S., Schmidt, M., Martin, E. R., Pericak-Vance, M. A., & Chung, R.-H. (2013). Pathway-PDT: A flexible pathway analysis tool for nuclear families. *BMC Bioinformatics, 14*(1), 267. doi:10.1186/1471-2105-14-267 PMID:24006871

Pascanu, R., Mikolov, T., & Bengio, Y. (2013). On the difficulty of training recurrent neural networks. *Proc. 30th International Conference on Machine Learning*, 1310–1318.

Pearce, R. P. (2002). *Meteorology at the Millennium* (Vol. 83). Academic Press. doi:10.1016/S0074-6142(02)80150-4

Peng, M., Li, Y., Zhao, Z., & Wang, C. (2015). System architecture and key technologies for 5G heterogeneous cloud radio access networks. *IEEE Network, 29*(2), 6–14. doi:10.1109/MNET.2015.7064897 PMID:26504265

Phan, J. H., Young, A. N., & Wang, M. D. (2013). omniBiomarker: A web-based application for knowledge-driven biomarker identification. *Biomedical Engineering, IEEE Transactions on, 60*(12), 3364–3367. doi:10.1109/TBME.2012.2212438 PMID:22893372

Piatetsky-Shapiro, G., & Tamayo, P. (2003). Microarray Data Mining: Facing the Challenges. *SIGKDD Explorations, 5*(2), 1–5. doi:10.1145/980972.980974

Poese, I., Uhlig, S., Kaafar, M. A., Donnet, B., & Gueye, B. (n.d.). IP Geolocation databases: Unreliable. *Computer Communication Review, 4*(2), 53–56.

Prasad, K. K., & Aithal, P. S. (2015). *Massive Growth of banking technology with the aid of 5G technologies.* International Journal of Management. *IT and Engineering, 5*(7), 616–627.

Pream Sudha, V., & Kowsalya, R. (2015). a survey on deep learning techniques, applications and challenges. *International Journal of Advance Research in Science and Engineering, 4*(3).

Productivity Commission. (2009). *Government drought support.* Inquiry Reports.

Raina, A. M. A. N. R. (2009). Large-scale deep unsupervised learning using graphics processors. *Proc. 26th Int. Conf. Mach. Learn.* doi:10.1145/1553374.1553486

Rajkumar, R., Lee, I., Sha, L., & Stankovic, J. (2010). Cyber-Physical Systems: The Next Computing Revolution. *Proceedings of Design Automation Conference,* 731-736.

Ranzato, M., Boureau, Y.-L., & Yann, L. (2007). *Sparse Feature Learning for Deep Belief Networks.* Adv. Neural Inf. Process. Syst.

Rappaport, T. S. (2012). *Wireless Communications* (2nd ed.). New Delhi: Pearson Education.

Rathore, M. (2016). Real time intrusion detection system for ultra-high-speed big data environments. *The Journal of Supercomputing,* 1–22.

Rathore, M. M. U., Paul, A., Ahmad, A., Chen, B. W., Huang, B., & Ji, W. (2015, October). Real-Time Big Data Analytical Architecture for Remote Sensing Application. *IEEE Journal of Selected Topics in Applied Earth Observations and Remote Sensing, 8*(10), 4610–4621. doi:10.1109/JSTARS.2015.2424683

Ratti, S., Frenchman, D., Pulselli, R. M., & Williams, S. (2006). Mobile landscapes: Using location data from cell phones for urban analysis. *Environment and Planning. B, Planning & Design, 33*(5), 727–748. doi:10.1068/b32047

Richthofen, B. F. (1882). II.—On the Mode of Origin of the Loess. *Geological Magazine, 9*(07), 293–305. doi:10.1017/S001675680017164X

Rivera, Vakil, & Bader. (2010). NeMo: Network module identification in Cytoscape. *BMC Bioinformatics, 11*(S1), 61.

Roy & Madhu Viswanatham. (2016). Classifying Spam Emails Using Artificial Intelligent Techniques. *International Journal of Engineering Research in Africa, 22.*

Roy, Abhinav, Rishab, Obaidat, & Krishna. (2017). *A Deep Learning Based Artificial Neural Network Approach for Intrusion Detection*. Springer. DOI: 10.1007/978-981-10-4642-1_5

Roy, S. S., Biba, M., Kumar, R., Kumar, R., & Samui, P. (2017). A New SVM Method for Recognizing Polarity of Sentiments in Twitter. In *Handbook of Research on Soft Computing and Nature-Inspired Algorithms* (pp. 281–291). IGI Global. doi:10.4018/978-1-5225-2128-0.ch009

Roy, S. S., Mittal, D., Basu, A., & Abraham, A. (2015). Stock market forecasting using lasso linear regression model. In *Afro-European Conference for Industrial Advancement* (pp. 371–381). Springer International Publishing. doi:10.1007/978-3-319-13572-4_31

Roy, S. S., Viswanatham, V. M., & Krishna, P. V. (2016). Spam detection using hybrid model of rough set and decorate ensemble. *International Journal of Computational Systems Engineering*, 2(3), 139–147. doi:10.1504/IJCSYSE.2016.079000

Rumelhart, D., Hinton, G., & Williams, R. (1986). Learning representations by back-propagating errors. *Nature*, 323(6088), 533–536. doi:10.1038/323533a0

Salakhutdinov, G. H. R. (2006). Reducing the dimensionality of data with neural networks. *Science*, 313(5786), 504–507. doi:10.1126/science.1127647 PMID:16873662

Sander, J., Ester, M., Kriegel, P.-H., & Xu, X. (1998). Density-Based Clustering in Spatial Databases: The Algorithm GDBSCAN and its Applications. *Data Mining and Knowledge Discovery*, 2(2), 169–194. doi:10.1023/A:1009745219419

Scherer, A. M. S. B. D. (2010). Evaluation of pooling operations in convolutional architectures for object recognition. *Proc. Int. Conf. Artif. Neural Netw.* doi:10.1007/978-3-642-15825-4_10

Schumacher, A., Pireddu, L., Niemenmaa, M., Kallio, A., Korpelainen, E., Zanetti, G., & Heljanko, K. (2014). SeqPig: Simple and scalable scripting for large sequencing data sets in Hadoop. *Bioinformatics (Oxford, England)*, 30(1), 119–120. doi:10.1093/bioinformatics/btt601 PMID:24149054

Security Intelligence With Big Data: What You Need to Know. (2013). *Security Intelligence*. Retrieved 26 June 2016, from https://securityintelligence.com/security-intelligence-with-big-data-what-you-need-to-know/

Shah, S., Horne, A., & Capella´, J. (2012, April). Good data won't guarantee good decisions. *Harvard Business Review*.

Shalev-Shwartz, S. (2012). Online learning and online convex optimization. *Foundations and Trends in Machine Learning*, 4(2), 107–194. doi:10.1561/2200000018

Shalev-Shwartz, S., Singer, Y., Srebro, N., & Cotter, A. (2011). Pegasos: Primal estimated sub-gradient solver for SVM. *Mathematical Programming*, 127(1), 3–30. doi:10.1007/s10107-010-0420-4

Sheperdson, J.C, & Sturgis, H.E. (1963). Computability of recursive functions. *ACM Digital Library*, 10(2).

Simard, P., Steinkraus, D., & Platt, J. (2003). Best practices for convolutional neural networks applied to visual document analysis. *Proc. 7th ICDAR.* doi:10.1109/ICDAR.2003.1227801

SINTEF. (2013). Retrieved from https://www.sciencedaily.com/releases/3013/05/130522085217.html

Smith, A. B., & Katz, R. W. (2013). US billion-dollar weather and climate disasters: Data sources, trends, accuracy and biases. *Natural Hazards, 67*(2), 387–410. doi:10.1007/s11069-013-0566-5

Srivastava, N., & Salakhutdinov, R. (2014). Multimodal Learning with Deep Boltzmann Machines. *Journal of Machine Learning Research, 15*(1), 2949–2980.

Stefanidis, A. (2012). Harvesting ambient geospatial information from social media feeds. *GeoJournal*, 1–20.

STIX, TAXII and CybOX Can Help With Standardizing Threat Information. (2015). *Security Intelligence*. Retrieved 26 June 2016, from https://securityintelligence.com/how-stix-taxii-and-cybox-can-help-with-standardizing-threat-information/

Stokes, T. H., Moffitt, R. A., Phan, J. H., & Wang, M. D. (2007). chip artifact CORRECTion (caCORRECT): A bioinformatics system for quality assurance of genomics and proteomics array data. *Annals of Biomedical Engineering, 35*(6), 1068–1080. doi:10.1007/s10439-007-9313-y PMID:17458699

Subhedar, M., & Birajdar, G. (2011). Spectrum Sensing Techniques in Cognitive Radio Networks: A Survey. *International Journal of Next Generation Networks, 3*(2), 37–51. doi:10.5121/ijngn.2011.3203

Sugiyama, S. (2008). Fundamental Behavior In Communication Method. IEEE/SOLI, Beijing, China.

Sugiyama, S., & Suzuki, J. (2012). Accumulation and Integration in Seamless Knowledge. *International Journal of Asian Business and Information Management*.

Sugiyama, S. (2013). *Intangible Capital Management Method As Dynamic Knowledge Wisdom. In Intellectual Capital Management For Knowledge-Based Organizations*. IGI Global.

Sutskever, I. (2012). *Training Recurrent Neural Networks* (PhD thesis). Univ. Toronto.

Sutskever, I., Martens, J., & Hinton, G. E. (2011). Generating text with recurrent neural networks. *Proc. 28th International Conference on Machine Learning*, 1017–1024.

Suzuki, J. (2009). *Gshop*. PITS.

Suzuki, J. (2013). *Multi Publications*. PITS.

Tallaksen, L. M., & Van Lanen, H. A. J. (2004). Hydrological drought: processes and estimation methods for streamflow and groundwater. Elsevier.

Tambe, P. (2012). *Big data know-how and business value*. Working paper. NYU Stern School of Business.

The Four V's of Big Data. (n.d.). Retrieved May 08, 2016 from http://www.ibmbigdatahub.com/infographic/four-vs-big-data/

The Global Risks Report 2016, 11th Edition, Insight Report. (2016). World Economic Forum, REF: 080116.

Thikshaja, U. K., Paul, A., Rho, S., & Bhattacharjee, D. (2016). An adaptive transcursive algorithm for depth estimation in deep networks. *IEEE Conference Publications*. doi:10.1109/PlatCon.2016.7456783

Threat Exchange | Threat Exchange - Facebook for Developers. (2016). *Facebook Developers*. Retrieved 26 June 2016, from https://developers.facebook.com/products/threat-exchange

Tibshirani, R., Hastie, T., Eisen, M., Ross, D., Botstein, D., & Brown, P. (1999). *Clustering methods for the analysis of DNA microarray data (Tech. Rep.)*. Stanford, CA: Department of Statistics, Stanford University.

Toffler, A., & Toffler, H. (2010). *40 for the next 40*. Toffler Associates.

Tseng, Y. L. (2015). LTE-Advanced enhancement for vehicular communication. *IEEE Wireless Communications*, *22*(6), 4–7. doi:10.1109/MWC.2015.7368815

TwitterMAPD. (n.d.). Retrieved from http://tweetmap.mapd.com/

Tzanis, Berberidis, & Vlahavas. (n.d.). *Biological Data Mining*. Department of Informatics, Aristotle University of Thessaloniki.

Vaillant, R., Monrocq, C., & LeCun, Y. (1994). Original approach for the localisation of objects in images. Proc. Vision, Image, and Signal Processing, 141, 245–250. doi:10.1049/ip-vis:19941301

van Iersel, M. P., Kelder, T., Pico, A. R., Hanspers, K., Coort, S., Conklin, B. R., & Evelo, C. (2008). Presenting and exploring biological pathways with PathVisio. *BMC Bioinformatics*, *9*(1), 399. doi:10.1186/1471-2105-9-399 PMID:18817533

Vasilev. (2015). *An introduction to deep learning from perceptrons to deep networks*. Toptal.

Vincent, H. L. Y. B. P.-A. M. P. (2008). Extracting and composing robust features with denoising autoencoders. *Proc. 25th Int. Conf. Mach. Learn.* doi:10.1145/1390156.1390294

Virvilis, N., Serrano, O., & Dandurand, L. (2014). Big data analytics for sophisticated attack detection. *ISACA Journal*, *3*, 22–25.

Waller, L. A., & Gotway, C. A. (2004). *Applied Spatial Statistics for Public Health Data* (Vol. 368). Hoboken, NJ: John Wiley & Sons. doi:10.1002/0471662682

Wang, B. (2006). *The Asian monsoon*. Springer Science & Business Media.

Wang, J., & Shen, X. (2007). Large Margin Semi-supervised Learning. *Journal of Machine Learning Research, 8*(8), 1867–1891.

Wang, K., Shao, Y., Shu, L., Zhu, C., & Zhang, Y. (2016). Mobile big data fault-tolerant processing for eHealth networks. *IEEE Network, 30*(1), 36–42. doi:10.1109/MNET.2016.7389829

Wang, Q., Shi, P., Lei, T., Geng, G., Liu, J., Mo, X., & Wu, J. et al. (2015). The alleviating trend of drought in the Huang-Huai-Hai Plain of China based on the daily SPEI. *International Journal of Climatology, 35*(13), 3760–3769. doi:10.1002/joc.4244

Weinberger, K. Q., Blitzer, J., & Saul, L. K. (2005). Distance metric learning for large margin nearest neighbor classification. *Advances in Neural Information Processing Systems.*

Weinberger, K. Q., & Saul, L. K. (2009). Distance metric learning for large margin nearest neighbor classification. *Journal of Machine Learning Research, 10*, 207–244.

West, T. O., & Post, W. M. (2002). Soil organic carbon sequestration rates by tillage and crop rotation. *Soil Science Society of America Journal, 66*(6), 1930–1946. doi:10.2136/sssaj2002.1930

Whishart, D. S. (2002). Tools for Protein Technologies. In Biotechnology: Vol. 5b. Genomics and Bioinformatics (pp. 325-344). Wiley-VCH.

Wirth, R., & Hipp, J. (2000). CRISP-DM: Towards a standard process model for data mining. *Proceedings of the 4th International Conference on the Practical Applications of Knowledge Discovery and Data Mining*, 29–39.

Wolfe, T. (2016). 6 Tips for Using Big data to Hunt Cyberthreats. *Dark Reading*. Retrieved 26 June 2016, from http://www.darkreading.com/analytics/6-tips-for-using-big-data-to-hunt-cyberthreats/a/d-id/1278970

Wood, Nisbet, Egan, Johnston, Haley, Krishnappa, … Hittel. (2012). *Symantec internet security threat report trends for 2011*. Symantec.

Wu, C., Buyya, R., & Ramamohanarao, K. (2016). *Big Data Analytics= Machine Learning+ Cloud Computing*. arXiv preprint arXiv:+1601.03115

Xia, R. CityBeat: real-time social media visualization of hyper-local city data. *Proc. of WWW Conference.*

Xu, Y., Zeng, M., Liu, Q., & Wang, X. (2014). A Genetic Algorithm Based Multilevel Association Rules Mining for Big Datasets. *Mathematical Problems in Engineering*, 1–9.

Yang, P., Patrick, E., Tan, S.-X., Fazakerley, D. J., Burchfield, J., Gribben, C., & Yang, Y. H. et al. (2014). Direction pathway analysis of large-scale proteomics data reveals novel features of the insulin action pathway. *Bioinformatics (Oxford, England), 30*(6), 808–814. doi:10.1093/bioinformatics/btt616 PMID:24167158

Yeung, Y. K., Medvedovic, M., & Bumgarner, R. E. (2003). Clustering GeneExpression Data with Repeated Measurements. *Genome Biology*, *4*(5), R34. doi:10.1186/gb-2003-4-5-r34 PMID:12734014

Zambon, A. C., Gaj, S., Ho, I., Hanspers, K., Vranizan, K., Evelo, C. T., & Salomonis, N. et al. (2012). GO-Elite: A flexible solution for pathway and ontology over-representation. *Bioinformatics (Oxford, England)*, *28*(16), 2209–2210. doi:10.1093/bioinformatics/bts366 PMID:22743224

Zeng, Y., Liang, Y., Hoang, A. T., & Zhang, R. (2009). A Review on Spectrum Sensing for Cognitive Radio: Challenges and Solutions. *EURASIP Journal on Advances in Signal Processing*, *2010*, 15.

Zhanga, Y. (2016). Image Region Forgery Detection: A Deep Learning Approach. *Proceedings of the Singapore Cyber-Security Conference (SG-CRC) Cyber-Security by Design*, 14.

Zhang, Q., Yang, L. T., & Chen, Z. (2016). Deep Computation Model for Unsupervised Feature Learning on Big Data. *IEEE Transactions on Services Computing*, *9*(1), 161–171.

Zhang, W., Mallik, R. K., & Lataeif, K. B. (2009). Optimization of Cooperative Spectrum Sensing with Energy Detection in Cognitive Radio Networks. *IEEE Transactions on Wireless Communications*, *8*(12), 5761–5766. doi:10.1109/TWC.2009.12.081710

Zhao, S., Prenger, K., & Smith, L. (2013). *Stormbow: a cloud-based tool for reads mapping and expression quantification in largescale RNA-Seq studies* (Vol. 2013). International Scholarly Research Notices.

Zhao, S., Prenger, K., Smith, L., Messina, T., Fan, H., Jaeger, E., & Stephens, S. (2013). Rainbow: A tool for large-scale whole-genome sequencing data analysis using cloud computing. *BMC Genomics*, *14*(1), 425. doi:10.1186/1471-2164-14-425 PMID:23802613

Zheng, Y., Chen, Y., Xie, X., & Ma, W. (2009). GeoLife 2.0: A location-based social networking service. *Mobile Data Management: Systems, Services and Middleware 2009, MDM'09, Tenth International Conference on*, 357-358.

Zhu, Q. Y., Bushnell, L., & Basar, T. (2013). *Resilient distributed control of multi-agent cyber-physical systems. In Control of Cyber-Physical Systems*. Springer.

Zien, A., Ratsch, G., Mika, S., Scholkopf, B., Lengauer, T., & Muller, R.-K. (2000). Engineering Support Vector Machine Kernels that Recognize Translation Initiation Sites. *Bioinformatics (Oxford, England)*, *16*(9), 799–807. doi:10.1093/bioinformatics/16.9.799 PMID:11108702

Zook, M., Graham, M., Shelton, T., & Gorman, S. (2010). Volunteered geographic information and crowdsourcing disaster relief: A case study of the Haitian earthquake. *World Medical & Health Policy.*, *2*(2), 7–33. doi:10.2202/1948-4682.1069

About the Contributors

Anand Paul received the Ph.D. degree in Electrical Engineering from the National Cheng Kung University, Tainan, Taiwan, in 2010. He is currently working as an Associate Professor in the School of Computer Science and Engineering, Kyungpook National University, South Korea. He is a delegate representing South Korea for M2M focus group and for MPEG. His research interests include Algorithm and Architecture Reconfigurable Embedded Computing. He is IEEE Senior member and has guest edited various international journals and he is also part of Editorial Team for Journal of Platform Technology, ACM Applied Computing review and Cyber–Physical Systems. He serves as a reviewer for various IEEE /IET/Springer and Elsevier journals. He is the track chair for Smart human computer interaction in ACM SAC 2015, 2014. He was the recipient of the Outstanding International Student Scholarship award in 2004–2010, the Best Paper Award in National Computer Symposium and in 2009, and International Conference on Softcomputing and Network Security, India in 2015.

* * *

Awais Ahmad received the Ph.D. in Computer Science and Engineering from Kyungpook National University, Daegu, Korea. He is currently working as a Foreign Assistant Professor in the Department of Information and Communication Engineering, Yeungnam University Korea. His research interest includes Big Data, Internet of Things, Social Internet of Things, and Human Behavior Analysis using Big Data. His serves as Guest Editor in various Elsevier and Springer Journals. He is invited reviewer in IEEE Communication Letters, IEEE JSTAR, IEEE Transactions on Intelligent Transportation Systems, and several other IEEE and Elsevier Journals. He is also published more than 63 research papers (Journals and conferences) and also several book chapters related to big data and IoT. Dr. Ahmad is also guest editor in various Elsevier and Springer Journals, including Future Generation Computer Systems Elsevier, Sustainable Cities and Society, Elsevier, and Real-time Image Processing, Springer. Dr. Ahmad was the recipient of three prestigious awards: (1)

Research Award from President of Bahria University Islamabad, Pakistan in 2011, (2) best Paper Nomination Award in WCECS 2011 at UCLA, USA, and (3) best Paper Award in 1st Symposium on CS&E, Moju Resort, South Korea, in 2013.

P. Bhargavi is working as Assistant Professor in the Department of Computer Science, Sri Padmavati Mahila University, Tirupati. Received her Ph.D. from Sri Padmavati Mahila University, Tirupati. She has 19 years of professional experience. She is member in IEEE, CSI, ISTE, IASCIT, IAENG, and MEACSE. Her areas of interest are Data mining, Soft Computing, Big Data Analytics and Bioinformatics.

Ankumoni Bora has received her M.Tech degree in Signal Processing and Communication from the Department of Electronics and Communication Engineering, Gauhati University, Assam. She is currently working as project associate in the Department of Electronics and Communication Technology. Her research areas of interests are wireless communication and signal processing.

Punam Dutta Choudhury has completed her M.Tech. degree in Electronics and Communication engineering from the Department of Electronics and Communication Technology, Gauhati University, Assam. She is currently working as project associate in the Dept. of Electronics and Communication Technology. Her areas of research interests include wireless sensor network and communication.

Manjaiah D. H. is currently working as a Professor in Department of Computer Science at Mangalore University. He holds more than 23 years of academic and Industry experience. His area of interests includes: Advanced Computer Networks, Cloud and Grid Computing, Mobile and Wireless Communication.

Shalinie Deepak completed B.E. CSE in 2006 affiliated to Anna University, completed M.E. CSE with specialization in networks at Anna University Regional Office Coimbatore, India and now working as Assistant Professor at United Institute of Technology, Coimbatore, India.

Ezz El-Din Hemdan has received his B.S. and M.Sc. degree in Computer Science and Engineering from Faculty of Electronic Engineering, Menofia University, Egypt, in 2009 and 2013 respectively. Currently, he is working towards his Ph.D. degree in Department of Computer Science, Mangalore University, Mangalore, India. His research area of interests includes: Computer Networks, Network and Information Security, Cloud Computing, Digital Forensics, Cloud Forensics, Internet of Things/Nano-Things and Big Data.

S. Jyothi is a Professor in Computer Science. She worked as Director, University Computer Centre, Head, Dept. of Computer Science, Head (I/C), Dept of Computer Science and Engineering, BOS Chairperson, BOS member and so on. She has 25 years teaching experience and 30 years research experience. She is handling core and electives subjects of Computer Science for post graduate and graduate level. 9 Ph.D., 7 M.Phil were awarded and 8 Ph.D. scholars are being guided under her supervision. She is senior member of IEEE & IACSIT, fellow of RSS, ISCA & SSARSC, member of ACM, IET & IAENG and life member of CSI, ISTE and ISCA. More than 80 papers published in International and National Journals and 60 papers presented in International and National conferences. 8 books were authored and edited by her. She has conducted 2 national and 1 international conference and 1 to be conducted in last week of March, 2016. She has completed one UGC major Project and she is handling one DBT major project and to be handled two more DBT projects. Her areas of interest in Image Processing, Soft Computing, Data Mining, Bioinformatics and Hyperspectra.

Murad Khan is working as an Assistant Professor in Sarhad University of Science and Information Technology, Peshawar, Pakistan. He completed his Ph.D in Kyungpook National University in the year 2017. His research areas include Computer Networks, Networking, Cryptography and Deep learning.

Pulkit Kulshrestha is a final year BTech (Computer Sc & Engg) student in VIT University Vellore. He has the interest in deep learning and pattern recognition.

Uthra Kunathur Thikshaja completed her bachelor in Computer Science Engineering from Sri Sivasubramaniya Nadar College of engineering, Tamilnadu, India and worked in Infosys Limited for 2.5 years (2012-2015). She is currently doing her master in Kyungpook National University in the school of Computer Science and Engineering, South Korea. Her research topics include Deep Learning, Artificial intelligence and Ambient Intelligence.

M. Newlin Rajkumar has completed his Bachelor of Engineering Degree in EEE in the year 2001 from Karunya Institute of Technology, Barathiyar University, Coimbatore; he did his Master of Science by Research (M.S) in Electrical and Control Engineering from National Chiao Tung University, Taiwan in 2007. During his studies in Taiwan, he was a recipient of International Student Scholarship from the Ministry of Education, Taiwan Education Bureau, Taiwan. He was awarded Academic Excellency award during his tenure. He was recognized as One of the Outstanding International Alumni Student and was honored by the President of the University, the first Indian Student to receive this Honor. He has served as the

Vice President of Foreign Student Association and International Students Union of the University. Later, He pursued Master of Business Administration M.B.A in International Business Management from Anna University in 2009. He has guided more than 150 M.E / M.Tech students and 40 U.G students. He has published many papers in reputed International Journals, Participated and presented his papers in various International and National Conferences. He has Chaired and organized several Conferences and served as Guest Speaker in many events. He has pursued his Ph.D with Specialization in Cloud Computing in Anna University, Chennai in the year 2014. He is a Professional Member of ACM, IEEE India Council, IACSIT, IAENG, INEER, AIRCC, IAARC, SCIEI USA, IIC USA, NAFSA USA, BSA U.K, CSTA, WASE Greece, EGA India, Tech Republic, USA, CCA USA, WEA U.K, IAIP USA, IAEST Senior Member USA, ISOC USA, ICGST, SDIWC, UACEE, PASS USA. His area of interest includes Cloud Computing, Big Data Analytics, Network Security and Networking. He has more than Eleven years of teaching experience in his career. Presently, He is working as Assistant Professor in the Department of Computer Science and Engineering, Anna University Regional Campus Coimbatore, Tamilnadu, India.

Priyanka Pandey is working as Assistant Professor in Computer Science and Engineering Department at L.N.C.T Group of College Jabalpur, M.P. India. She received B.E. in Information Technology from TIE Tech (RGPV University), Jabalpur, MP, India, in 2013, M. Tech. in Computer Science and Engineering from TIE Tech (RGPV University), Jabalpur, MP, India. She published many research papers in international journal and conferences including IEEE. She attends many national and international conferences, her researches areas are Computer Networks, Data Mining, wireless network and Design of Algorithms.

Prasant Kumar Pattnaik, Ph.D. (Computer Science), Fellow IETE, Senior Member IEEE is Professor at the School of Computer Engineering, KIIT University, Bhubaneswar. He has more than a decade of teaching research experience. Dr. Pattnaik has published numbers of Research papers in peer reviewed international journals and conferences. His researches areas are Computer Networks, Data Mining, cloud computing, Mobile Computing. He authored many computer science books in field of Data Mining, Robotics, Graph Theory, Turing Machine, Cryptography, Security Solutions in Cloud Computing, Mobile Computing and Privacy Preservation.

Muhammad Mazhar Ullah Rathore received his Master's degree in Computer and Communication Security from the National University of Sciences and Technology, Pakistan in 2012. Currently, he is pursuing his Ph.D. with Dr. Anand Paul at Kyungpook National University, Daegu, South Korea. His research includes Big

Data Analytics, Network Traffic Analysis and Monitoring, Remote Sensing, IoT, Smart City, Urban Planning, Intrusion Detection, and Computer and Network Security. He is an IEEE student member. He is also a nominee of Best Project Award in 2015 IEEE Communications Society Student Competition for his project "IoT based Smart City". He is serving as a reviewer for various IEEE, ACM, Springer, and Elsevier journals.

Sabitha R. received the Ph.D. degree in Computer Science & Engineering from Anna University, Tamil Nadu, India in 2016. Currently an Assistant Professor in Computer Science and Engineering Department, SNS College of Technology, Coimbatore, Tamil Nadu, India. Her primary research area is unsupervised data mining techniques used in Customer and Market Segmentation. Her other interests include Data Mining, Data Structures & Artificial Intelligence.

Pijush Samui is an associate professor in the department of civil Engg, NIT PATNA. He graduated in 2000, with a B.Tech. in Civil Engineering from Indian Institute of Engineering Science and Technology, Shibpur, India. He received his M.Sc. in Geotechnical Earthquake Engineering from Indian Institute of Science, Bangalore, India (2004). He holds a Ph.D. in Geotechnical Earthquake Engineering (2008) from Indian Institute of Science, Bangalore, India. He was a postdoctoral fellow at University of Pittsburgh(USA)(2008-2009) and Tampere University of Technology(Finland)(2009-2010). At University of Pittsburgh, he worked on design of efficient tool for rock cutting and application of Support Vector Machine (SVM) in designing of geostructure. At Tampere University of Technology, he worked on design of railway embankment, slope reliability and site characterization. In 2010, Dr. Pijush joined in the Center for Disaster Mitigation and Management at VIT University as an Associate Professor. He was promoted to a Professor in 2012. Dr. Pijush's research focuses on the application of Artificial Intelligence for designing civil engineering structure, design of foundation, stability of railway embankment, reliability analysis, site characterization, and earthquake engineering. Dr. Pijush has authored or co-authored 7 books, 14 book chapters, 118 journal publications, and 29 conference papers. Dr. Pijush is the recipient of the prestigious CIMO fellowship (2009) from Finland, for his integrated research on the design of railway embankment. He was awarded the Shamsher Prakash Research Award (2011) by IIT Roorkee for his innovative research on the application of Artificial Intelligence in designing civil engineering structures. He was selected as the recipient of IGS Sardar Resham Singh Memorial Award – 2013 for his innovative research on an infrastructure project. He was elected Fellow of International Congress of Disaster Management in 2010. He served as a guest in the disaster advance journal. He also serves as an editorial board member in several international journals. Dr. Pijush is active in a variety of professional organizations including the Indian Geotechnical Society, the Indian Science Congress, the Institution of Engineers, the World Federation of Soft Computing, and the Geotechnical Engineering for Disaster Mitigation and Rehabilitation. He has organized numerous workshops and conferences on the applications of artificial intelligence in civil engineering design.

Kandarpa Kumar Sarma, currently Associate Professor in Department of Electronics and Communication Technology, Gauhati University, Guwahati, Assam, India, has over seventeen years of professional experience. He has covered all areas of UG/PG level electronics courses including soft computing, mobile communication, digital signal and image processing. He obtained M.Tech degree in Signal Processing from Indian Institute of Technology Guwahati in 2005 and subsequently completed PhD programme in the area of Soft-Computational Application in Mobile Communication. He has authored/co-authored/edited ten books, several book chapters, several peer reviewed research papers in international conference proceedings and journals. His areas of interest are Knowledge-aided design, Soft-Computation and its Applications, Mobile Communication, Antenna Design, Speech Processing, Document Image Analysis and Signal Processing Applications in High Energy Physics, Neuro-computing and Computational Models for Social-Science Applications. He is the recipient of IETE N. V. Gadadhar Memorial Award 2014 for contributions towards wireless communication. He is senior member IEEE (USA), Fellow IETE (India), Member International Neural Network Society (INNS, USA), Life Member ISTE (India) and Life Member CSI (India). He serves as an Editor-in-Chief of International Journal of Intelligent System Design and Computing (IJISDC, UK), guest editor of several international journals, reviewer of over thirty international journals and over hundred international conferences.

Sanjiban Sekhar Roy is an Associate Professor in the School of Computer Science and Engineering, VIT University, Vellore, Tamilnadu, India since 2009. His research interests include machine learning, data science, and big data. He has to his credit various articles published in the international journals and conferences.

Madhvaraj M. Shetty has received his B.Sc. and M.Sc. degree in Computer Science from Mangalore University, in 2011 and 2013 respectively. Currently, he is working towards his Ph.D. degree in Department of Computer Science, Mangalore University, Mangalore, India. His research area of interest include: Computer Networks, Networks and Information Security, Bigdata Security.

Shigeki Sugiyama has been working on various fields from Industrial Engineering, Control, Artificial Intelligence, Neural Networking, Virtual Reality, E-learning, Embedded Technology, Computer, to Consciousness Studies for more than 30 years and has presented more than 70 papers. He also puts much attention on Service Science, especially on a network behavior in a scalable situation. And he had touched upon setting up a science park project about the matters of IT during 1994 – 1999 and he had done some cooperative research works with Universities in US and in Europe in Information Technologies. He had been a lecturer at Gifu Univ. and at Nagoya Management Junior College for years. Dr. Eng. from University of Gifu (Retired).

Index

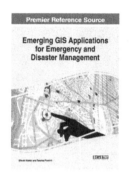

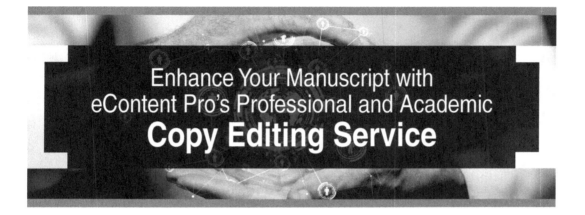

Printed in the United States
By Bookmasters